MEAT MARKET

Inside the Smash-Mouth World of
College Football Recruiting

MEAT MARKET

Inside the Smash-Mouth World of College Football Recruiting

By Bruce Feldman

ISBN: 978-1-933060-39-2

ESPN books are available for special promotions and premiums. For details contact Michael Rentas, Assistant Director, Inventory Operations, Hyperion, 77 West 66th Street, 11th floor, New York, New York 10023, or call 212-456-0133.

FIRST EDITION

10 9 8 7 6 5 4 3

ESPN BOOKS
a division of
ESPN publishing

CONTENTS

Introduction: **BANGING THE DRUM**   1

1. **MEASURING UP**   13

2. **SNAP DECISIONS**   23

3. **BÉBÉ—PART ONE**   32

4. **BÉBÉ—PART TWO**   43

5. **RAGS AND RICHES**   54

6. **LORD OF THE INTERNET**   65

7. **SPRING CLEANING**   82

8. **SUMMER CAMP**   112

9. **THE OKOLONA KID**   133

10. **THE JAILER**   154

11. **FACE TIME**   176

12. **PLAN B**   199

13. **SECOND SEASON**   218

14. **ROAD SHOW**   236

15. **HOME STRETCH**   255

16. **COUNTDOWN**   273

Epilogue: **THE FUTURE IS NOW**   305

Acknowledgments   311

BANGING THE DRUM

A GRIZZLY SOUND surges through the hallways of the Indoor Practice Facility on the University of Mississippi campus. It's as if someone were trying to start an old lawn mower. The noise grows louder as, rounding a corner about thirty paces away, a bear of a man with short black hair and the build of a refrigerator appears. He stalks his way toward you, a silver aluminum bat dangling from his hand.

"A new day has come for da Ole Miss Re-bels, Bay-beh!" he huffs in a husky Cajun accent to no one in particular. *"A new day!"*

This is Ed Orgeron. And he is *not* just making noise. A native of Louisiana, the 44-year-old had just finished his first year as the head coach of the Ole Miss Rebels. Their record in 2005: 3-8. Just plain awful, especially to someone whose previous coaching stop was USC.

For decades Ole Miss football has been better known for its pregame tailgate parties than for anything that took place after kickoff. In the college game's roughest, most competitive league, the 74-year-old Southeastern Conference, the Rebels have been a perpetual doormat, drifting from one lousy season to the next.

Orgeron (pronounced O-ZHUR-on) was brought in to turn that around by doing what he does better than any coach in the business: identify, and recruit talent. He was given a four-year contract. In return, he was to make Ole Miss a legitimate SEC title contender.

This was Orgeron's first head-coaching assignment, and it began in a swirl of controversy.

Shortly after Ole Miss announced his hiring in 2004 to replace David Cutcliffe (44–29 in six seasons), reports surfaced about alcohol-related, off-the-field behavior problems that had cost Orgeron his assistant coaching job at Miami a dozen years earlier. Then, in his first three months on the job in Oxford, Orgeron had to fire two assistant coaches for alcohol-related incidents. Rival coaches whispered that Orgeron wasn't cut out to be a headman. They told anyone who would listen—coaching buddies, the media, high school recruits—that this was a train wreck waiting to happen.

Orgeron's Cajun caveman persona had already proven to be great fodder for the fans of other SEC schools. They quickly developed a taste for mocking his halting speech patterns and gruff exterior.

But Orgeron was no punch line in the world of college recruiting. His rep in coaching circles was legendary. And so was his toughness.

Once, while he was at Miami, he allegedly threw Warren Sapp out of practice because he didn't like the lineman's attitude. Orgeron said that if Sapp really thought he was so tough, he should show up behind the UM practice field at midnight, where Orgeron would take him on. And at Ole Miss, in his first meeting with his new team in Oxford, "Coach O" supposedly tore his shirt off and challenged every single one of his new Rebel players to try him.

Some of Orgeron's closest buddies in the game say they're not sure what's true and what isn't. (Some admit they're afraid to ask, just in case more of the "wildman" tales are true than they figured.)

But no one who's ever worked with him disputes the fact that this guy is the best recruiter working in college football today. It was on

Orgeron's watch as USC's recruiting coordinator-defensive line coach that the Trojans amassed a stash of talent that spawned two national championship teams and had NFL personnel people giddy. His former boss, USC head coach Pete Carroll, marveled at what his burly assistant could do. He said Orgeron was as responsible for the rebuilding of the Trojan empire as anyone. Called him a one-man recruiting whirlwind.

It was Orgeron who, in 2000, while working for a then-rebuilding USC program, beat Notre Dame to land Shaun Cody, the nation's most sought-after high school defensive lineman. Orgeron sold Cody's dad, a lifelong Fighting Irish fan, that he could turn his son into a surefire NFL player and spark a USC renaissance.

Orgeron also discovered an unheralded 5'11", 280-pound introvert named Mike Patterson at a summer football camp. Orgeron loved Patterson's quickness and his ability to use his hands. He dubbed him Baby Sapp, a perfect nickname since Patterson idolized the former Miami star. Unfortunately, then-Trojans head man Paul Hackett thought Patterson was too short and too round and didn't want to offer him a scholarship. But when Hackett got fired, Orgeron sold his Baby Sapp to new coach Pete Carroll.

Baby Sapp and Cody, along with two other recruits during Orgeron's reign as recruiting coordinator—Reggie Bush and Matt Leinart—became the backbone of two national title teams. (Bush was the shining star of USC's recruiting class of 2003, later hailed by Rivals.com as the greatest in modern college-football history. The class of 2003 was literally worth a fortune to USC. The year before this crew arrived, the school reported making $38.6 million in football revenue, roughly what it had made in 2002. By 2005, that number had swelled to $60.7 million.)

Patterson was a first-rounder (Eagles) and Cody a second-rounder (Lions) in 2005. Bush and Leinart were first-rounders (Saints and Cardinals, respectively) in 2006.

Unearthing and signing gems like Patterson is the surest way to build a team. The challenge, of course, is identifying such prospects. Most major college programs begin their recruiting year with 1,000 or so names, gleaned from a variety of sources. From that shopping list, they sign up to 25 players to binding letters of intent on the first Wednesday in February, better known as National Signing Day.

To football-crazy fans in some parts of the country, National Signing Day has become practically a holiday.

To Ed Orgeron, it is the day that will make or break his career.

Orgeron would be the first to say that the recruiting game is tricky to read, even for coaches who have spent decades in the business.

Basketball recruiting is a whole different ball game. Well before signing time in college hoops, virtually all of the nation's top 500 prospects will have displayed their talents *against each other* at AAU tournaments and at summer camps. The best of the best can be seen competing in actual games. The sneaker-camp circuit was where a young Kobe Bryant distanced himself from Tim Thomas, the other guy vying for top-dog honors in his class.

In football, you essentially have just a prospect's game footage to study. But even that's a trickier proposition to translate once you consider the variety of different systems employed in high school football.

Otherwise, colleges make do with some 40-yard dash times and reports written up from Internet fan sites. "I remember hearing about this one linebacker from a combine in terms that made it sound like he was ready for the NFL," recalled one ACC assistant. "They wrote about how he could do this and that, and how his muscles bulged out from that spandex stuff he was wearing, and how he moved great. But when we screened his game tape, he may have been the biggest pussy in shoulder pads I've ever seen."

Projecting makes the football evaluation process even murkier. Basketball scouts seldom have to do much projecting to see how a high school power forward may look at "the next level." Try doing that with a fleet-footed but weak-armed quarterback/kick returner, who simply gets categorized as an "athlete."

Where do you line that kid up when he arrives? Too often the answer has to be "We'll figure it out. Just get him in the boat."

Understanding the recruiting world and its complex, confusing, and sometimes confounding rules isn't easy. It operates on its own calendar independent of the football season and has its own language. While the dates vary from year to year, the NCAA regulates the recruiting process in four different stages:

THE QUIET PERIOD: Most of the year is considered to be the Quiet Period, during which college coaches are allowed to speak in person with a recruit only if he is on their campus. A coach may call a senior prospect no more than once a week.

THE DEAD PERIOD: Similar to the Quiet Period, except that schools may not host a recruit on their campus. For the class of 2007 recruiting cycle, there were two Dead Periods: one from December 18-January 4, and another from January 8-11.

THE CONTACT PERIOD: A window in the winter that permits coaches to make in-person visits with recruits away from the campus, which is often the easiest way to meet-and-greet the player's parents and coaches. In 2006 the Contact Period began on November 26 and ended on February 3, sandwiched around the two Dead Periods.

THE EVALUATION PERIOD: This takes place for six weeks in the spring, during which the coaches may visit the recruit's high school, watch him practice, and talk to his coaches and teachers. But speaking to the recruit in person? A no-no. And no recruiting on Sundays. In 2007, the Evaluation Period—more commonly, Eval Period—was from April 15 to May 31.

Sounds pretty cut-and-dried, right? Think again.

Start with the "Bump Rule." That's a little NCAA loophole that allows a coach who encounters a prospect unexpectedly—as in "bumps" into him—to say hello and exchange pleasantries. But that's all it's supposed to be. Sometimes a high school coach unaware of the rules might bring a kid right over to the college coach. The college coach doesn't want to be rude, and he didn't initiate the contact, so maybe he takes advantage of the situation and gets in a little soft-core recruiting under the cover of politeness.

Then there's the "Third Party Non-Conversation." Say a college coach, a high school coach, and a hot prospect are in a room, and the two coaches have a conversation about Jimmy Bluechip. If it's not directly college coach-to-prospect, it's allowable under NCAA rules. That it's also a farce doesn't seem to bother anybody involved, although things can get messy.

During the last few years, the text message became an essential recruiting tool since a text was not a telephone call, at least according to the NCAA Manual, which contained detailed restrictions on telephone calls to recruits but not a single word about text messages. Coaches interpreted that omission as a green light to text-message recruits all they wanted. And if a coach texted "CALL ME NOW," it was certainly within his rights to accept the recruit's calls.

In April 2007, the NCAA approved legislation to ban *all* text-messaging beginning in August 2007. A little late, but the letter of the law finally caught up to the spirit. Or so the NCAA hopes.

The lingo of the scholarship-offering process is slightly easier to grasp, although it does require a reevaluation of two key terms: *offer* and *commitment*.

THE OFFER: How the scholarship offer is extended varies from college to college. Some coaches simply call a recruit and tell him he is "officially" being offered a scholarship to play football. In the last few years, most programs have chosen to send out a formal offer letter on official letterhead with the head coach's signature.

Most recruits are "offered" during or after the Evaluation Period, which takes place the spring of their junior year. The Ole Miss Rebels' official scholarship offer letter, approved by the university's legal counsel, comes with two important stipulations: first, that the recruit's academic performance and test scores must be adequate for him to gain admission to Ole Miss; and second, that his level of play does not slip below the Rebels coaches' expectations.

Other colleges employ different stipulations. Some explain that they're going to take only a certain number of players at a position and that once they're filled up, the offer letter is invalidated. In most cases, colleges have an out clause so that they don't get stuck with someone they've changed their mind about come Signing Day.

THE COMMITMENT: In the minds of 17-year-old high school football players, the word doesn't quite measure up to how Noah Webster intended it to be understood and used. Instead, it's "I'm 75% committed to Old State U.," or something even less.

Every year dozens of blue-chippers waffle on commitments, often "de-committing" more than once before making their decisions official on Signing Day. Many recruits say they opt to commit early just to stem the flood of calls they're getting from the hundreds of Internet recruiting reporters looking for a scoop.

Determining which other programs have offered a recruit is not easy. Recruiters often rely on information from a player's high school coach, although that's hardly an airtight indicator since the coach might just be trying to entice the action around his kid.

The other possibility is going online to check out one or more of the Internet recruiting services that track such things. Coaches know better than to read too much into what the fan sites are reporting. Still, every program in the country has someone in its office monitoring the two biggest online networks, Rivals.com and Scout.com for rumors.

With the possible exceptions of auctions and porn, no other business is better suited to the Internet than college football recruiting.

Jim Heckman, a Seattle-based entrepreneur, founded Rivals.com in 1998. His plan was for every program to have its own team site with a reporter covering recruiting, and an active message board. Better still, the team sites would be connected, to share relevant information pertaining to a certain recruit.

Within three years, Rivals.com went bankrupt.

In 2001, Bobby Burton, a Texan who'd been the editor-in-chief of *National Recruiting Advisor*, a magazine geared toward recruiting, scarfed up Rivals. He and his two partners repackaged the network by beefing up their recruiting database to include everything from a recruit's 40-yard dash time to his GPA to which schools were recruiting him. For $9.95 a month, a fan could learn about the players his team was recruiting, what the kids thought of their official visits to Old State U., *and* download highlights of the players.

Heckman, meanwhile, turned around and created a competitor to Rivals called Scout Media, which he later sold to Fox for a reported $60 million.

The two networks, hubs to hundreds of satellite sites such as GatorBait.net, IrishEyes.com, and OMSpirit.com, hit a nerve just like fantasy sports did a decade or so ago.

Evidence? On Signing Day in 2007, Rivals.com claimed a staggering 74.5 million page views—almost five times the number MSNBC.com had drawn on its Election Night coverage a few months earlier.

Most college coaches say the people doing the evaluating there are no more qualified than their mailman to judge football players. And they're right, at least about the qualifications thing. In fact, you rarely hear of anyone grading talent for an Internet site who has ever actually worked for a college or pro team.

Then there are the professional recruiting services that colleges pay thousands of dollars to each year for lists of prospects and, most important, game film. Many of these services are run by former high school coaches like Dwight Thomas (Florida) and Dick Lascola (California), who canvass their territory every year to provide schools with a thick catalogue of game tapes.

Ole Miss subscribes to a half-dozen services, ranging from Lascola's California JC Report (cost: $800 per year) to the Texas Film Service, which provides info on every high school of note in the Lone Star State (cost: $5,000 per year) to Thomas' LRSSports.

According to a January 2007 article in the Memphis *Commercial Appeal*, Ole Miss' recruiting budget for 2006-07 was $375,000, eighth highest in the SEC. In fact, it was ninth: Alabama (which spent more) and Vanderbilt (which spent less) didn't respond to the survey. Tennessee was No. 1 at $900,000.

Orgeron believes what his program lacks in funds will be made up in effort. The nerve center of that effort is an 800-square-foot office in the middle of the football complex, the Indoor Practice Facility (or IPF), at 1810 Manning Way. The address honors the program's two most famous products, quarterback legends Archie and Eli Manning. (Archie wore 18; Eli wore 10.)

The Rebels "war room" is the hub for the rebuilding of a gridiron powerhouse, and with it, the not-so-subtle overhaul of the landscape of SEC football. Here, every blip on the local and national recruiting radar is analyzed. Here is where Orgeron will live up to his reputation—or, as he would say, bust his ass trying.

Every major college football program has its own version of the war room and would rather post the game plan for its annual rivalry game online than let anyone know what is discussed inside it. For years, despite the booming interest in the recruiting game, the process—going from 1,000 prospects to 25 signees—has been the most clandestine operation in sports. That's in part due to the mind-numbing strictness of NCAA rules, and in equal measure to the paranoid personality of most college coaches.

But Orgeron wasn't shy about providing unprecedented access inside an actual college football recruiting machine: his.

"When we turn this thing around," he told me two years ago, "this is gonna make one helluva story."

Coach Orgeron provided me with a unique perspective from which to watch that story unfold.

For more than a year of the recruiting cycle that culminated in the selection of the 2007 recruiting class, he let me be a fly on the wall in the war room and throughout the IPF. Most mornings, I would meet him in the war room before the sun came up. By 6:00 a.m., Coach O was already a bundle of energy. And just in case anyone else in the IPF wasn't, from time to time the head coach would bang on a massive bass drum lest anyone try to grab 40 winks.

Much of the information, insights, and perspectives in this book come from the conversations, reactions, and debates around the IPF. Other details were culled from interviews I had done to flesh out the story of the recruiting class. It was an eye-opening experience for someone who thought he knew a lot about the recruiting process.

And Ed Orgeron was right: It does make one helluva story.

Chapter 1

MEASURING
UP

THE AIM OF all college football recruiting programs is straightforward: find the right guys and get on them before everyone else does. Sounds easy, right? It's not.

To Ed Orgeron, the key to beating everybody else to those right guys is fearlessness—and he demands that his staff be every bit as fearless as he is.

Since arriving at Ole Miss, Orgeron had not worried once about recruiting a kid who already had scholarship offers from USC, LSU, Notre Dame, or some other big program. Nor did he have qualms about recruiting someone with no offers at all. Orgeron was quick to say he wasn't afraid to be the first one into the deep end of the pool. His thinking ran like this: "Offer him now, and he's an instant billboard ad for your program over the Internet."

Revving up a positive vibe was critical, seeing as how Ole Miss couldn't exactly point with pride to its 3–8 record in 2005. Worse still, the season was punctuated by a blowout 35-14 loss to Mississippi State in the Egg Bowl, the annual showdown between the two archrivals.

But while all football fans in the Magnolia State knew which team had dominated the 2005 Egg Bowl, many high school studs across the South were more aware of the high-profile recruits who kept mentioning Ole Miss in interviews on the Internet recruiting sites.

Besides, to sign 25 to 30 kids next February, Orgeron would need to cast a wide net, which meant offering 200 or so. "At USC, we didn't have to do that," he said, spelling out the difference between a couple of national titles and a 3–8 record. "Maybe we'd have offered only 20 by Signing Day."

To get to 200 offers, Orgeron understood that Ole Miss might have to throw the dice and go for a few kids they'd scouted only on film. His rule on film-only offers: "He'd better damned well be a no-brainer."

Another Orgeron rule: He was the only one allowed to make the actual offer. At many other schools, the position coach or the area coach in charge of a certain recruiting turf could do it. Orgeron adopted this MO from Pete Carroll. This way, Orgeron said, his was the only butt on the line, and there were no political ties to any particular assistant coach to worry about when the player arrived.

Like most coaches, his thought process when studying a recruit on tape differs from that of the average person watching a football game. The No. 1 rule in the evaluation business: "Don't get caught up in following the ball." Instead, focus solely on what the man you're evaluating is doing at all times. That's a day at the beach for Orgeron—and most college coaches, for that matter—who truly loves the games within the game of football.

The first thing Orgeron looks for when scouting a defensive lineman is how quickly he moves off the snap. "Get off" when the ball's snapped is a must. Doesn't matter how big and strong a defensive lineman is if the blocker gets there first.

Orgeron says he learned how important that is when he was a young assistant at Miami under Jimmy Johnson and had what he called "the privilege" of coaching two future NFL first-round draft picks, Cortez Kennedy and Warren Sapp.

Among the questions he always asks in evaluating a D-lineman:

Does the guy he hits get rocked back upon impact? (Nothing's more telling than insufficient "pop.")

How quick are his hands? (D-linemen who can't disengage from blockers are *dead*, Orgeron says.)

Is he stiff in the hips, or can he change direction effortlessly?

Does he pursue the play downfield?

Does he keep his feet?

The last point became an issue with a certain D-lineman as the Ole Miss staff studied his tape in the war room early on in the class of 2007 recruiting cycle. "See, watch him hit—*boom!*" Orgeron said to the room. But then the downside: "Thing I don't like is I keep seeing him going to the ground. He's gotta be able to stay out of the trash."

February 1, 2006, was National Signing Day for the recruiting class of 2006, but the primary focus in the Ole Miss war room had long since shifted to the recruiting class of 2007, the one just 371 days away from becoming Ole Miss Rebels. The coaches were still waiting on a few faxes from recruits, but the Rebels had been boring in on the 2007 crop for months.

Ole Miss already had four commitments for *next* year's class, including middle linebacker Chris Strong, who Orgeron was saying would be the nation's top linebacker prospect in his class. Strong was a shockingly nimble 255-pounder. His uncle Eddie had been a star LB at Mississippi in the 1990s.

Just the day before, the Rebs had gotten a commitment from small-town tailback Robert Elliott, a long-striding glider who'd been unearthed by former Rebels assistant George DeLeone. "That's why you gotta go to every school in the state, no matter how small, because you never know," Orgeron told his staff after the good news about Elliott.

15

Orgeron, dressed in a red Ole Miss golf shirt and blue slacks, held court with rows of video tapes separated by position lined up in front of him. Normally the recruiting meetings would be more formal and organized, with the entire staff seated around the table. (The Rebels meet in the war room to go over recruiting at 8:00 a.m. every Wednesday during the entire year.) But since today was Signing Day, things were a bit more chaotic.

For most of the morning, there'd been between 6 and 10 assistants seated around the table watching the film. Almost always present were Dave Corrao and Grant Heard, the Rebels' two graduate assistants; Kent McLeod, the slender 28-year-old coordinator of football operations, who looked more like a golfer than a football man; and Barney Farrar, a former Clemson coach in his late 40s, who had just joined the staff as an assistant athletic director.

Also omnipresent was Hugh Freeze, a baby-faced, slightly graying, 36-year-old former high school coach from Memphis who was the Rebels' recruiting coordinator in 2005. A yes sir/no sir kind of guy, Freeze was Orgeron's right-hand man, and now his tight ends coach as well. Freeze also handled many of the peripheral details that kept Ole Miss football humming.

That very day, for example, he'd talked with the caterer about what kind of shrimp would be served at Friday's celebration dinner to thank everybody who'd helped land the class of 2006. Freeze told Orgeron he could get a deal on popcorn shrimp for $17 a head. Or else it'd be $22 per if they opted for jumbo shrimp.

Orgeron paused for a few heartbeats and then told him to go for the jumbos: "We're going to run a first-class program, and we're going to do it first-class."

Many of the tapes the Rebels would see that morning would be of prospects targeted as defensive players. With the lights dimmed, a red introduction panel appeared on the big screen in front of the room: Golden Tate–5'11", 185, 4.4–Hendersonville, Tennessee.

Every tape was labeled with an intro like this, although about the only things Orgeron took for granted were the kid's name and his hometown. As for height, weight, and time in the 40-yard dash, Orgeron would believe it when he or a member of his staff measured it. He had seen more than his share of times when high schools and the recruiting services overinflated a kid's dimensions or speed.

The Rebels saw Golden Tate as a cornerback. His tape, however, began with a series of dazzling offensive plays. He was juking would-be tacklers, leaving them staggering into each other. He was spinning. He was cutting. He was stopping and starting. His ability to regain top speed, going from first to fourth gear, was startling. That kind of quickness was critical for a defensive back who had to break on the football after a receiver had made his cut. Tate also was showing go-the-distance speed, running away from everyone on the field. A few other clips displayed that he had good hands and could make catches in traffic.

"We sure he's not a running back?" Orgeron asked.

"I talked to him," responded Freeze, the coach who recruits Tennessee, "and he says it doesn't matter."

Orgeron: "Only thing we gotta figure out is, what's our strategy? I know he says it doesn't matter, but somebody somewhere is going to sell this kid on something."

Freeze: "Tennessee's also offered him."

Orgeron: "You're not afraid of Tennessee, are you?"

Freeze: "No, sir, I am not."

The son of a former Mississippi high school football coach, Freeze comes across as a polar opposite of Orgeron. A math major at the University of Southern Mississippi, Freeze never played college football. While in school, he did missionary work in Russia and Australia. Now, he said, coaching was his "calling."

Freeze arrived at Ole Miss in 2005 as the former boy wonder coach from Memphis who had taken over the Briarcrest Christian

School program at age 26 and led the Saints to two state championships in football and four more in girls' basketball. He brought with him former Briarcrest Christian star Michael Oher, whose improbable ride to the SEC from homelessness was the subject of Michael Lewis' best seller *The Blind Side*.

Orgeron said he was impressed not only by Freeze's moxie and coaching savvy but also by his strong connections in the Memphis area, always fertile soil for SEC football programs.

Two months before coaching his first game at Ole Miss, and with Freeze at his side, Orgeron vowed at a Rebels booster meeting at the Memphis Botanic Garden that he planned to "build a fence around Memphis" to lock up the city's top recruits. He even guaranteed it.

That comment didn't sit too well with Memphis head coach Tommy West or with Tennessee's Phil Fulmer, both of whom took jabs at Orgeron's big talk. Locally, some newspaper columnists and radio talk-show hosts had fun with it too. But neither West nor Fulmer, whose Vols were coming off an embarrassing 5–6 season, were laughing when Signing Day rolled around in 2006 and the Rebels landed a half-dozen of the top players in the Memphis area.

As Freeze glanced back to the video screen to observe the next recruit, Orgeron turned to secondary coach Chris Rippon, who was seated on the other side of the table: "We may need to go to the JUCOs to get us some corners."

Orgeron clicked through three other defenders, none of whom kept his attention, before he came to Johnny Brown, a six-foot, 180-pound DB with 4.59 speed, from Charleston, Mississippi. As the tape started, Corrao, sitting in the front of the room by the screen, started nodding: "This kid's a stud. He's awesome."

Brown proceeded to make the assessment look good, running down ball-carriers on the tape's first four plays. Your first thought was that if this guy ran only a 4.59 forty, most of the other guys were probably three-tenths slower than the times they claimed.

Rippon: "He's got great balance. His change of direction is the best we've seen."

Orgeron: "Good. Listen up, everybody. If you see something you like or something you don't like when we're watching, say it, loud and clear. We can all learn from each other."

(Later, after the staff had left the war room, Orgeron explained that he *really* wanted to hear his coaches' observations. He was still trying to get a read on their evaluation skills. He said there was no one right answer or way to evaluate, but he felt pretty confident in his own eye, and he was just as interested to get a read on theirs.)

"He's fast-twitch," added offensive coordinator Dan Werner. Fast-twitch refers to the muscle fibers connected with explosive movements. Long-distance runners are said to be more wired with slow-twitch fibers, while sprinters are charged with fast-twitch.

Orgeron: "Okay, we gotta get him in the boat early because everybody is gonna come after him."

Brown had visited Oxford the previous summer with his high school team for a 7-on-7 passing league tournament, a passing-game simulation in which an offense runs plays with no linemen against an opponent's linebackers and defensive backs. He'd also been to another 7-on-7 tournament in Starkville, home of Mississippi State. Brown had been on the Rebels' radar for a year, but Orgeron knew that once other schools scrutinized Brown's tape, he would have to battle to keep the kid in-state.

Next up was a DB from a small out-of-state school. The first five plays were all run away from the player's side of the field. Another clip showed him sprinting in to jump on a pile. He did *look* athletic. Later he darted in front of a receiver running an out pattern, but the quarterback threw the ball way behind the play. "He's 5'11" and ran a 4.62 at a combine," Orgeron read from some notes McLeod had given him. "I'm not offering if he's 5'9", but if he's 5'11" we might take him."

"I saw him," one of the coaches chimed in. "He's probably 5'10" coming out of the locker room."

Orgeron's decision was to label the kid as a "prospect." They'd try to get him to their summer camp for a closer look. If not, somebody else could go jump on him. The feeling was that he might not be any better than people already in the program. Or maybe they just needed more film showing him doing *something*.

Next on the screen: Harrison Smith–6'3", 215, 4.5–Knoxville.

Smith was a virtual one-man team: LB, S, RB, and TE were listed under "Position." Indeed, the two-minute tape showed Smith doing everything from making open-field tackles to running guys down. During one five-clip sequence he looked like John Lynch, the Broncos' hard-hitting All-Pro safety. The next sequence, he looked like a white Eric Dickerson, gliding downfield past tacklers. He also made a bunch of highlight-worthy catches and runs-after-catch. The last shot was of Smith making a diving TD grab.

Freeze: "That was with six seconds to go in the state playoffs."

Orgeron: "Everybody like him?"

"Yes!" the entire room responded in unison.

Without missing a beat, Freeze flipped open his cell and called an assistant in the Ole Miss recruiting office: "Get Coach Pemberton on the phone please."

"Hey Coach," Freeze said into the phone 30 seconds later. "We're having a great day here. Coach O is ready to offer Big Harrison a scholarship."

Orgeron in a whisper to Freeze: "Have him call my cell phone."

Freeze's voice lowered as he asked Pemberton, "They already offered him?"

Freeze chatted just enough to satisfy the demands of politeness, said good bye, and turned to the room: "UT offered him last week."

And then, in a softer, more upbeat tone: "That's okay. They'll take for granted that they got him, and we'll out-recruit them."

Two feet away, Orgeron was smiling as he stared at the blank screen and offered a parting message to his staff: "Alright now, don't go out there trappin' and come back without no furs!"

One of the truisms of player evaluation: Everybody good must look like somebody else good. Coaches subconsciously use this comparison technique to reassure themselves, or perhaps to try and make objective something that is inherently subjective. This is, after all, an industry completely in love with its tape measures and stop watches and percentages.

So that swift, hard-nosed white linebacker? He *was* Dan Morgan. Harrison Smith, the white defensive back *was* John Lynch. And so on, right down the list of potential blue-chippers. Not good enough that they looked like they could be good. They had to remind you of somebody else who you knew *was* good.

Sometimes the fit seemed natural and sometimes not. But almost always, if you looked closely enough, you'd find somebody who made it big to put next to a prospect you liked and make your guy look even better.

The trouble with this sort of cross-comparison is that coaches sometimes get a little gun-shy if they can't ID an antecedent for a prospect under review.

That had been Karlin Brown's bad luck. For the LB from Tallahassee's Lincoln High, the Rebels video screen flashed these vital stats: 5'8", 200, 4.4. The 5'8" evoked a collective groan.

"Uh, 5-foot-8?" one of the assistants in the front of the room muttered in feigned disbelief. "Oh, jeez."

But only two plays into the film the mood of the room shifted from skeptical to intrigued. A squat, pit bull-like hitting machine, Brown played at a different speed than the other players in the film, and this was an elite level of high school football. Brown's game was powered by leverage and explosiveness. His low center of gravity turned out to be an advantage, almost as much of one as his speed burst. He didn't appear to have just first-step quickness; it was more like *five-step* quickness. He was constantly in attack mode. Clip after clip showed Brown flying into the frame and blasting ball-carriers and blockers backwards.

During the 1990s, Miami had a 5'8", 200-pound linebacker named Rohan "the Rat" Marley, the son of reggae legend Bob Marley. Rohan was a lights-out hitter too, but he didn't seem to be this fast.

Maybe Brown was the next Rohan Marley.

Orgeron: "I loved the Rat."

Matt Lubick, the recruiter who handles north Florida for the Rebels, announced to the room that Brown also ran the anchor leg on Lincoln's nationally ranked 4x100 relay team. So in essence, Karlin Brown with his short strides didn't just appear to be fast, he now *was* fast. *Officially* fast, as in legitimate speed.

That's what comes with a track background: speed cred.

Orgeron: "Show of hands, who thinks we should *not* offer him?"

Half the hands in the room went up.

Orgeron: "Okay, who thinks we *should* offer him?"

This time, maybe three-fourths of the hands went up. Obviously, a few people from the first group had been on the cusp. The basic breakdown: The offensive coaches wanted the little linebacker, the defensive guys were still skeptical.

Orgeron: "I don't know. If he's listed at 5'8", that probably means he's more like 5'6.""

Offensive line coach Art Kehoe: "How about we say, 'If you can ride the roller coaster in Tallahassee, we'll take you.'"

Orgeron: "Or if you're tall enough to try and walk under this table and you hit your head, we'll take you."

The verdict: Call the folks at Tallahassee Lincoln and tell them their little linebacker was going to be offered a scholarship by the Ole Miss Rebels.

Chapter 2

SNAP
DECISIONS

THERE WERE TWO certainties about the class of 2007: Quarterback Jimmy Clausen was, by far, the most celebrated recruit in the country; and yet, despite all the hype—or maybe because of it—Clausen was a long shot to end up as the top college QB in the class.

Clausen, who grew up in Southern California, was a product of good genes, shrewd planning, and deep pockets. He didn't start kindergarten until he was 6, and he repeated the sixth grade. "We held him back so he could gain maturity," his mother, Cathy, explained to *Sports Illustrated*, which profiled him in 2005 under the headline "The Kid with the Golden Arm."

The kid's father, Jim, a one-time football assistant at Cal State-Northridge, had spent well over six figures having his three boys tutored since grade school in the fine art of quarterbacking by a former Canadian Football League QB named Steve Clarkson. The tutor did well by Jimmy's older brothers, Casey and Rick, who became starting quarterbacks at the University of Tennessee. But Clarkson's main claim to fame? He groomed Matt Leinart into a future Heisman Trophy winner and first-round NFL draft pick.

As one would expect, the list of all-world quarterback prospects who flopped in college is probably three times as long as the list of those who flourished. Conducting any postmortems on the supposed failures is tricky, because even the ones who made it—even the great ones—have flaws. Joe Montana had a weak arm. Brett Favre had the throwing mechanics of a drunk trying to win his girlfriend a stuffed gorilla at the county fair. And Dan Marino's IQ, legend has it, didn't register much higher than any of his receivers' jersey numbers. All three QBs thrived in college and later in the NFL in spite of what any top recruiter would call major blemishes.

Except when referring to John Elway, the word "pure" doesn't get thrown around much anymore. Maybe that's because folks are looking a lot closer these days.

"Recruiting quarterbacks is such an inexact science," says Minnesota Vikings QB coach Kevin Rogers, the man who developed Donovan McNabb at Syracuse. "With quarterbacks, the things that really make them great players are the intangibles, the things you can't measure. You gotta go a lot on what high school coaches tell you. Problem is, most have never had a great one before, so they don't know what a great one really is."

Regardless of all that, college football coaches pursued Jimmy Clausen like so many Ahabs on the trail of Moby Dick. A year from the day he could officially sign scholarship papers, Clausen was already the epicenter of their recruiting world. It's doubtful that any single player has ever been more coveted by so many.

Quarterback isn't the toughest position to evaluate, says USC's Pete Carroll. The toughest position is cornerback, because it's harder to get good film on corners, which often forces coaches to project a high school wide receiver or a running back as a college corner. Of course, if you make a mistake on projecting a corner, no one outside the football complex notices. Whiff on a couple of quarterbacks, and the whole staff may get fired.

Quarterbacks also have to be recruited differently. Blue-chip QBs commit earlier than other prospects. Most pop (recruiting lingo for the moment a blue-chipper announces his college choice) by the spring of their junior year. Because it's become rare for top programs to take two quarterbacks in the same recruiting class, schools usually tell prospects their scholarship offers are extended on a first-come, first-served basis. That means that if another QB snatches up the offer first, the store is closed.

What this boils down to is that the top QB in each year's recruiting class usually makes the first move, and then the rest of the country falls in line. Coaches call it the Domino Effect, and Clausen was a domino the size of a cinder block in the 2007 class. The buzz had him down to four schools: USC, Notre Dame, South Carolina, and Tennessee, where his brother Rick had just got a job working for the Vols' football program as a graduate assistant.

To help show Jimmy its commitment, USC didn't pursue any top quarterbacks a year *ahead* of him. At Notre Dame, Coach Charlie Weis went so far as to say no to Mitch Mustain, the top-rated QB prospect in the class of 2006, after the Arkansas native expressed second thoughts about his initial choice, the home team Razorbacks.

Going against the current norm, Ole Miss had signed two quarterbacks in the class of 2006: Brent Schaeffer, a junior college All-America, and Michael Herrick, a narrow-shouldered, dead-eye 165-pound Californian. The Rebels took two QBs rather than the customary one per recruiting class because their depth chart had become perilously thin. The plan was that Schaeffer would be Ole Miss' present and Herrick the future. But having a plan never stops coaches from trying to upgrade.

That's why, at the first big recruiting meeting of the year on January 31, 2006, the topic of QBs was high on Ed Orgeron's agenda.

The Rebels' war room is a hexagon with two doors on opposing sides. Dominating the room is a round, glossy, cherry-wood table whose top is as thick as the New York City yellow pages. Around the table are 15 high-back, black leather swivel chairs, each with the blue-and-red script Ole Miss logo on the headrest. All of the Rebels coaches and support staff have an assigned seat. Orgeron's seat is directly opposite a projection screen where the Rebels view all their recruiting tapes. Behind the projection screen is the board on which the team depth chart is kept.

Around the room are four boards, each with magnetic nameplates in different colors neatly aligned. The boards flanking the screen are marked "In-State Offense" and "In-State Defense." The boards on Orgeron's side read "Out-of-State Offense" and "Out-of-State Defense." Each is broken down by positions. An orange nameplate means the player is committed to Ole Miss. A blue plate means the player has been offered a scholarship by Ole Miss. A green plate means the player is considered a "prospect" and needs more evaluation before he can be offered.

Next to the In-State Offense board is a list scrawled on a dry-erase board of the priorities for the 2007 class:

1. O-Line
2. D-Line
3. QB
4. Safety
5. CB

The scene here often resembles a gridiron version of the movie *Boiler Room*. There is a constant flow of anxious men gabbing into cell phones, walking and talking, entering and exiting, laughing and shouting.

"Here, I'm going to let you talk to Coach O," someone will say, then whisper the kid's name to Orgeron, hand off the cell, and nervously walk away. At some point during each call, Orgeron will hold the phone in the air, and on cue everyone in the room—coaches and grad assistants—will belt out the Rebel Yell, a primal howl that is an indecipherable jumble of "GO REBELS!" and "OLE MISS REBELS!" and the kid's first name.

Today, as the Rebels focused on Priority No. 3, several of the assistant coaches around the table were busily thumbing away at their Blackberries trying to get recruits to call in.

The tapes in front of Orgeron weren't aligned in any special order. The first one he grabbed bore the name of Nick Foles, a 6'5", 240-pound quarterback from Austin, Texas. The Rebels had already offered a scholarship to Foles, but Orgeron kept the tape handy so he could check it now and then to be sure, in an ever-fluid situation, exactly where the big Texan ranked on Ole Miss' QB wish list.

To Orgeron, the evaluation process is always on-going during recruiting season. The key is to get as much tape and other information as possible, and to review it as often as possible. That is the only way, he feels, to be sure you are targeting the right people.

The video clips showed Foles standing tall in the pocket, effortlessly flicking deep outs to wide open receivers. "Big, strong kid, eh, Dan?" Orgeron said to Dan Werner, the Rebels' quarterbacks coach/offensive coordinator.

Werner, like OL coach Art Kehoe, was new to Oxford. Six weeks earlier he'd been fired by Miami after working five years as the Canes QB coach and two seasons as their offensive coordinator. Miami imploded in the Peach Bowl, losing to LSU in a 40-3 rout. Werner and Kehoe were among four long-time assistants canned shortly thereafter by head coach Larry Coker. Combined, the four assistants had 11 national championship rings.

Not a day had passed that Werner, a father of two small children, hadn't thought about what he'd just lost. A year earlier, he believed he was on the verge of landing a head coaching job of his own, but that was before the Canes "fell" to a 9–3 record, while ranking in the bottom half of the Atlantic Coast Conference statistically.

Werner watched three more plays. "I think he's at the bottom of the top guys," he said matter-of-factly. "Sometimes his ball floats a little." Foles' tape ran for another 90 seconds. The rest of the room fell silent. This had been one of their top-five QB targets.

Orgeron: "What's our timetable here, Dan?"

Werner: "Usually quarterbacks commit in May, right after the Nike combine."

Another silence, only this time shorter.

Orgeron clicked the Foles tape off and popped in Clausen's tape. The first two plays showed two picture-perfect touchdown passes, beautifully lofted to closely covered receivers. Each evoked a rolling "Wow!" from around the room.

Werner: "Look at that—bam-bam-bam! See that zip out of his hands? That's what you like to see. Everything you coach, he's showing. See how he gets his hips around?"

Werner pointed to the screen as Clausen fired a zinger on a comeback pattern. "Wow!" he said, shaking his head.

"What?" asked Orgeron.

"Go back to that comeback," Werner said.

Orgeron rewound the tape to a play where the receiver ran downfield before turning and darting back toward the quarterback.

"See how he's nice and smooth back there?" Werner said. "Not like he's struggling at all."

"I don't wanna put a damper on all this," Orgeron announced in response to the enthusiasm, "but his old man told me for sure that he ain't comin' to Ole Miss."

Ryan Nielsen, the Ole Miss recruiter for California, seconded his boss: "His high school coach said he's going to Notre Dame."

Orgeron clicked off the tape: "Well, it's good to study him to have something to compare the others to."

Next up was film of Mike Paulus: 6'5", 220 from Syracuse. "He's the younger brother of the basketball player," one of the assistants said, referring to Greg Paulus, a record-setting high school quarterback *and* point guard who'd decided to play basketball for Duke.

Paulus' footage impressed everybody in the room. It showed him connecting on deep passes and deep outs that not only displayed his arm strength but also his timing.

"Nice release!" Kehoe blurted out. "That was a sweet-ass throw."

The film also showed a few nice scrambles. The ability to feel the pass rush coming from the blind side is a must for good quarterbacks, and Paulus showed he had it. Coaches call it "pocket presence," and it's one of those intangibles that's not always easy to identify in the recruiting process.

"Out of all the guys, this might be the guy we're closest to," Orgeron said as he turned to Werner. "Bombard him about Eli."

Eli, of course, is Eli Manning, the former star Rebels quarterback now starring in the NFL. Eli Manning gives Ole Miss football cred.

The message: If Oxford, Mississippi, was good enough for Archie and Olivia Manning to send their youngest boy here, and if he could blossom into the first pick of the 2004 NFL draft here, then it damned well oughta be good enough for Mike Paulus—or any other high school quarterback in the country.

The problem: USC and Notre Dame were both bird-dogging Paulus just in case they lost Clausen.

"Tell Paulus he can come in and learn the system for a year and then he's the starter for four years," Orgeron said to Werner.

The fourth quarterback viewed was Stephen Garcia: 6'3", 190, from Tampa.

Clearly the wild card of the class of 2007 quarterbacks, the long-haired Garcia seemed to everybody to have a little Brett Favre, a little Kenny Stabler, and a touch of Bill Walton in him. He watched the movie *Braveheart* before every game. He was writing a blog for the *Tampa Tribune* about his recruitment (signature: Stephen Achilles Garcia #5). The person he most admired, he wrote, was Alexander the Great, for his courage, leadership, and ability to conquer everything in his path.

Two of Garcia's older brothers played football at Harvard. His father, Gary, was a self-made millionaire who'd hit it big in the investment world and was proud to tell one and all that he was a product of the "Harvard of the South"—Hillsborough County Community College in Tampa.

Garcia's tape was more of a combination of throws and scrambles than the others. Fewer big plays than in the Paulus tape. Less polish than Clausen displayed. But Garcia did offer up some laser-beam throws and demonstrate a linebacker's bravado. And the kid exuded the "it" factor. It was easy to see why he'd earned a rep as a natural leader.

Werner: "He's got a cannon. The only thing I don't like about him is that he winds up a little."

Orgeron: "What's his background?"

Werner: "His dad's real rich."

Orgeron: "It says here he's 6'3". Is he?"

Kehoe: "Easy, at least 6'3". He runs real good. He's a better athlete than Paulus, but not a better thrower."

Like Paulus and Foles, Garcia already had a Rebels offer, although nobody thought he trumped Paulus in the Ole Miss ranking order. But Werner had a solid relationship with Garcia's coaches at Tampa's Jefferson High, so he was considered a more realistic target.

One potential stumbling block: a rumor on the recruiting trail that Garcia was one of the quarterbacks Steve Spurrier was going to make a run at. That was disturbing, because the South

Carolina Gamecocks head coach still enjoyed legendary status back in Florida.

QB No. 5 was Matt Simms: 6'2", 200, from Franklin Lakes, New Jersey. This was the youngest son of former Giants' Super Bowl hero Phil Simms and the younger brother of Tampa Bay QB Chris Simms. Matt was being touted by some of the online recruiting analysts as a top prospect. Two swing passes left the room quiet.

The tape showed about 45 seconds of side-arm throws, which drew no other reactions, before Orgeron clicked it off. Still silence.

Orgeron: "He's real hyped because of his name. He's not any better than Garcia or Paulus." (You got the feeling that the coach really meant "not as good.")

After viewing three more quarterbacks, Orgeron popped out of his chair and glanced at the stack of tapes on the table. "C'mon, we gotta go get us some studs!" he roared. "This class has *got* to measure up to LSU and Auburn! Got to!"

Then he turned to his quarterbacks coach: "Dan, you watch the rest of the tapes. Then bring me the offers and the prospects."

Werner: "Wait! Quarterbacks get only 45 minutes?"

"Yup," Orgeron replied as he strode from the room.

The rest of the coaching staff stayed in their seats. Some fiddled with their PDAs. Werner just rubbed his eyes and laughed.

"You know, I heard this story about Ed from a buddy about when he got introduced at Syracuse," Werner said to his colleagues. "He steps up and he goes, 'I'm Ed *O-jer-un* and I am da *D*-fensive line coach, and I *hate* quarterbacks. And so do my players.' My friend says the place went nuts."

Werner paused for a minute: "Never did I dream that someday I'd be quarterbacks coach for a guy who hates quarterbacks."

Chapter 3

BÉBÉ— PART ONE

J UST DAYS AFTER the December 16, 2004 announcement by the University of Mississippi of Ed Orgeron's hiring, the new Rebels head coach became an Internet phenomenon.

The initial cyber-accounts of his first team meeting read like something out of a Dan Jenkins novel. Consider this posting, which originated on the Rebels fan site OMSpirit.com and then popped up on virtually every college football message board in the country:

> *Orgeron came into the locker room and imme- diately started yelling at his new team that this 4–7 shit wasn't going to cut it.*

> *He talked about how the last game he coached was for the national championship and screamed that it was a goddamn embarrass- ment to win anything less than 10 games.*

> *He went on yelling about how he recruited Matt Leinart and Reggie Bush and that he didn't come to Ole Miss to have a goddamn losing sea- son or even to go to this bullshit Cotton Bowl and get goddamn thirteenth place. Thirteenth place was bullshit! He came here to win.*

He said that his team was going to play defense and hit hard. Goddammit, his team was going to play with goddamn passion! They were going to whip some asses!

He then passed a box around the room and said he wanted every goddamn earring in the room in the box. He wasn't going to have any fucking pussy girls on his team and wanted every piece of bullshit earring in that box right now.

Coach O started to walk toward the door ...

Only he wasn't done.

... but then he stopped. He looked back at the team as they passed around the box and said, "I'm going to walk out of here right now, and when I come back in here, I'm going to have my shirt off, and I want everyone of you motherfuckers to have your shirts off too."

He walked out and everyone, confused, started taking their shirts off. Sure enough, Coach O walked back in, bigger than a lot of the guys on the team, without his shirt on. He started yelling and telling the team that they needed to get loud.

He said, "When I point to this side of the room, I want you to yell 'Ole Miss!' When I point to this side, I want you to yell, 'Wild Boys!'"

Standing there with no shirt on and with every guy in the room shirtless, he started pointing to each side of the room. Half the team would yell, "Ole Miss!" then the other would yell

"Wild Boys!"

Apparently it got pretty crazy, and guys started flipping chairs, yelling, and throwing coolers across the room while chanting "Ole Miss! Wild Boys! ... Old Miss! Wild Boys! ..."

Coach O then stopped and said, "One more thing. If any of you motherfuckers thinks you can take me, you can come up here and get a piece of me right now."

He gave everyone an opportunity to come up and fight him and said, "That's what I thought," and walked out of the room.

Orgeron and the Ole Miss brass were evasive in their responses to press queries once this posting surfaced:

"We don't disclose what goes on in the locker room, but it was a very emotional meeting," Orgeron said. "We wanted to set the standard. But I never hit anybody or challenged anybody to take me on. Things got way out of hand on the Internet."

When a reporter for *The Atlanta Journal-Constitution* asked Ole Miss athletic director Pete Boone about the meeting, Boone conceded that they were in the ballpark: "There's a ring of truth. And even if it's not true, you might not want to deny it."

Some people present for Orgeron's little get-acquainted speech say that the "Come get a piece of me" challenge was embellished, but that the rest was pretty accurate. The "Wild Boys" chant was something current Jacksonville Jaguars RB coach Kennedy Pola had started back when he held the same position at USC.

Two years later, Orgeron regretted the fiery speech. He believed that within the bond of a team, his message wouldn't have seeped out: "If I had to do it all over again, I wouldn't do it, because I couldn't trust that team. I didn't know them."

Orgeron said he was surprised by the amount of "negative publicity" his pep talk had generated: "It all blew up into something it wasn't supposed to be. At SC, we'd done that sort of thing for years. But it taught me that criticism comes with the territory."

Still, the Internet noise made Orgeron sound like a Cajun boogeyman with a coach's whistle. Problem is, Orgeron's image is being shaped in a much different era than when Bobby Knight, Woody Hayes, and other firebrand coaches were throwing chairs and bullying players. In a sound-bite, YouTube, message-board world, everything is known by everybody the minute after it happens.

The elder of Bébé (pronounced Buh-BAY) and Coco Orgeron's two sons, Edward Jim Orgeron Jr. grew up in a remote corner of Bayou country, about an hour's drive southwest of New Orleans, smack in the gut of the gumbo belt.

Down in Lafourche (pronounced la-FOOSH) Parish, you can drive for miles along a slender swath of water past floating bridges, beat-up trawlers, and houses resting on cinder blocks. The towns have names like Golden Meadow and Grand Isle and Cutoff (as in "cut off from the rest of civilization," as locals are quick to tell you). The Orgerons lived in a tiny town called Larose.

Orgeron—who, like his old man, is known as Bébé by everyone in South Lafourche—traces his roots on his mother's side back six generations. He and his younger brother Steve were raised in a house his parents rented for $25 a month right on the bayou. His old man was a foreman for the phone company.

Orgeron's father always tried to make time to coach Little Bébé and the other neighborhood kids in their backyard football games. But Little Bébé quickly grew too big to play with the kids his age; by the time he was 6, he was playing with the 12-year-olds. The games were played on a gravel driveway littered with shells and rocks, with a sewer ditch used as the 50-yard line. Orgeron says he and his mates didn't know from "touch" football. Almost every game ended with a fight. Bébé rarely lost, either a game or a fight.

Like pretty much everyone else in Louisiana, Orgeron lived for LSU Tigers football. Saturdays were spent glued to WWL Radio, listening to LSU games. Even now, he can't seem to go a day without humming "duh-DA-duh-DAH!" or "Hold that Ti-Gah!" approximating the strains of the Tigers' battle cry.

At 13, Ed Jr. stood 6'1"and weighed 220 pounds. From the beginning, he loved not only the physical nature of football but also the tactical side of the game. He'll tell you now that even when he was in high school he found beauty in the way every individual battle on the field worked to make a play successful—or not.

Someday, he thought, he would be a coach.

At 6'1" and 245 pounds by the time he finished high school, Orgeron was seldom the biggest or fastest lineman on the field, but he believed in his heart that he could "out-tough" his opponents. He played both ways, dominating on offense and defense. It didn't take him long to realize that football is, in its purest sense, a game about will, and that the guy who never backed off had a damned good chance of winning. Orgeron never backed off.

"Bébé was just flat-out mean," says former teammate Bryan Arceneaux. "He loved getting after it." Along with future NFL QB Bobby Hebert, Orgeron led South Lafourche to the state championship in 1977, his junior year. The next season, he made All-State.

Off the field, Orgeron and his buddies partied as hard as they played. Around Lafourche, it wasn't uncommon for teenagers to belly up to the bar and chug beers with the grown-ups, something Orgeron and his pals started doing when he was 13.

"We're Cajuns. Everybody believed in having a real good time," says Arceneaux. "It was pretty crazy growing up then."

Orgeron parlayed his mean streak into a scholarship to LSU. Tigers coaches told him he would play D-line. But in his first week of practice, they shifted him to center. They decided he wasn't fast enough to rush the passer for them.

Orgeron tried for two weeks to convince himself the move was the right thing for him. But when he watched the defensive line practicing, he stewed. He was homesick, too. At the end of two-a-days, he bolted for Larose, where he got a job working with his father at the telephone company. He spent his free time pumping iron and drinking with his buddies.

That little vacation lasted three months. After Christmas, he and Arceneaux headed up I-49 to join Hebert at Northwestern State in Natchitoches. The 1-AA Demons were delighted to have Orgeron rushing the quarterback for them.

Orgeron started at defensive end all four seasons (1980-1983) for Northwestern State. Former teammates say that he raised plenty of hell off the field, as well as on. "Bébé is just so damned intense," says Hebert. "It's unreal how intense the guy is. He is definitely someone you'd want to have in your foxhole."

"Unblockable." That's how Larry Dautrieve, the former offensive coordinator at rival Louisiana Tech, describes Orgeron. "He was so aggressive, you had to scheme your whole game plan around him. He was undersized, but you still had to double-team him. The passion he played with was unbelievable. He never took a play off."

After Northwestern State, Orgeron got a one-day tryout with the USFL's Memphis Showboats. Orgeron's curt self-assessment: "Too small, not fast enough."

On the way back home to Larose, Orgeron stopped off to call his father. "I'm done," he told his old man. "Well, then," his father said, "I guess now you'll start coaching."

Orgeron dialed up John Thompson, the Northwestern State defensive coordinator, who invited him back to Natchitoches to work for defensive line coach Bill Johnson. Problem was, the Demons didn't have a big enough budget to hire another full-time coach. The best Thompson could offer was a graduate assistantship at something south of $2.25 per hour.

Says Orgeron: "I started at 7 a.m. the next morning."

After spending the 1984 season at Northwestern State, Orgeron followed Johnson to McNeese State, again as a graduate assistant. He was only there one season before landing a job at Arkansas as an assistant strength coach. It wasn't exactly X's and O's, but it was a way to get his foot in the door at an established program.

Only he didn't keep it there long.

Orgeron was in Arkansas less than two years when he called up old pal Bill Johnson, who was a graduate assistant at Miami. Tommy Tuberville, another UM grad assistant, answered and told Orgeron that Johnson had just taken a job at Louisiana Tech.

Orgeron: "You mean y'all got a grad assistant job open?"

Turbeville:"Yeah, we're meeting in 15 minutes. You want it?"

Orgeron: "Yes!"

Twenty minutes later, Tuberville called back and told him the job was his. Orgeron threw a pillow in his car and headed toward South Florida: "I couldn't get down there fast enough."

Miami was the ultimate, the top of the heap, the promised land of college football at the time. The Canes had just won a national title. Orgeron had witnessed firsthand what the Canes were capable of when Miami came to Arkansas and smashed the 10th-ranked Razorbacks, 51–7. Led by the brash Jimmy Johnson, UM's coaching staff was a collection of colorful characters, all seemingly cut out for future greatness. Four of the assistants would end up coaching their own teams in the pros or at the college level.

Orgeron says that he felt like he'd died and gone to heaven.

He arrived in 1988, at the apex of the Canes' bad-boy run, during which the program not only won national titles and cranked out first-rounders, but also led the country in police blotter headlines. Still, for all of the criticism, UM was an awesome force on Saturdays.

In Orgeron's first game with the Canes, Miami pounded top-ranked Florida State, 31-0. Ho-hum. The Canes expected to win—big—every time they stepped on a football field.

It didn't take Orgeron long to scope out the secret to Miami's success: talent. *Lots* of talent. Starters were understandably reluctant to come off the field in practice because they feared their understudies might never surrender the position again.

Orgeron marveled at how Johnson, a guy with a psychology degree, always seemed to know which buttons to push. He knew how to stoke people, so Orgeron paid close attention to Johnson's behavior with the team and with his coaching staff.

Most important, Orgeron hung on Johnson's every word whenever JJ evaluated a player. From the outset, Orgeron realized that he was in the presence of a master talent scout. Indeed, when Johnson ran the Dallas Cowboys from 1989 through 1993, he was all but universally acknowledged to have the game's keenest eye for talent.

Johnson detested stiff athletes. He was one of the first coaches to value speed and quickness over size and strength. Consequently, he was never afraid to turn safeties into linebackers, linebackers into defensive ends, and defensive ends into defensive tackles.

All the while, Orgeron was taking mental notes.

Whenever Johnson screened tape, he knew what kinds of reactions within each portion of a play might reveal whether a kid had "it" or not. He was big on change of direction. Can a kid turn and run? Or is there wasted motion before he gets cranked up? Johnson sought physically explosive players with explosive attitudes. And he had an uncanny eye for potential. If a kid "flashed," he had Johnson's attention, and that could be enough, since the coach figured he could get the kid to play hard once he got him.

Johnson was also never afraid to tell his coaches "No." He didn't need to hear then-defensive line coach Butch Davis whine about why the Canes should take a certain prospect. If Johnson didn't believe in his gut that the player could excel, he wouldn't bring him onto his team. Period. No way. End of discussion.

"It was fantastic watching how Jimmy ran that team," Orgeron says now. "He was the absolute master."

In 1989, Johnson decamped for the Cowboys. Dennis Erickson, from Washington State, was hired as Miami's new head coach. Erickson named Orgeron as his DL coach, giving the 27-year-old Cajun his first full-time coaching job.

Back when Orgeron first dreamed of a career in coaching, his big goal was to become a Division I assistant by the time he was 35. Now he was ahead of his dream.

By then, most people around the UM program had already been sold on Orgeron as a natural D-line coach. He had a booming voice, he had a blunt delivery, he liked working with his hands—and he had an insatiable passion for *Dee*-fense. To a man, his players not only respected him, even feared him, but also connected with him because they believed he was absolutely straight with them. Nothing about Coach Orgeron was an act.

(Years later, one of Orgeron's former linemen at Miami, a reserve defensive tackle named Dwayne Johnson, became a pro wrestler. Johnson based part of his ring persona on one of his old coach's bombastic speeches. He even adopted Orgeron's signature principles—"Know your role and shut your mouth"—as his own mantra. Johnson went on to fame and fortune as The Rock.)

Under Orgeron's prodding, Miami's five-man D-line rotation of Cortez Kennedy, Russell Maryland, Greg Mark, Willis Peguese, and Jimmy Jones became the most dominant defensive front in college football history, sparking the Canes on a national title run. The defense set a school record with 52 sacks.

Even with JJ no longer around, Miami fed off his legacy of swagger, relishing the black-hat image he left behind. Orgeron fit in perfectly. Perhaps too perfectly.

South Florida turned out to be one big adrenaline rush, and Orgeron jumped in head first. Competitive to the core in everything, he had to chase women, belt down booze, and party at a harder, faster pace than anyone. *Had to.*

"It was wild, Bro," Orgeron says now, looking away, seemingly caught in the moment. "So wild you probably wouldn't believe it. I can't hardly believe it myself. Hell, I was 29 and we were winning national championships. I had a false sense of reality."

In 1991 Miami went 12–0 and won another national title. The Canes held eight opponents to 10 points or fewer and didn't give up more than 20 points to anyone. Maybe the most amazing part was that the Miami D did all that despite having to play two defensive ends, Eric Miller and Anthony Hamlet, inside as tackles. Orgeron's stock as a D-line coach was soaring.

Off the field, his life spiraled out of control. A whirlwind marriage didn't last much longer than spring practice. In 1991, after a Miami woman accused him of domestic violence, Orgeron was placed under a restraining order and required to complete a 26-week treatment/counseling program. The demons lurking whenever Orgeron got drunk seemed to be getting the best of him.

Erickson, whose own reputation for drinking was well-known in the coaching business, referred to Orgeron in the *South Florida Sun-Sentinel* as "the wild man of the staff, fired up all the time."

On July 25, 1992, two nights before his 31st birthday, Orgeron went out drinking with some buddies. One thing led to another, and he got thrown out of a Baton Rouge bar. As he neared the door, someone got in his face. Orgeron reacted by smashing his forehead into the other guy's nose. Blood spattered everywhere. Turned out that Orgeron had head-butted the bar manager. Bouncers pinned Orgeron on the ground till the police arrived. He was charged with second-degree battery. (The charges were later dropped and Orgeron settled out of court with the bar manager.) Less than a week after the incident, Erickson placed his "wild man" on probation for the rest of the year.

Orgeron continued to coach for the Hurricanes that fall, but on October 18 he announced that he was taking a voluntary leave of absence for personal reasons. Erickson said Orgeron needed time away from work to "get some personal things in order."

Orgeron returned in mid-January, 1993. But, seven months later, he abruptly resigned. The announcement cited "personal reasons" again, but Orgeron subsequently admitted that Erickson had forced him to resign or be fired. That's all he'll say about what was obviously an immensely painful time in his life.

In four years as coach of Miami's defensive line, Orgeron had groomed three first-round NFL draft picks as the Canes won two national titles. Suddenly, in an instant, it was all gone. Orgeron had drunk himself out of his dream job. With nowhere else to go, Orgeron went home to his parents' house in Larose.

"Those were the longest steps of my life," he says. "I was back to sleeping in my old bedroom with the same basketball league trophies in there after having just lived in Miami on Brickell Key. For those first couple of days, I couldn't even get out of bed."

His mother was "crushed," says Orgeron, "but my father kept telling me, 'You stick with it. You're gonna come back better than ever. Just get it together. You're alright.' Those words meant a lot to me, and there was no pressure when I was back living at home."

No pressure except the sinking feeling that, at age 31, his college coaching career was over.

Chapter 4

BÉBÉ–
PART TWO

A FTER LEAVING MIAMI in disgrace, Orgeron spent a lot of days sitting on his parents' stoop in Larose, thinking about all he had squandered. He says it wasn't the money or the lifestyle he missed, or even coaching those games on national TV. Instead, he says, he kept thinking about the drills he ran during practice, challenging his players to do better. He missed studying film with his buddies. Maybe most of all, he missed going into high schools and presenting himself as a Miami Hurricanes coach, knowing that statement put him in the hunt.

"I was really worried about him," says Arceneaux, his childhood pal. "Football was everything in his life. And he was so devastated."

Orgeron dreaded the thought of having to go into some other line of work: "I really didn't know if I was gonna get another shot."

Then, one night in March, 1994, Orgeron got a call from another old buddy, Henry Lafont, a lawyer in Larose who was a booster of Nicholls State, a 1-AA school in Thibodaux, just 40 miles away. Lafont asked Orgeron what he was planning on doing.

"Henry, I got nothing," Orgeron said.

Lafont asked if he'd consider working as a volunteer coach. Orgeron said he'd take anything. The next day he got a call from

Rick Rhoades, the Nicholls State head coach. Orgeron was back in the game. It didn't matter that he wasn't getting a penny for it.

Every morning, Orgeron got in his mother's old station wagon and headed out, arriving on campus at dawn. After the sun went down, he'd drive back to Larose. "I was the first one in the office and the last one to leave," he remembers. "It was humbling, but I was so happy just to be back in a locker room again, putting on a pair of coaching shoes, and getting out there on the field."

Back amid the clatter of shoulder pads colliding and the smack of tackling dummies getting blasted, Orgeron started to feel like he was back in his element. And he wanted more.

After about a month with the Colonels, Orgeron told Rhoades he wanted to go on the road and recruit. Rhoades explained that Nicholls didn't have enough travel money in the budget. "Don't worry about that," Orgeron replied. All he needed was a Nicholls State golf shirt, and he'd make do. He'd borrow his father's Chevy S-10 truck and pay for the gas himself. Rhoades gave him a shot and assigned Orgeron the Lafayette area, Cajun country.

"I had to take some steps back to regain my career," Orgeron says. "And one of those steps was to prove I could still recruit."

On May 1, 1994, the first day of the year that NCAA regs permitted coaches to hit the recruiting road, Orgeron climbed out of bed at 5 a.m. He hadn't slept much because he was so pumped up. He'd been going over and over in his mind what he would tell folks when he entered their schools. He couldn't wait. His mother, awakened by her son's bouncing around the house, noticed that he couldn't stop smiling. "Why are you so happy?" she asked him.

"Because I'm getting the greatest gift," he told her. "Today, I get to recruit."

Orgeron says he didn't realize it that morning, but recruiting carried a much deeper meaning to his soul than he imagined. He now believes it stirred his lust for The Chase, whether for the best time, the best high, or the hottest woman in the bar.

Years later, after many long conversations with experts on addiction, with friends, and with his second wife, Orgeron says he came to understand that many of the same feelings he is hardwired for in recruiting operate within the same emotional circuitry that powered The Chase in Miami.

By the time he had settled in at USC in the late 1990s, after a three-year stint at Syracuse, Orgeron had a much better grasp on his own psyche. He says that he saved his own life by trading in one addiction (the wild life) for another (recruiting).

"That's where the magic is," he said. "Turning bad things that are rooted in weakness and making them into a strength. People always knew I had a wild side, and it came out when I drank. That stuff did it to me. I also had a side of me that was fairly normal, but in my drinking days you could never tell what was inside."

A loud, boisterous bear of a man clearly driven by emotions, Orgeron can also be surprisingly selective in choosing his words. And there's one thing that he's dead sure about: "Recruiting isn't some kind of heavy-duty hobby. It's my lifestyle."

Make no mistake, Bébé Orgeron loves being on the practice field. He loves teaching and prodding and charging the guys up. He loves examining practice tape and drawing up defenses. But the recruiting game taps into a different part of his brain. It taps into who he is. He says that when you get down to the lick log, there's nothing like the thrill of discovering a player before everyone else does and then leading the subsequent chase.

"The whole competitive thing about recruiting gets me going," he says. "But I just flat love going out and meeting people. Before I got sober, that really wasn't the case. Now, I feel better about where I'm at, and where I'm headed. I know that I have some good things to give. I love going into those homes where you can see people who need help other than football, and you can give them that help."

Orgeron says he knows he doesn't have his drinking problem licked. Counseling has taught him that he'll battle that until the day he goes into the ground. There was a time, he says, when he thought he had overcome his demons, but then his life spiraled out of control again, with more wild nights blurring together.

"Now, I know," he says. "It's always there. Once you go through something like that, and when you have children, you are so motivated about not going back."

He pauses, as if groping for the right words.

"You know," he says finally, "it's all about telling *yourself* the truth. When you're young and doing all those things, you think everybody is your friend. Then, all of a sudden, something happens and you're lucky to have three or four real people in your life. In my world now, it's to the office and then to my home, to the office and then to my home, every day the same. Then it's church on Sunday, and if we do something, we'll go to the beach as a family."

Getting to that point wasn't easy. In 1995, Orgeron left the Bayou for another crack at big-time college football after just 10 months at Nicholls State. Syracuse coach Paul Pasqualoni, a Joe Paterno protégé, was looking for ways to put some teeth into his defense. Pasqualoni had asked some colleagues who was the best defensive line coach he could hire. Orgeron's name kept coming up. They met, and Pasqualoni decided he had his man.

In 1995, Orgeron's first season with the Orangemen, the team's sack total went up almost 50%, and Syracuse led the Big East in turnover margin. The next season, the Orangemen were on the brink of an Orange Bowl berth, but first they had to get by Orgeron's old team, the Miami Hurricanes. But Syracuse committed five turnovers and lost to the Canes, 38-31, and got the Liberty

Bowl instead. And yet, the heartbreaking defeat proved to be the best thing that ever happened to Orgeron.

The Orangemen headed down to Memphis for the Christmas holidays. While there, Orgeron got a call from David Saunders, a coach he'd worked with at Nicholls State, who had since moved on to Arkansas State. Saunders had been after Orgeron to meet one of his wife's friends, a woman named Kelly Owens, for weeks.

The couple went out three days before the Liberty Bowl, and again the day after Syracuse beat Houston. Two months later, they were married.

"How about that for recruiting?" Orgeron says now. "She's a rock. She's so tough. I told her the whole deal before I married her. She's totally into what I'm doing. In 10 years, she has never asked me one time where I'm at. All those nights sleeping in the office at USC, all of those nights out on the road recruiting? Not once was it, 'What are you doing? Where are you going?' Not once. She is so confident in herself. She has given me confidence."

As Orgeron tells this story he has no doubt told dozens of times, he still can't hide amazement at the set of circumstances that had to fall perfectly into place for him to meet his future wife: "If I hadn't left Miami, I never would've met David Saunders, and then if we had beaten the Miami Hurricanes and gone to the Orange Bowl instead of the Liberty, I probably would never have met Kelly."

Following the 1997 season, USC had an opening for a defensive line coach. Former Miami assistant Bob Karmelowicz, one of the men who had recommended Orgeron to Pasqualoni, suggested Orgeron to his buddy, Trojans head coach Paul Hackett.

The Trojans had long-since tumbled from their old perch atop West Coast football. USC hadn't beaten its archrival UCLA in almost a decade. The perception was that USC was a dilapidated old wreck that had been left for dead by the Florida schools. Worse still, it was an image that other schools were able to sell to many blue-chip recruits from California.

Under Hackett, USC struggled to get out of its own way. Orgeron, it seemed, was the only one fired up to be there. After three years at USC, during which the Trojans went 19–18, Hackett was fired at the end of the 2000 season.

His career again in limbo, Orgeron did the one thing he knew best. He kept recruiting. No matter that he probably wouldn't be retained by Hackett's eventual successor. No matter that while he was out visiting local high schools, most of the other USC assistants were out looking for jobs. Orgeron figured this was a chance to prove something. If he could land quality prospects now, for a program that didn't even have a head coach, he could land anyone.

One day in early December, just days after Hackett was canned, Orgeron went to a high school playoff game in Los Altos to check out Shaun Cody, a sacking machine who'd been tabbed by *USA Today* as the nation's top defensive player.

Cody still hadn't committed anywhere, so at halftime Orgeron approached Mike Cody, Shaun's father, and introduced himself. In no uncertain words, the lifelong Fighting Irish fan made clear that he wasn't interested in hearing any pitch from Orgeron.

"I don't want you recruiting my son," the elder Cody told Orgeron. "You don't even have a job."

The rebuff just made Orgeron want to land Shaun Cody all the more. Now he was determined to make sure that Mike Cody's boy knew that he was the guy who had coached all of those first-round draft picks at Miami, and that he was someone who could teach him how to be more than just a pass-rusher.

After Orgeron left the stadium for another high school game, he bumped into Pete Carroll. The former New England Patriots head coach told Orgeron he was about to be named USC's next head coach. Carroll was looking for a right-hand man, someone who loved competing, loved the chase as much as he did. Carroll figured out after that first meeting that Orgeron was that guy. Together, they made Cody their top priority.

Orgeron's relentless pursuit and positive attitude finally wore Mike Cody down. The turning point, the elder Cody now says, was a two-hour talk he had with Orgeron on the Manhattan Beach pier. Orgeron sold Cody on a vision that had more to do with where a college football program was headed than with its immediate past or even its legacy. Before the two men left the pier, Orgeron had Mike Cody convinced that Shaun was going to be the first building block in the rebirth of a football dynasty at USC.

Orgeron's sales pitch proved prophetic. Reeling in Shaun Cody turned out to be the most significant recruiting development for USC football in two decades. It re-established the Trojans as a presence, setting the tempo for the new Carroll regime, and demonstrated to the new head coach what kind of drive his new recruiting coordinator had.

The next four years, Carroll and Orgeron dominated college football recruiting like it had never been done before. Their efforts produced the 2003 national championship team. And eleven months later, Orgeron would find himself in a place most in the coaching world never would've imagined he'd be: interviewing to be the head coach of an SEC program.

By the end of the 2004 season, the University of Mississippi brass had lost faith in head coach David Cutcliffe. A longtime Tennessee assistant, Cutcliffe had been Peyton Manning's quarterback coach. After he was named as Rebels head coach in 1999, his big move was getting a commitment from Manning's younger brother, Eli. The younger Manning shined in Oxford, just as his dad Archie had three decades earlier, leading Ole Miss to a 10-win season in 2003.

But after Eli moved on to the NFL, the program sagged. The next season, Ole Miss plummeted to 4–7. Cutcliffe was fired, despite a 44–29 career record.

Pete Boone, the Ole Miss athletic director, favored hiring an established coach. But when he and Ole Miss chancellor Robert Khayat met with Orgeron in Dallas, they were blown away by the 10-page plan the USC assistant presented to them. Orgeron had written it while sitting in the back row of the flight to Texas.

"I showed them all the organizational things I picked up from Jimmy, Coach Pasqualoni, and Pete," Orgeron says. "I showed them how we would recruit, the type of football we would play, how we'd involve the alumni, and the kind of staff I'd bring in."

Having Carroll's stamp of approval didn't hurt either, now that the Trojans headman had come to be perceived as the leading mind in college coaching. Said Carroll in a *Los Angeles Times* story: "My faith in Eddie to do whatever he needed to do was as strong as I've ever had with any coach I've ever worked with."

Orgeron's approach, most notably his energy and preparation, ultimately won him the job. On the morning of December 16, 2004, he became the University of Mississippi's 35th head football coach.

"Today's probably the biggest day of my life," Orgeron told the assembled media. "We are going to teach our young men to compete. We're going to compete from the time we get up in the morning until the time we go to bed."

The press conference wasn't all about Orgeron trying to get his message out. He—and Khayat and Boone—were forced to address his past run-ins with the law in the early 1990s, which the *Northeast Mississippi Daily Journal* reported also included the domestic violence conviction 13 years earlier.

Orgeron's response? "All I'm going to say is this: I'm completely comfortable with the steps I've taken to correct the mistakes in my life, and they're no longer part of my daily living."

Khayat and Boone added that, yes, background checks had indeed been conducted on Orgeron and all the other candidates.

"One item I want to address up front," Khayat said, "is that in the press, you have read that at one point, many years ago in coach Orgeron's career, he had an unpleasant experience that involved behavior of which he is not proud, and of which we fully checked out, thoroughly reviewed with him, and with others. And we know that that is something in his past. I will just remind all of us that those among us without sin should cast the first stone. Pete Boone and I and the athletics committee are totally comfortable and confident that coach Orgeron is going to provide the kind of role model, and be the inspiring, challenging leader, that we want for our football program."

Orgeron's rough past instantly became a hot topic all over talk radio. It was hardly the welcome Orgeron had hoped for, but by lunchtime, he was on the road recruiting for Ole Miss. Orgeron says now that he was surprised his problems got so much attention in the wake of his hiring.

"When I went to Syracuse, there was a little bit about it," he says, "and then when I went to USC, after those three years at Syracuse, there was a little bit. But when I came here, the media made it sound like it all just happened yesterday. They brought back everything. That really was such a long time ago. It was hard on Kelly because her family had to listen to it, and she wasn't even with me when that stuff happened. I thought it was really unfair."

Being a head football coach at a major college is akin to being a presidential candidate. Your past is an open book—or soon will be. If you're not married (with 2.5 kids), a churchgoer, and a scrubbed-and-polished pillar of the community ... well, you probably aren't a head coach in the first place. After all, the job description requires cozying up to well-heeled alumni, coddling local fat cats, and cuddling up to the school administration.

Oh, and winning games.

Orgeron, by his own admission, isn't big on warm and fuzzy. He also knows that for his own good, as an alcoholic, he can't hobnob with the boosters at the local restaurants and pubs down by the Square to build up equity within the Ole Miss family. Plus, he had his own battles with the Rebels brass to deal with. Once, during one of his moments of frustration in the middle of his second year at Ole Miss, he said defiantly, "They will *not* put me in a box."

Much as he might not like it, the box comes with the whistle hanging around his neck.

The demon recruiter's career, both as a player and as a coach, has been built on a manic-level of intensity. Even in his settled-down, non-boozing days, he comes across as a Red Bull-guzzling ball of fire as he barrels down the coaching corridors of life, seemingly on a collision course with something.

Says one coach who had worked with Orgeron on an earlier stop in Bébé's career: "I truly believe in my heart that he may be crazy. I might be wrong, but there is the thought in the back of all our minds, he could get pushed past his edge and then it's, *'Oh Shit! Look out!'* But the older he gets, you also kinda wonder, maybe he really is the smartest guy in the room. Maybe he really does know exactly where he is at all times and exactly how to play people. I do know this: kids, especially competitive kids, love him because they know he'll make them better. Does he scare the shit out of me? Hell, yeah, but the guy is a great coach. That part I am sure of."

Those reactions, the murky details about his past, the man's imposing size, that deep Cajun accent, his emotional outbursts— together, they have combined to create an intimidating aura around Ed Orgeron Jr.

"We've built an entire mythos about 'The Orgeron,'" says Spencer Hall, who writes one of the most trafficked football blogs on the Web, EverydayShouldBeSaturday.com. "He is The Orgeron. It's the voice, that odd accent. Even his name—OR-*JUR*-ON—it sounds like the name of an emperor or some medieval form of torture. He's this very large, very charismatic figure, and he's very easy to spoof. You could hear almost anything and people would think, 'Wow, from what I know about him, that's not that far-fetched.'"

You get the impression Orgeron doesn't mind his menacing persona. You go back to his now-legendary initial meeting with his players, and you ask if he really did challenge everyone in the room that day. And what you get is a mischievous expression that spreads across his face, his chin jutting out in a devilish smirk, and his eyes rolling ever so slightly.

It's probably the same look you'd get if you asked him whether he believes he's the smartest guy in the room.

Or just the craziest.

Chapter 5 ▶

RAGS AND
RICHES

IT DIDN'T TAKE long for the mud to start flying. Orgeron knew it would happen sooner or later. When you start becoming a threat, he says now with a sly grin, your rivals start to get nervous. Still, he didn't expect the attacks against him and the Ole Miss program would show up the way they did—in the mailboxes of Ole Miss recruits.

Toward the end of January 2006, Rebels staffers started hearing from high school juniors on their prospect lists who had received packets of "information" about Ole Miss football: newspaper columns critical of the direction the program was headed in, printouts of web postings speculating about the Rebels' "shady dealings," personal attacks on Orgeron that were slanderous, veiled (and not-so-veiled) allegations of just about everything this side of devil worship in Oxford.

The source? A post office box in Memphis. And that was only the beginning. On May 28, 2006, a story in the Memphis *Commercial Appeal* reported that "one coach currently in the league was turned in by seven different schools (and not all in the SEC) for alleged recruiting violations." Almost in unison, talk radio hosts, college football bloggers, and message-board jockeys pointed the finger at the prime suspect: Ed Orgeron.

"I know it's not us," countered Orgeron. "And if anyone's cheating on my staff, I don't know anything about it."

As Orgeron sat in the Rebels war room in late spring, he didn't appear rattled by the hailstorm of allegations and innuendos. He said he felt good about what the Rebels staff was doing. He knew, of course, about Ole Miss' history with the NCAA cops. He said he understood what he was up against. Despite his pedigree and his four national championship rings, Orgeron realized critics and self-appointed experts thought there was no way, at least no legitimate way, that he could woo blue-chip recruits to Ole Miss, a school that hadn't won an SEC title since a week after JFK was assassinated.

Fact is, the Rebels program, like all the others in college football, lost any benefit of the doubt years ago. At the core of today's universal suspicion of college football recruiting is a rich legacy cluttered with bagmen, loose women, and overzealous, ego-driven boosters, not to mention a small army of corrupt politicians.

Stories about rogue recruiting and outright bribery in the bad old days may sound outrageous, but a generation or so ago, before the NCAA encoded strict rules governing things like booster involvement and the number of times coaches could visit prospects, they were neither startling nor uncommon. In fact, many of the practices forbidden today were perfectly legal a couple of decades ago.

Ken Dabbs, a former recruiting coordinator at Texas (1973-84), once stayed at a Ramada Inn in Tyler for 17 straight nights while staking out a single prospect in early 1974. Seeing as that prospect was Earl Campbell, and he was being courted by Oklahoma (among many others), the vigil was well worth the $12 a day that Dabbs' room cost.

At least Dabbs didn't have to get a second job. In the 1970s, an Oklahoma assistant coach spent so much time hanging around the high school in Hooks, Texas, where Billy Sims was a senior, that he actually worked there a few days as a substitute teacher.

Recruiting also wasn't just a job for the coaching staff. Back in 1978, after word spread around Oklahoma that Rodney Tate, the state 100-yard sprint champion from a town of 4,000, was thinking of signing with arch-rival Texas, Governor David Boren not only called the prized running back to urge him to stay at home, but even called a press conference to urge Oklahomans to call and write Tate to get him to change his mind. (It didn't work.)

"We had boosters who practically kidnapped some recruits to make sure we'd get them," says one retired coach, who requested that he not be identified. "You did whatever it took because you knew the other guys would, and you really never thought twice about it. It was like the Wild, Wild West."

Eventually, lawlessness gutted the old Southwest Conference. Arkansas decamped for the SEC in 1992. Texas, Texas A & M, Texas Tech, and Baylor turned the Big 8 into the Big 12 in 1993. And in 1996, after 82 years, the Southwest Conference disbanded.

It didn't take very long for the SEC to grab college football's black hat. "It was pretty comparable," says Pat Forde, a former columnist for the Louisville *Courier-Journal* and a senior writer at ESPN.com. "And that open secret that they used to say in the SEC about how 'If you ain't cheatin', you ain't tryin'? That was pretty much true."

The SEC's most intense rivalry, Auburn-Alabama, took an especially nasty turn off the field, setting the tempo for the rest of the conference, when the "Tape Recording Wars" broke out in 1991. First former Tigers player Eric Ramsey made public tapes he'd made of then-Auburn coach Pat Dye speaking to him about gifts and even cash payments. That was followed up by Auburn boosters helping to coax one-time Crimson Tide captain Gene Jelks to come forward with incriminating recordings of his own that would put Alabama under the NCAA microscope.

"You had guys going to any depth to destroy each other," says long-time Birmingham-based radio commentator Paul Finebaum. "It was nuclear war."

The incidents landed both schools on NCAA probation. But the two SEC heavyweights weren't the only ones to get in the NCAA's crosshairs. The "cheating within the rules" modus operandi, in which everybody pretty much attended to their own business, had changed. Now programs jockeyed to turn each other in. The running joke among people who covered college football was that SEC actually stood for "Sure, Everybody Cheats."

Whether there was more cheating going on was impossible to say. There certainly were more NCAA rules to navigate—or circumnavigate. One thing was certain: There was more reason to cheat, thanks to a staggering jump in coaching salaries. According to a 2006 *USA Today* study, at least 42 of the 119 1-A coaches made $1 million or more, up from five in 1999. At several schools coaches made five times what their university presidents earned in salary.

Since 1989, the conference has been busted a record 21 times for major violations.

"You learn to believe anything is possible," says one former SEC coach. "Too much crazy stuff happens in recruiting, especially in the South. It's like because people are conditioned to believe crazy shit happens, they are prone to doing crazy shit. You know, when in Rome ... "

The Ole Miss letterhead that Orgeron and his staff use for their notes to recruits touts three national championships. Truth is, none of the three titles was awarded by the Associated Press, the gold standard in the college game. The Rebels' three "national" championships (1959, 1960, 1962) were bestowed by ratings outfits like Berryman, Dunkle, and the Litkenhous Ratings.

The Rebels' heyday, under coach John Vaught from 1947-70, came during the era of segregation. It was a time when the NCAA had no scholarship limitations and had few academic restrictions. Fueled by in-state talent, Ole Miss had 10 top-10 finishes in the AP poll, including five consecutive seasons from 1959-63. But once the NCAA imposed new rules and incorporated standardized tests such as the ACT and the SAT, Ole Miss got broadsided. The state, which traditionally ranks last in the country in education, suddenly didn't have the talent pool to sustain one college football program, much less two or three.

Worse still, Vaught and folk hero Archie Manning rode off into the sunset—Vaught into retirement, Manning to the NFL. Ole Miss struggled to find a suitable successor to Vaught. The rise of Bear Bryant at Alabama also helped shove the Rebels onto the college football outskirts.

The hardest thing of all to overcome for the Rebels was the stigma that Ole Miss was a place where race was a problem, an issue that rival coaches didn't mind bringing up on home visits. After all, it was one of Oxford's own, William Faulkner, who wrote of Mississippi, "The past is never dead. It's not even past." Ole Miss recruiters to this day suspect their competitors of using the implied perception of Mississippi as a state mired in the past against the Rebels.

It's a fact, after all, that the Rebels won their last SEC title in 1963, just one year after James Meredith arrived on the Ole Miss campus. The presence of the first black student to enroll at Ole Miss sparked riots on campus in 1962. Two people died and 166 federal marshals and 40 soldiers were injured by the time 30,000 combat troops called in by President Kennedy could quell the violence.

The image of "that" Ole Miss has been hard for many people to get past, especially since it's reinforced by fans flying the Rebel flag and singing "Dixie" during Ole Miss football games.

During one 12-season stretch starting in 1972, the Rebels didn't make a bowl appearance. Even worse, Ole Miss fell further behind the rest of the SEC in terms of facilities and support programs.

The Rebels didn't get within a sniff of respectability until Billy "Dog" Brewer, a former standout Ole Miss player on the glory teams of the late 1950s, took over as head coach in 1983. In his 11-year run as the man in charge, Brewer led Ole Miss to six winning seasons and five bowl games. But Brewer's tenure was scarred by recruiting scandals that twice landed Ole Miss on NCAA probation.

The first time, the Rebels were banned from postseason play and live television for the 1987 season after a two-year investigation found that recruits had received cash and other benefits from Ole Miss boosters. That episode proved to be a huge embarrassment for then-chancellor Gerald Turner, who previously had been the head of the NCAA's President's Commission. At a news conference following the announcement of the sanctions, Brewer vowed never to "be in this situation again."

A few weeks after the 1993 regular season ended, Ole Miss was rocked by another recruiting scandal after a lengthy investigation by *The Clarion-Ledger*. The NCAA nailed Ole Miss for 15 infractions, most of them of the eye-popping variety, such as boosters taking recruits to strip clubs in Memphis.

Sometimes the strippers weren't even the principal enticement. In 1992, a booster took four Rebel recruits to a Memphis strip club and asked what it would take for them to sign with Ole Miss—before offering a player a new Ford Mustang to sign. On another occasion, an Ole Miss assistant coach offered a defensive back prospect cash and airline tickets to come play football in Oxford.

The NCAA determined that Ole Miss coaches knew all of the violations were taking place, thereby demonstrating the dreaded "lack of institutional control" over the football program. In the wake of the scandal, Ole Miss athletics director Warner Alford, another former Rebels football hero, resigned in July 1994. The following day Turner, the school chancellor, fired Brewer.

Then, in January 1995, Turner announced he was done at Ole Miss too. The chancellor had resigned to become SMU's new president.

Ole Miss was barred from postseason play in 1995 and 1996. The stiffest penalty was in scholarship reductions; the Rebels lost 13 in the 1995 and the 1996 classes. It was among the harshest punishments the NCAA had ever levied upon a school not named SMU.

The recruiting scandals prompted Ole Miss to create a compliance director position, a sort of ombudsman for the athletic department. Again, Ole Miss was playing catch-up ball; many other SEC schools had hired compliance directors in the late 1980s.

Ole Miss hired David Wells, another former John Vaught player, to be its first compliance director. He still holds the job today. The Rebels' repeat stints on the NCAA bad boy list gave Wells a substantial role in Ole Miss athletics right from the start. "In that sense, it was good," says Wells, "because people were more responsive."

Wells had previously been an assistant football coach at Ole Miss and Kentucky. He left coaching for the administrative side of college athletics in the late 1970s, working in academics. Since being appointed as the school's compliance man, Wells has worked with three different head football coaches: Tommy Tuberville, David Cutcliffe, and now Orgeron.

Wells refuses to discuss the different approaches of the three men. He says only that, "I have good experiences with each of them," and that "Coach O is a very hard worker," and that "My primary concern is to the University of Mississippi."

The length of his tenure makes Wells a rarity in his field. Most compliance directors don't last more than a decade at one school. "There is a high burn-out rate," he says, primarily because the job is inherently adversarial. Millionaire coaches are rarely told "no" in their fiefdoms on college campuses. But saying no is a big part of

Wells' job, and for someone who says he doesn't even make enough to live in Oxford, that makes for some tense situations.

In preparation for the class of 2007, Wells and AD Pete Boone began taking a much more active role in the Rebels' recruiting process. After a spring meeting of the SEC's presidents and chancellors, the league approved a new system requiring each school to have a committee to examine questionable students. Grounds for suspicion include a big jump in test scores, too many correspondence courses, and school transfers midway through senior year.

The tension between Orgeron's new regime and Wells' office had been palpable at the outset. Orgeron had come from a USC program that enjoyed a cozy relationship with its compliance department. Pete Carroll knew that the Trojan brass was on his side. Orgeron recalls that the USC AD, Mike Garrett, once placed a midnight call to the provost in support of the coach's desire to get nose tackle Mike Patterson admitted. It helped. Patterson went on to become a two-time All-America.

Wells, despite what Orgeron and others in the war room may think, says he doesn't relish saying no. As he's quick to point out, it's one thing to breeze in from out of town with a briefcase like an NCAA representative, do some digging, and then go home and file a report. Being an employee of the school and having an office inside the athletic department is another thing altogether.

What both sides admit is that most schools stretch the boundaries of the rules as far as humanly possible to bring in top prospects who are academically marginal. Wells' instincts are to adhere to the letter of the law, but he concedes he hears a lot of "everybody's doing that." That doesn't necessarily mean the rules have been broken, at least not technically, but rather that some schools found a loophole, and now everyone else is playing catch up.

"And no," Wells interjects, anticipating the next question, "I don't want our coaches to be at a professional disadvantage."

One of the Orgeron's assistants has a somewhat harsher view of the current situation: "David Wells and Pete Boone are out of touch. Pete doesn't even know what he's looking at with high school kids, and it only plays into Ed's paranoia. He sees them as trying to work against him when he's going after certain kids."

Kent McLeod, who oversees the academic profiles of all the recruits, understands Boone's thought process. "Pete's not worried about us getting the kids in here. He's more about, 'Can they survive in college once they do get here?'"

In truth, Orgeron is working out of a hole he dug for himself with his first recruiting class at Ole Miss. He and his staff had only six weeks to pull together a class, and they did so while Orgeron was spending half that time getting USC ready for its national title game against Oklahoma. The major Internet recruiting sites hailed the group of new Rebels they signed as a top-30 class, quite a coup considering the tight turnaround. SI.com rated Ole Miss among its winners when labeling winners and losers on the recruiting front.

Trouble is, the rushed-together class didn't have much in terms of character checks. There simply wasn't time for an exploration of intangibles, such as whether a kid was coachable, a hard worker, or whether he would require a lot of baby-sitting. "There were so many kids that we took that we really never had a great feel for," says McLeod, one of the few holdovers from the Cutcliffe regime.

The class of 2005 included 27 signees. By the spring of 2006, nine of them were gone, and seven more were floundering academically. (The highest rated signee, nose tackle Jerrell Powe, never qualified academically and spent 2005 at Hargrave Military Academy in Virginia. Orgeron signed Powe again in the winter of 2006, but the Ole Miss administration was still skittish about his prospects too, wondering if the 340-pound lineman's transcript would get past the NCAA's Clearinghouse.) The mere mention of the dismal spring classroom performances of many holdovers from that class still sends Boone's blood pressure up.

Orgeron's second recruiting class, the class of 2006, has proven in its first two semesters to be more diligent academically. Good thing, too, because 2006 was the first year the NCAA was imposing scholarship reductions on low-performing teams based on their Academic Progress Rate (APR).

The NCAA adopted the APR to measure the retention and eligibility of a school's student-athletes. It is a complicated formula, with each student-athlete getting assigned two points per semester: one for staying with the school, another for staying academically eligible. An athlete who flunks out thus would count as 0-for-2. From that, a team's APR is computed by dividing its points earned by its total possible points and is placed on a 1,000-point scale. Eventually, each year's APR will be based on rolling four-year data.

Any team with an APR below 925 loses a scholarship. Penalized teams cannot re-award that scholarship to another player for one year. In 2005, the Rebels' APR was 976, the sixth highest in all of Division 1-A football. A year later, it had dipped to 958.

Boone was worried about the team's slumping APR in 2006, and he also ripped into the football staff in a meeting in late spring for such things as players blowing off study-hall sessions. (The offense that ticked Boone off the most seemed to have been the $900 in parking tickets that JC defensive lineman Hayward Howard amassed in just the three months since his arrival on campus.)

The meeting left Orgeron stewing, but he said he understood there was merit to what Boone and Wells were driving at. "Marginal guys who are marginal players drain the blood out of the program and out of us," he told the staff—*after* the administrators left the war room.

There's an important distinction between the shaky character guy and the shaky student guy, McLeod later explained. The Rebels can live with the kid who will go to all his classes and tutoring sessions and shows up for everything on time and practices hard. It's the player who is lazy and requires baby-sitting or has to have his position coach track him down when he doesn't show up for something who causes so many headaches. In most cases those high-maintenance players aren't starters or even contributors. Instead, they become distractions in the locker room and in position meetings.

But deciphering a prospect's character is never automatic and rarely easy in the recruiting process, and the temptation to roll the dice is always strong if the talent is there. Just a few hours before the meeting with Boone, Orgeron and the Rebels coaches were watching the evaluation tape of an offensive lineman. The guy's fluidity and grace dazzled them. From a strictly athletic standpoint, the kid had everything the NFL covets in an offensive tackle.

But he was also a special education student, with a severe learning disability, and in the staff's limited dealings with the lineman, that was a cautionary flag. "It's not that he's a bad student or doesn't try," Orgeron told one of his coaches. "It's that I don't know if this kid is capable of learning."

Orgeron added that they might be able to get the kid past the NCAA eligibility standards, but what then?

Maybe last year, the Rebels would've fought for the kid. Heck, maybe early that morning they would've. But not now. Orgeron plucked the lineman's nameplate off the top of the recruiting board and flipped it onto the round table.

But who knows? Maybe in a month, he'd feel differently and the nameplate would manage to find its way back to the top of the recruiting board.

After all, recruiting's an art, not a science.

Chapter 6

LORD OF
THE INTERNET

O N APRIL 5, 2006, the first domino in the class of 2007 recruiting season toppled. It wasn't Jimmy Clausen. It was John Brantley, a wiry QB from Ocala with a born-and-bred-to-be-a-Florida Gator pedigree, who announced at a press conference at Ocala's Trinity Catholic High that he was excited to be a ... Texas Longhorn?

Part of Texas' winning sales pitch to Brantley had been a promise that he could redshirt his first season in Austin. His family, especially his father, a former Gator QB, liked that since it would give Brantley a chance to develop physically while also getting a better grasp on the Longhorn offense. The kind of thing that might push one guy away—in this case, a relaxed timetable—can be the exact thing that draws another guy in.

As any top salesman will tell you, it's all in the details.

Texas was now out of the quarterback-recruiting hunt, which meant that 6'7", 240-pound Ryan Mallett from Texarkana, Texas, who had reportedly been given a deadline by the Longhorns, would have to take his cannon arm elsewhere. Of course, the really big news would come two weeks later, when Jimmy Clausen would announce his college choice. But every time a major domino falls, everybody flashes to the others in line for any hint of movement.

Since the recruiting boom collided with the Internet in the late 1990s, press conferences for blue-chip prospects announcing their college choices have taken on a surreal quality. A wide-eyed teenager, clad in his high school football jersey, stands in front of a make-shift podium and, with what passes for a dramatic flourish, reaches into his duffel bag and pulls out a cap emblazoned with the logo of the college he's selected. If the kid is particularly cocky, maybe he extends the moment by trying on caps of the other finalists before finally settling on the lucky one. Or he yanks off his high school jersey to reveal the shirt of his new team.

Clausen's announcement on April 22, however, would take this mini reality-show format to another level, only without any pseudo suspense. Word had gotten out to members of the college football beat that Clausen was picking Notre Dame. The source was a Los Angeles-area PR firm, which sent out a cryptic e-mail saying: "A major college recruiting announcement will be made this coming Saturday ... at the College Football Hall of Fame."

See, the College Football Hall of Fame is in South Bend, Indiana, which happens to be the home of Notre Dame, and the day Clausen was going to announce where he was going to play college football was, not so coincidentally, the day the Fighting Irish were playing their spring football game.

On the big day, Clausen pulled up at the steps of the Hall of Fame in a white stretch Hummer limo accompanied by a 16-member entourage and with an ESPN television crew tracking his every move. About 50 folding chairs had been set up in a second-floor room that soon swelled with five times that many people. Behind the back row was a cadre of TV cameras. All around the room, Hall of Fame staffers were whispering into walkie-talkies. They must have done five sound checks into the microphone at the podium before Clausen, dressed in a charcoal suit, white shirt, and gold tie, entered the room to a half-minute of applause.

Three hundred die-hard Domers hung on (and then cheered) his every word. And Internet recruiting gurus hammered away at their keyboards trying to put the moment into some perspective.

"How big is Jimmy Clausen's commitment to Notre Dame?" Mike Farrell, the lead recruiting writer for Rivals.com, answered his own question: "It's A-Rod to the Yankees, TO to the Cowboys, and Shaq to the Heat. It's the Great One to the LA Kings, Tiger winning the Masters, Hagler-Hearns. In the college football recruiting world, this is as big as it gets."

Maybe even bigger.

The Clausen announcement kicked off a flurry of activity in college football's annual quest for the Holy Grail, *i.e.*, a can't-miss, surefire, quarterback who would guarantee a national title. Two days later, Ryan Mallett announced that he was going to Michigan. The same day, Virginia's Peter Lalich chose the home-state Cavaliers. Three days after that, Mike Paulus picked North Carolina, saying that he felt comfortable with the Tar Heels coaching staff and that it'd be great to be close to his brother Greg, a basketball player at Duke, just a few miles down the road.

Paulus's decision stung Ole Miss. The Rebels had been very high on the kid from Syracuse. Just a day before Paulus's announcement, Dan Werner had been up north trying to show interest.

Twenty-four hours later it was "Okay, who's next on the board?"

Within two weeks of Clausen's announcement, three more top quarterbacks declared their intentions: Aaron Corp and Samson Szakacsy, a pair of lanky Californians whom Ole Miss had also targeted, to USC; and Pat Bostick, the top high school quarterback in Pennsylvania, to Pittsburgh.

Just like that, the pool of elite QB targets had drained considerably. The only names still at the top of the Ole Miss quarterback board by the end of April were long-haired Tampa gunslinger Stephen Garcia and Nick Foles, from Austin.

The responsibility to land one or the other fell squarely on Werner. Alone among coaches on the Rebels staff, he had no other positions to monitor. Just quarterbacks. That's a little like saying a surgeon's responsible for "just brains," but at least Werner didn't have to worry about DBs or OTs. *Just* quarterbacks.

Werner had been text-messaging Garcia and Foles and their fathers weekly touting Ole Miss. At the very least, Werner and Orgeron would like to get them to come to Oxford for the Ole Miss summer camp so each side could get better acquainted with one another.

The Rebels liked Foles, but they *loved* Garcia. Those feelings had crystallized between February and April to the point that Orgeron conceded it might be Garcia or bust. He said he probably wouldn't sign a quarterback just to sign a quarterback. Most programs sign a QB in every class. Ole Miss however, had too many other needs, and because the Rebels' scholarship numbers were still far below the 85-man NCAA limit, Orgeron wasn't sure he wanted to spend one on a player he doubted would play before 2010—if at all.

Orgeron was still trying to build his scholarship numbers back after the attrition that, as with most coaching changes, came in the wake of his arrival in Oxford. While having that extra scholarship room sounds like a good thing, it's not. The NCAA caps the number of scholarship players each program can add at 25 per year, making it impossible to build back a program right away.

In Orgeron's first year at Ole Miss, his offensive coordinator/QB coach at the time sold him on a 6'5", 215-pound "sleeper" from St. Petersburg named Billy Tapp. Unfortunately, Tapp arrived on campus flinging wobbly ducks in summer workouts and was now a long shot ever to compete for the QB job. Meanwhile, the offense floundered, and Orgeron canned the offensive coordinator before the 2005 season even ended.

"I don't wanna just *settle*, Dan," Orgeron said to Werner in April as he flashed a red laser pointer at the bottom of the Rebels quarterback depth chart. "What we absolutely don't need is to get another guy who fits into *this* mode."

But what about the rule of thumb that you always take a quarterback in every recruiting class?

"Let's see how Herrick and Davis do before we take a guy who's only 'above average,'" Orgeron continued. He was referring to Michael Herrick, an undersized incoming freshman from California, and Cliff Davis, a former Alabama recruit set to arrive on campus in the summer after having spent the past three years playing minor league baseball for the Houston Astros.

Orgeron's command decision: "Let's go get Garcia!"

Werner, sitting three seats away, nodded his head, but the expression on his face was anything but assured.

From what the Rebels staff had seen on film, Garcia was more athletic than Foles and had a stronger arm. He was raw, but he had more "upside." Foles's stock had dropped in the winter, even though the kid hadn't played a game since November. It was just that other quarterbacks had emerged to overshadow him, and Garcia especially had surged—in their eyes.

And the word circulating that Steve Spurrier and the South Carolina Gamecocks apparently had also made Garcia a top priority after losing out on Jimmy Clausen? All the better—that just made Orgeron's recruiting juices flow even faster.

"We have *got* to beat the Spurrier mystique," Orgeron said after Werner left the war room. "It's gonna be tough, especially in Tampa. That's Gator country." And still Spurrier country, but he didn't need to add that.

Foles played for Westlake, a ritzy Austin high school with facilities better than at some Division I colleges. As a junior, the 6'5", 240-pound Foles had thrown for over 2,353 yards and had 23 touchdowns with just six interceptions. Foles hadn't taken the ACT yet, but he sported a 4.0 GPA, a huge plus in Werner's mind.

He believed top QBs were usually excellent students; it showed that they were hard workers and that they processed information well. Two of his former star quarterbacks at Miami, Steve Walsh and Ken Dorsey, were examples that Werner mentioned every time the subject came up.

The Rebels were the first school to offer Foles a scholarship and they felt like he was close to committing—although now, the way things had unfolded, that wasn't such a good thing for Ole Miss.

The Rebels had offered Foles in early January as part of Orgeron's "get in the boat" theory. He believed that to get on the radar of a top out-of-state prospect you needed to make some kind of early commitment to him. The strength of that commitment could (and often did) vary as the recruiting season unfolded. In this case, once the quarterback dominoes began to fall, the Rebels determined that Garcia was a viable option, and so they began to "slow play" Foles. This meant not texting him so often or writing him so many letters.

Ideally, the Rebels would have waited until the summer to accept any commitments from recruits. That way, they would have been able to bring Garcia and Foles to their summer camp, the better to evaluate them side by side. But quarterbacks were committing much earlier these days—witness Clausen—and the ensuing domino effect was making the "up close and personal" look all but a thing of the past. The ideal wasn't an option.

That's why Orgeron was driving his staff so hard to get earlier evaluations of prospects. At USC, it was important to be on the front end of the curve. At a rebuilding program like Ole Miss, it was vital to be the one establishing the curve. By April 1, 2004—the last year Orgeron was the Trojans recruiting coordinator—USC had offered 12 players. By April 1, 2006, Orgeron's Rebels had offered more than 10 times that number.

Nick Foles, a blue-eyed blond on the huge side as quarterbacks go, grew up a big Texas Longhorn fan and was disappointed that UT wasn't pursuing him. But he said that Ole Miss was intriguing, and that he was definitely interested. It didn't hurt that Foles's father, Larry, was originally from Pascagoula.

The elder Foles liked Orgeron's confidence and hands-on approach: "Coach O is a recruiting genius. He's going to have a great class. He really knows how to recruit."

The younger Foles admitted he found the recruiting process confusing. He was polite, and didn't seem to have any trace of ego or a sense of entitlement. He was more willing to stump for his buddy, the team kicker, than to talk about himself. He also chose his words carefully and occasionally tried to edit his parents to make sure nothing they said came across as inflammatory.

Foles claimed not to pay much attention to what was being written on the Internet about the recruiting season. "But, thankfully," he said, "Dad does."

Indeed. All spring, the elder Foles was up-to-date about everything written about all the other quarterback prospects, especially those linked to schools looking at his son. He knew all the scuttlebutt about Stephen Garcia and Mike Paulus and Jason Munns, a quarterback from Kennewick, Washington. Larry Foles had read that Arizona State, a school that was also recruiting his son, liked Munns, too. But Larry knew that Munns was more interested in a few schools closer to his home. (He was right: Munns ended up signing with Brigham Young University.)

Nick's father had also read that Garcia was the quarterback the Rebels really wanted.

In the first week of April, while the Rebels were in the middle of spring football, Nick Foles and his parents visited Ole Miss. The younger Foles was "blown away" by the Rebels' indoor facilities. Sitting in on Werner's quarterback meeting was "really cool." Still, the Foles family had a lot to process before Nick would make his decision. To help them do that, they hired a onetime Bristol-Myers exec turned college football coach turned entrepreneur.

Randy Rodgers is a folksy, 50-something-year-old former recruiting coordinator at Texas and Illinois. Since 1998, Rodgers has billed himself as a "Recruiting Consultant/Analyst." And in that role, he has essentially turned the domino effect in recruiting into a cottage industry.

His Austin-based business is called Randy Rodgers Recruiting. The home page of Rodgers' website (randyrodgersrecruiting.com) features a picture of the white-haired Illinois-native wearing a cowboy hat and a shirt designed to look like the Texas state flag. Rodgers works as a consultant to college programs, listing over 50 major universities as clients. He charges between $3,000 and $6,000 to the schools for his evaluation services, which include the names and contact information numbers of potential prospects in the state of Texas. The Rodgers operation is just one of dozens of such services. The twist is that he works the other side of the street as well, selling his expertise about the recruiting game to families like the Foleses.

Rodgers says he's counseling about 70 prospects, adding that two-thirds of them are not major college talents. One of his primary functions, he says, is to explain to the parents how the recruiting process works. "Most people receive form letters and think their kids are being recruited when they really aren't," he says.

For a fee—he doesn't disclose what he charges each family for his service—Rodgers crafts what he calls a "recruiting game plan that is straight, honest feedback of the prospect's ability and where he fits best." Rodgers says he does this by breaking down each school's situation as it relates to the quarterback, ranging from nuances in its depth chart to its offensive style.

"He'll tell you, 'They really don't throw the ball. They're more of an option team,'" said Larry Foles about a program that was sending his son a lot of letters. "Randy said we really want to go to a place with a lot of play-action passes."

Rodgers had tried to size up all of Nick Foles' suitors for his family. In the mix were Ole Miss, Arizona State, UTEP, and Duke, each with its own degree of attractiveness to the Foles family.

Of the four schools, only Ole Miss wasn't a Rodgers client. Rodgers told the family he wasn't sure how to read the Rebels' situation. He knew about Werner because Miami is one of his clients. And he knew that the current Ole Miss QB, junior Brent Schaeffer, "is a different kind of quarterback than Nick." But he quickly added, "Quite frankly, I don't know yet. Ole Miss isn't a client, so I don't pay too much attention to them."

Rodgers did have a strong opinion on what kind of fit would be best for his new client: "Nick isn't a West Coast Offense guy, dinking it out in the flat, spreading it around, and running. That's not him. He fits best in the vertical passing game. I think he fits what Dirk Koetter at ASU likes to do."

Rodgers, who enjoys a solid rep among college coaches, is adamant that he would never steer one of his quarterback clients to one of his institutional clients just because of his relationship with the latter. "I'm completely out of the solicitation business," he says. "And I don't lobby schools on a kid's behalf. I stay out of that."

The irony in all this was that Rodgers might have been helping most the one school that wasn't a client.

By early May, the Stephen Achilles Garcia Derby was primed to overtake the Jimmy Clausen Stretch Hummer Extravaganza for the title of most bizarre recruiting sideshow of the season.

On May 2, a tall, attractive 20-year-old brunette named Autumn Clark walked into the Ole Miss defensive staff room and handed Orgeron the day's recruiting scoop. Clark, a former shooting guard on a state title basketball team coached by Rebels tight ends coach

Hugh Freeze, was one of a half-dozen female student workers in the Ole Miss football office. Part of her job was surfing the Internet daily for stories related to the Rebels' recruiting world. She'd been given a list of websites like OMspirit.com and RebelSports.net to cover. In today's 30-page packet, the story that jumped out at Orgeron concerned Mike Shula's visiting Stephen Garcia's high school on the first day of spring football.

"Alabama head coach Mike Shula and coach Dave Ungerer were at the school today watching me practice," Garcia was quoted as saying by BamaOnLine.com. "It was pretty cool seeing Coach Shula there because he was the first head coach that has been out to see me. It was awesome having a head coach from a university with such a great tradition there watching me in person. I knew he was there, but I wasn't nervous. I just made sure I played my best."

Orgeron's expression didn't change as he glanced at the rest of the packet. In April, Garcia and his father had road-tripped to both Alabama and Ole Miss. The quarterback said he loved both places, but Orgeron had noticed that the younger Garcia seemed to talk up South Carolina and Florida more than Ole Miss in the Web reports. Maybe now Alabama was surging past the Rebels too.

Orgeron knew that as a consequence of the QB domino effect Garcia's stock was rising faster than that of any other quarterback prospect in the country. And the kid certainly appeared to be relishing the stage, which only complicated matters. He was even writing his own blog chronicling the recruiting season on the *Tampa Tribune*'s website. On the first day the blog was posted, it was the 10th-most-visited page on the newspaper's site. Much of the traffic was coming from South Carolina fans eager to sell their coaching savior Steven Orr Spurrier, a.k.a SOS. The user comments ranged from comical to mind-numbing to sad:

POSTED BY BIG JOHN L, LEXINGTON, SC, ON 05/05 AT 06:05 PM:

Can't wait to see you run out of the tunnel in 2007 playing for the best QB coach in the nation. Go Cocks!!! PS: Clemson Sucks!

POSTED BY TOM MEDLOCK, COLUMBIA, SC, ON 05/11 AT 01:00 PM:

Stephen, I submitted a post before mentioning my niece. She graduated from Plant last year and has just finished her freshman year at the College of Charleston. Her dad is Cuban and her mom Irish. She's loads of fun, very smart, and good lookin' to boot! When you enroll at USC, you'll have to meet her. Go Gamecocks!!

POSTED BY TOWNES MAXWELL, OXFORD, MS, ON 05/12 AT 03:46 PM:

Stephen, I think you should look harder at Ole Miss. We now have the offensive coordinator and offensive line coach from Miami. I know we have Brent Schaeffer, but we'll only have him for two years. You could come to Ole Miss and redshirt a year, enjoy the grove and the school that has produced more Miss Americas than any other university. Then you could start for the next four years.

POSTED BY AARON HOLLEY, LEXINGTON, SC, ON 05/12 AT 04:51 PM:

Man, Stephen, we need you in Columbia. We are gonna win championships, and you're gonna help us win them. If you commit to UF, you're just gonna be in the shadow of Tim Tebow your whole career, but if you come

*to South Carolina you have a chance to become
a hero.*

Garcia was amused about the following he was developing online, especially about his budding folk-hero status in South Carolina. Gamecocks fans even chanted his name when he showed up at their spring game. He said that he got a kick out of the crazy comments and added that "fan base will play a pretty big role" in his decision-making process.

His father wanted him to enjoy the recruiting process and not rush it, but he cringed when he heard that his son might be gauging a school's merits based in part on the comments posted on his blog. "I keep telling him, 'Don't you think that might be two or three different students writing in under different names?'" the elder Garcia said. And then he added, "I really hope his decision isn't going to be influenced by that stuff. He'll do his homework about it."

Stephen shrugged when asked about his dad's skepticism about the blog fan base: "I guess it's always a possibility, but I really don't think five guys would take all that time to post all that stuff. At least I hope not."

**POSTED BY JULIAN BARKER, EASLEY, SC, ON 05/17 AT 02:10
PM:**

*Yes congradulations on the offensive player of
the year award. Im sure Plants defense is shaking in their shoes just like every SEC defense
except the Gamecocks of course. I cant wait
until you are apart of the Carolina exteded
family. I have watched all of yours and Tebows
film and he is a great talent, but i know you
could beat him out at Florida, I know you have
the talent, but we need you to be a Gamecock.*

Be part of something big. It will also be a great battle between you and Chris Smelley at Carolina. There is nothing like a top qb battle under the greatest colleage coach ever! I already consider you family, just show the rest of the world whos family your in. Comon to South Carolina Stephen.

For Stephen Garcia and every other uncommitted college hopeful in the South, the most important day in the off-season was Saturday, May 20. That was the date of the Nike camp in Gainesville on the University of Florida campus.

Hundreds of college coaches swarm the sidelines at such camps each May for an up-close look as kids compete against each other in a variety of drills. The camp is a one-day open casting call for sophomore and junior prospects designed to mimic the NFL combine, with an array of timed sprints and shuttle runs, and a test to see how many times they can bench-press 185 pounds. In addition, there are lots of one-on-one drills in which players are tested against each other.

This year, Notre Dame's Charlie Weis, Florida's Urban Meyer, and Louisville's Bobby Petrino were on hand in Gainesville to check out the class of 2007 and perhaps get a jump start on 2008.

Orgeron was there too. He had spent the week evaluating players in Florida before joining Werner in Gainesville. The head coach went to scout the other positions and be noticed by the top players peeking at the sideline.

Werner's assignment was simpler: Focus hard on Garcia, and keep an eye out for other QB possibilities in case the Rebels have to go to Plan B.

Garcia's performance had the coaches on the sideline raving. Coaches could hear his ball whistling by. And he appeared to be having a blast. "He's got an aura," one of the coaches observed later. "I think players will want to play for him. He's got it."

Werner left Gainesville more convinced than ever that it was going to be a battle to land Garcia. But he also came away with the names of three other quarterbacks he liked.

Good thing, because the day Werner arrived in Gainesville for the Nike camp, Nick Foles committed to Arizona State.

The competition for Garcia kicked into high gear, and the object of it was having the time of his life. By the end of May, Garcia was saying in his blog that South Carolina and Florida were distancing themselves from Ole Miss, Alabama, and Louisville.

Garcia's father continued to tell reporters how impressed he was by Ole Miss. He said that he and Stephen really had taken the "side trip" to Oxford after visiting Alabama solely out of respect to Werner, but they came away pleasantly surprised by the Ole Miss campus, the state-of-the-art facilities, and the coaching staff. Plus, he said, it's close to some great hunting, and for him that would be a nice bonus.

"Everybody keeps asking us, 'Why is Stephen listing Ole Miss?'" said Gary Garcia in early June. "But I'll predict right here and now that they are going to win big there. That guy Orgeron just flat knows how to recruit." But that was Gary Garcia talking, not his son, who made it pretty clear in his blog that just because Ole Miss was on his list didn't mean the Rebels were in his dreams.

On the plus side for the Rebels, they didn't have a hair policy. Seems Alabama had made clear to Garcia that he'd have to trim his long hair, and he didn't like the idea one bit. The last time a coach had taken exception to the length of his hair, Garcia said, was when he was thinking of trying out for the high school baseball team: "Coach said you have to cut your hair and shave. I said we can forget about that. I'm just not a very traditional guy."

The Rebels told Garcia he could redshirt his freshman year (2007), which would be Brent Schaeffer's senior season. Then, when the QB job opened up in 2008, he would be ready to battle Michael Herrick for the vacancy. At South Carolina, QB Blake Mitchell would also finish up in 2007, but Spurrier had just signed another blue-chip QB, Chris Smelley. And at Florida, the Gators had just signed Tim Tebow, a local legend who was being hailed as the perfect fit for Urban Meyer's spread-option offense.

The younger Garcia didn't worry about any of that: "Wherever I go, there's going to be competition. I'm not afraid of competition. So, it's like, 'Whatever.'"

At first glance, Robert Marve looked like the flip side of Stephen Garcia.

Both would end their high school career in 2006 as three-year starting quarterbacks, both were from Tampa (Marve went to Plant High School, Garcia to archrival Jefferson High), both were 17 years old, and both were fielding multiple scholarship offers.

But Garcia had been on the scouting radar since his sophomore season, when he led Jefferson to the state title game. In his two seasons as a starter, he had thrown for over 5,100 yards and 50 touchdowns. By the spring of his junior year, he'd received scholarship offers from most of the SEC.

Marve, on the other hand, completed just 44% of his passes in his sophomore season, as his team went 3–7. But Plant improved to 9–3 in 2005 and upset Jefferson, 26–23. Marve threw for over 1800 yards on the year, completing 54%. By the spring of his junior year, the 6'1", 195-pounder was sifting through scholarship offers from Kansas, South Florida, and Buffalo.

Werner liked what he saw from Marve in Gainesville. He liked the zip on his passes, and he liked his nimble footwork. He also liked his speed: Marve ran a more than respectable 4.65 seconds in the

40-yard dash. Garcia opted not to run. Werner came away with a Plan B taking shape in his head.

It helped that Marve had his own personal cheerleader working the sideline. Robert Weiner, Marve's high school coach, spent the day telling anyone who would listen that his player was a keeper. Weiner also handed out detailed information sheets that listed the courses his protégé was taking as well as his stats on the field and in the weight room.

"Robert is the hardest-working player on my team and any team I have ever coached," Weiner exclaimed on the information sheet. "His leadership skills stem from this work ethic and his charisma. Robert has a way of getting along with every player—black/white, rich/poor, good/mediocre, smart/not-so-smart. Robert has a way of reaching everyone. In the off-season, Robert's dedication is unparalleled, including coming to my office every single day to study film and to study our offense. He makes me quiz him on our offense weekly. He wants to know every nuance. He comes from good stock. His dad Eugene was an NFL linebacker for 12 years for the Bills, Chargers, and Bucs."

The genetics-on-his-side angle was a factor in the résumés of two other Plan B possibilities Werner pursued after the Gainesville camp, Joe Weatherford and T.J. Borcky. Weatherford, a spindly 6'2", 165-pound Floridian from Land O'Lakes was the younger brother of Drew Weatherford, the starting QB for the Florida State Seminoles. Borcky, a 6'4", 175-pound five-sport athlete at a small Orlando private school, was coached by his dad Tim, a former Buffalo Bills offensive lineman.

Marve, Borcky, and Weatherford were all later told by Werner that Garcia was Ole Miss' first priority. "It's tough," Weatherford acknowledged, "but I understand where they're coming from. My film isn't that great."

In reality, the differences among them seemed trivial. Did it really matter so much that Marve was 6'1" and not 6'2". Or that Borcky ran a 4.8 not a 4.6? Ask that sort of question in just about any recruiting war room at any college football program and the resounding answer you'll hear is "Yes! You damned right!" Fractions of inches and tenths of seconds are objective data, and that data becomes hard evidence when coaches make projections about how good a 17-year-old will be by the time he turns 21.

You can't see every prospect in game conditions or even on film. And no matter how hard you try, you can't look into the heart and soul of a kid to find out, definitively, if he has character. But you can find out if he's a 4.8 or a 4.6 in the 40.

All three of Ole Miss' Plan B quarterback hopefuls had a hectic summer ahead of them. They would bounce from campus to campus to show their talents in the hope of getting more offers. All the while, they'd be waiting for Stephen Garcia to make his move.

But the Garcia family was in no hurry to pull the trigger.

"My parents' advice has been to get the most information possible," Stephen said, "and not to let anybody else pressure me." On his blog he reported that he, too, was going to have a busy summer itinerary: heading up to Boston to see his older brother graduate from Harvard, competing for his high school in some 7-on-7 tournaments, and taking a family vacation to the Bahamas.

In the delicate push-pull world of college recruiting, the Garcias realized they had the leverage, at least for the time being. But you got the sense that they knew the clock was ticking.

Chapter 7

SPRING
CLEANING

A T 5:27 A.M. on Monday, May 22, 2006, Ed Orgeron's black Hummer was already parked in the first space next to the Ole Miss football offices. Inside the Rebels' war room, Orgeron sat alone at the big table, jotting down notes on a yellow legal pad, prepping for an 8 o'clock recruiting meeting with his staff. He said with a grin that he'd pulled in just five minutes earlier, but gauging from the near-empty 16-ounce coffee cup in front of him, you got the idea he was fudging.

"Man, it is gonna be a *great* day!" Orgeron shouted, leaning way back in his chair and stretching his arms above his head. He seemed way more fired up than any person in his right mind could possibly be this long before dawn on a sticky-hot Mississippi morning. He and his staff had been out on the recruiting trail the past month—officially, the Spring Evaluation Period—and this was the first time everybody would come together as a group to share findings.

Obviously, the thought of sitting down with his people and swapping stories about prospects was making Orgeron downright giddy.

Most head coaches, including Orgeron's predecessor, David Cutcliffe, spend a big chunk of the annual four-week evaluation period working the booster circuit or polishing up their short games, leaving most of the actual scouting to their assistants. Not Orgeron. A makeshift calendar on a dry erase board on the other side of the war room showed that he'd been on the road scouting talent every single day, save for the Sundays the NCAA puts off limits.

In Week 1, he'd started in northern Mississippi and worked his way throughout the state in a five-day trek that covered over 1,800 miles and included 21 stops. Orgeron then went to New Orleans and Miami to conclude a hectic opening week.

By the start of Week 2, on May 1, Orgeron was back in Mississippi, before making stops in Tennessee, Mobile, Atlanta, and Arkansas, then returning to Mississippi to wrap up the week by speaking at a clinic and getting more face time with high school coaches.

Weeks 3 and 4 were spent in Louisiana, Alabama, and Florida.

"It was awesome," he said. "Friggin' *awe*-some!"

Saying that Ed Orgeron loves the chase is like saying that the Mississippi River is wet. The chase for talent feeds his lust for competition. And though he didn't say so right out, you got the feeling he was even more wired about recruiting now, as an underdog, than he had been in the glow of USC's dominance.

A clear, early sign of Orgeron's passion for the chase came in the pre-Pete Carroll era at USC. Back in 2000, after USC fired head coach Paul Hackett, Orgeron continued to recruit even though the Trojans program was leaderless. One day, he showed up a local high school at the same time as UCLA assistant Gary Bernardi. "What the fuck is he doing here?" Bernardi asked a high school coach within earshot of Orgeron. "He doesn't even have a fuckin' job." Orgeron wanted to tear Bernardi's head off, but instead he just gritted his teeth. A few days later, after Carroll was hired as the new Trojans head coach, he named Orgeron his recruiting coordinator and asked him which area he wanted to recruit personally.

"I want Bernardi," Orgeron answered.

Orgeron wanted to recruit the San Fernando and Santa Clarita schools, traditionally UCLA strongholds, just so he could go head-to-head with Bernardi. And from that day on, Bernardi never beat Orgeron for single player. Two years later, UCLA canned Bernardi.

In Orgeron's mind, every visit to scout a prospect was game day against the rest of college football. He believed with all his heart that he could outwork, outcharm, and outsmart the competition. The keys, he always said, were preparation and mind-set—same as with a football game.

"It's all about *com-pe-tin'!*" might as well be tattooed on his chest. During an impromptu 10-minute dissertation after the spring evaluation on how to work the road, Orgeron used the word "compete" eight times. On his final recruiting foray, to a high school football jamboree capped by two two-quarter games, he and receivers coach Matt Lubick outlasted Florida State assistant Kevin Steele and were the last to leave the field. They jawed with high school coaches until 11:30 p.m. "They'd already turned the sprinklers on," Orgeron said proudly.

Orgeron hoped that his passion for recruiting had rubbed off on his staff. He even held a contest for his assistants: Whoever came back with the most visitor passes from high schools won $100. Defensive line coach Ryan Nielsen, the winner of Orgeron's one-day recruiting derby back in the winter, again snagged first place by averaging 10 schools per day.

The Ole Miss road map for the spring evaluation period covered 13 states, with each coach assigned a tightly programmed itinerary. For instance, the 27-year-old Nielsen, a former defensive lineman for Orgeron at USC, was the primary recruiter in California. Aside from his one-day trip with Orgeron to Georgia—mainly to see defensive tackle prospect Ted Laurent—Nielsen spent all his road time in the Golden State. Meanwhile, Werner was in Virginia,

Florida, New York, New Jersey, Ohio, and Pennsylvania, following the combine circuit where he studied quarterbacks.

While on the surface it might seem inefficient to double up as the Rebels did whenever Orgeron accompanied one of his assistants on the road, it was valuable to have that second set of eyes at scrimmages and combines, where so many things are going on at once. Orgeron also felt that since he was going to have the ultimate say in whether Ole Miss chased a prospect, he needed to eyeball as many of them as possible.

Typically, college programs use the monthlong evaluation process to identify the players they want to pursue for their next recruiting class. In the Rebels' case, it was more of an opportunity to get updates on many of the prospects they'd already targeted for the 2007 class. "I felt like when I walked into a school, it was November," Orgeron said with pride, referring to how far ahead of schedule he believed the Rebels were with regard to National Signing Day on February 7, 2007.

Orgeron's plan to get ahead of his competitors this spring included a new twist for the college scouting circuit: camcorders. Orgeron was looking for a way for his whole staff to see and study as a group what each coach saw while on the road. One of his assistants had told him that he'd noticed an assistant using a camera on the road, and Orgeron's interest had been piqued. After checking with the Ole Miss compliance office to make sure filming prospects was permissible under NCAA rules, Orgeron had the Rebels' video coordinator go to the local Wal-Mart and buy eight camcorders.

A few of the assistant coaches weren't too keen on the idea of adding cameraman to their scouting duties, but Orgeron had obviously convinced himself that video evidence would help fine-tune the evaluation process, so they kept their reservations to themselves.

"It was an, uh, interesting idea," Lubick said. "But it worked out great."

Seeing coaches in Ole Miss garb at high school spring football practices with camcorders drew some puzzled looks from rival assistants. "Most coaches thought we were filming to nab cheaters," Orgeron said. "But this was going to give us a big-time advantage."

Orgeron joked that he would be handing out an Oscar to the assistant who came back with the best film: "That is what they give out, right?"

The Rebels' four-person video staff had spent much of the previous two weeks working on the collection of tape, editing out blurry video and random close-ups of elbows, pylons, and pretty women in the stands to get the film ready for this morning meeting.

The camcorder videotape had been added to the plays compiled on tapes from players' junior seasons. In most cases, this close-up footage would give the Rebels an almost 3-D view of their prospects, focusing on position-specific movements.

Sitting proudly behind a stack of cassettes neatly aligned on the table in the war room, Orgeron could hardly contain himself as he grabbed the first tape. It was of Bradley Sowell, a mammoth 6'7", 350-pound offensive lineman from Hernando, Mississippi, about 60 miles north of Oxford. Sowell hadn't been highly touted by the Internet recruiting sites, but the Rebels were intrigued enough by his size and agility to offer him in the winter. Sowell, a lifelong Ole Miss fan, reported to Rebelsports.net in February that it took all of 10 seconds for him to commit.

Like most offensive linemen, Sowell was a long-range project. He probably needed to shed 35 pounds before he'd have a prayer of cracking the Rebels' two-deep depth chart. Offensive tackle is the position with the highest washout rate. Offensive line coach Art Kehoe had just left a Miami program with more than a half-dozen OL misfires still on scholarship.

Orgeron hoped he'd done the right thing in pulling the trigger on the young giant. In the back of his mind, he knew better than to jump early at local kids, especially ones who grew up attending all of the college's home games. You could throw out an early scholarship offer to some blue-chipper 2,000 miles away in California just to "get in the boat." But offering the local guy early meant you were offering to buy the boat.

As Orgeron popped in Sowell's tape, he looked for a second as if he might be feeling a touch of buyer's remorse. He took a gulp from the cup of coffee and pushed Play on the remote, then leaned forward in his chair as the camera framed a close up Hernando's spring drills.

"There he is, *Big Bradley Sowell!*" Orgeron bellowed.

The tape showed Sowell, alongside other offensive linemen on his team, lined up under a four-foot high cage during a blocking drill designed to teach the players to stay low while firing out of their stances toward the defenders. "*Wooooo!*" Orgeron yelped as Sowell uncoiled out of his stance, took a jab step to his left, then busted through the chute.

"That right there is one of the biggest human beings I've ever seen," Orgeron exclaimed to the room, "and just you wait 'til we get him down to 315. *Look at dat big boy!*"

Clips like this, of Sowell displaying not only toughness and tenacity but also uncanny flexibility for a man his size, would get any football coach in America excited. Orgeron, just more so. The clip had come from "Freeze-cam"—that is, it was filmed by tight ends coach Hugh Freeze, who had also brought back footage of other Hernando High spring football drills. Without the camcorder, Orgeron would've had to rely on Freeze's description. Thanks to the video, the whole staff could see what Freeze had seen.

Over the next hour, Orgeron buzzed through a dozen more tapes while polishing off another big coffee, a can of Red Bull, and a 16-ounce, caffeinated, chocolate-covered protein bar.

The videos featured an array of athletic maneuvers: Chris Walker, a blue-chip linebacker from Memphis, gliding around a basketball court, effortlessly flipping his hips and shuffling his feet doing defensive drills, and later showing off a variety of dunks as a little bonus ... Mike Harris, an unheralded, 310-pound offensive lineman from Duarte, California, exhibiting surprising agility as he moved laterally with his hands held behind his back while walling off a teammate in a pass-rush drill ... Gary McClellan, a 6'4", 315-pound D-lineman from Arkadelphia, Arkansas, swiftly running circles around bags lined up on the ground.

Orgeron, devouring every frame, kept up a running commentary. He liked McClellan's quickness. He didn't like how McClellan came out of a three-point stance and leaned into a blocking sled. "He doesn't know how to work hard," Orgeron decided on the spot, adding that McClellan might make a better offensive guard than defensive tackle.

And then: "Man, I *love* this. It's just like having him at camp."

By 7:50, nearly the entire staff was assembled around the big table in the war room. Missing: Dan Werner and Art Kehoe, who had been recruiting in Florida and were now in Memphis for a Rebels booster gathering. Orgeron told his assistants that he'd already had a sneak preview of their camerawork and was ecstatic about what they'd brought back. "Everybody is going to have to start doing this," Orgeron beamed. "How do you like that, Coach Rippon?"

On the other side of the table, Chris Rippon, the Rebels' veteran secondary coach, arched his eyebrows and nodded his head. A more usual response to an Orgeron proclamation would have been "Sounds great, Coach." Rippon wasn't ready to give that to his boss this early.

"I bet every assistant coach in the country is hating your guts right now," Rippon said with a grin.

He was probably right. Rebels assistant AD for internal affairs Maurice Harris had already told Orgeron that University of

Memphis offensive coordinator Randy Fichtner had said the Rebels were "invading kids' privacy."

"You tell Randy Fichtner that we're fixing to invade his back-field with Jerrell Powe," replied Orgeron, referring to the Rebels' blue-chip defensive tackle prospect who was awaiting clearance from the NCAA.

Orgeron wasn't going to admit that pissing off his rivals was a nice bonus of the camcorder experiment, but you could tell it wasn't exactly breaking his heart.

The recruiting meeting formally opened with Orgeron's leading his staff through their board reports. The nameplates of the recruits—categorized as Committed (orange), Offered (blue), and Prospects (green) and aligned in two columns, In-State and Out-of-State—had been updated to reflect current heights, weights, and 40-yard-dash times. Most of that data had come courtesy of the spring combines and camps conducted all over the country by recruiting websites. The Rebels put one asterisk next to info gleaned from a combine and two next to stats that had been gathered during Ole Miss' own summer camp.

Orgeron insisted that the board be frequently updated because the info would help him prioritize how hard the program should be chasing certain recruits. He repeatedly prodded his assistants to chime in with their thoughts, but as always, he did most of the talking. Virtually every prospect on the Ole Miss recruiting list got assessed over the next hour, some in greater detail than others.

First up: In-State Linebackers.

Linebacker hadn't been designated as one of the program's top five priorities in January. Back then those priorities had been, in descending order of greatest need, O-line, D-line, QB, Safety, and CB. But now, since watching the Rebels' spring practice, Orgeron had become worried. Ole Miss had returning All-America middle linebacker Patrick Willis, a senior; strong-side linebacker Garry Pack, a junior, who was struggling academically; and a motley crew of unproven underclassmen who hadn't impressed Orgeron this spring on or off the field. The Rebels were hoping for contributions from Rory Johnson, a speedy junior college weak-side linebacker, and Jonathan Cornell, an incoming freshman from California, whom they saw as a possible heir apparent to Willis at middle linebacker. But in Orgeron's mind, they were still only maybes.

The LB situation had started unraveling in March, when Stevan Ridley of Natchez, Mississippi, who had committed to Ole Miss in January, announced that he'd changed his mind and was going to LSU. Now, two months later, two of the three remaining LB recruits Orgeron had been counting on looked increasingly doubtful.

Chris Strong, a 6'2", 255-pounder from nearby Batesville, Mississippi: Already committed to the Rebels, Strong was the star of a high school juggernaut that hadn't lost a game in three years. Unfortunately, he was also a poor student and no sure thing to being admitted to Ole Miss without first spending a year at a prep school or junior college. "This guy is a bona-damn-fide first-round pick!" Orgeron practically screamed. *"Ho-ly shit!* Big Chris can flat-ass get it! He's raw-dog tough! We can't let him go to no Hargrave Military Academy! We'll go to bat for him!"

Chris Donald, a 6'2", 220-pounder from Tennessee: "He's a great-looking player on film," Orgeron said. "Everybody in the world is after him. It's gonna be us and Tennessee." Back in January, Hugh Freeze, the Rebels recruiter in Tennessee, said he thought he could land Donald, but now word through the grapevine was that Donald was thinking it might be nice to spend his next four autumns in Knoxville. (Donald and a few other players from outside Mississippi were listed on the In-State board because either they had already committed to Ole Miss or they were from the Memphis area, which the Rebels believed was as good as home turf.)

Johnathon Frink, a 6'1", 220-pound honor student at Oxford High: Only Frink still appeared to be a mortal lock to sign with the Rebels. He was best friends with Rebels DB recruit Jamison Hughes, the son of Ole Miss cornerbacks coach Tony Hughes. The Rebels staff was familiar with Frink because Rippon and LB coach David Saunders had sons who played for Oxford High. "I love him, big time," Rippon said. "He knows plays before they happen." "I love his intangibles," Saunders added. "The only thing I wonder about is his pure speed." But Frink hadn't committed yet. What was he waiting for?

A few months before, Orgeron had planned on signing three linebackers in the class of 2007. Now he was thinking about upping it to five.

Orgeron nodded his head at the praise for Frink and pointed to the words "SIZE-SPEED RATIO," which were written in six-inch-high capital letters on the dry erase board beside the In-State Defense list. "Remember, that's our deal," he said. "The Florida guys are going to come in and tell us who they have, and we can be a little choosy."

The Florida guys were Kehoe and Werner, who'd been recruiting in the southern part of the state, and Lubick, who handled the northern half. Florida usually cranked out about 30 major college linebacker prospects a year, and with the ties Kehoe and Werner had brought from their days at Miami, Orgeron was hoping to cash in.

Strong, the highest-profile player among the 16 already committed to the Ole Miss program, had been certified as a learning disabled student, meriting "accommodations" (a term employed by the NCAA) that allowed him to take an untimed ACT exam. That figured to boost Strong's performance, but Orgeron knew he still might need to lean on the Ole Miss administration to get Strong's admission approved.

At many top-25 programs, blue-chip prospects who would normally be rejected because of substandard academic records sometimes (make that often) get admitted after intervention (make that supplication) by the head coach. The more clout a head coach has, the greater the chance of marginal students making it in. For instance, at Notre Dame, a program that used to lament not being able to pursue many of the nation's top prospects because of its stern admissions policy, Charlie Weis was suddenly getting the green light on some players Clemson couldn't take. At USC, such cases were called Presidentials, and Pete Carroll had enough support from the Southern Cal brass to get a handful admitted each year. The formula was simple: The more the Trojans won, the more green lights Carroll earned in dicey admissions cases.

Orgeron, of course, hadn't been at Ole Miss long enough to have a sense of how much leeway he'd get for marginal blue-chippers categorized as at-risk students. But in trying to get Strong into the 2007 freshman class, he knew he'd find out soon enough.

Willis, Orgeron's All-America linebacker, would actually be his best selling point if he had to press the university administration on Strong. Willis had come to Oxford in 2003 from Bruceton, Tennessee (pop: 1,554), labeled an at-risk student. His high school grades were acceptable (if below average), but he scored poorly on his ACT exam, leading Tennessee and a few other SEC schools to pass. But Ole Miss had taken a chance on him, and it paid off big time.

The road to Oxford was all uphill. Willis' mother had abandoned the family when Patrick was 4. Raised with his three younger siblings by an alcoholic father, Willis spent his summer vacations from the time he was 10 chopping cotton for $110 a week. At 16, he and his three siblings were taken from their father—his sister had filed allegations of physical abuse—and were placed in a foster home by the Department of Children's Services.

Given his background, doing homework and studying for tests didn't come easy for Willis. But at Ole Miss, helped by tutors and buoyed by a stable, nurturing structure for the first time in his life, he excelled in the classroom, making the honor roll as a freshman. He was on pace to graduate in three and a half years.

Orgeron would enthusiastically cite Willis as a golden example of what an at-risk student could accomplish, but Chris Strong's high school transcript wasn't as good as Willis's, and the coach knew the kid needed to score well on his ACT exam if he was to have a prayer of suiting up in Ole Miss colors in the fall of 2007.

The worst-case scenario? Strong wouldn't make it past the admissions committee, Donald would go to Tennessee, and Frink wouldn't feel enough love from the Rebels and would opt to go to Stanford.

One day chicken, the next day feathers.

The only solution, obviously, was to find more LB prospects.

"I don't feel good about the linebacker board," Orgeron said, staring at Saunders, his new linebackers coach. "Take care of your position. Come on, now. I ain't bitchin' at you. I'm just talking at you."

Orgeron didn't wait for a response before moving on to the next list: In-State Defensive Linemen.

The top name in the DT column was that of a committed prospect from Atlanta, Ted Laurent, who had been born in Quebec and moved to Georgia when he was in eighth grade. Orgeron loved defensive tackles so the mere act of reading Laurent's name aloud brought a smile to the coach's face. Miami, Auburn, and Georgia loved Laurent too, but Orgeron had been the first to give chase, selling the 6'1", 290-pounder on his gift for molding D-linemen into first-rounders. It also didn't hurt that Laurent's mom spoke little English and Orgeron was able to talk to her in French.

"Guys, Ted is a fantastic player, and he loves us," Orgeron said. "I watched some tape of him this morning and saw him snatch this guy up like a friggin' cobra."

At that point, Orgeron dropped into a weightlifter's squat position, hefting an imaginary barbell across his shoulders. "I saw him squat 585 and go deep," Orgeron said just before springing upright. "*Boom!* It was friggin' great!"

The bad news was that Laurent was also struggling academically and (according to his high school coaches) was mired in a particularly bad semester. Orgeron told Nielsen and Saunders, the assistant in charge of Georgia, that they needed to monitor his progress.

Orgeron wasn't as enthusiastic about the rest of the defensive line prospects. Drake Nevis, a defensive tackle from Louisiana on the In-State board because he'd already committed to the Rebels, figured to spark a battle with LSU once the home-state Tigers offered a scholarship. Orgeron commended assistant Tony Hughes for getting a commitment from Stanley Porter, an end from the delta. The rest of the high school DE prospects, however, were either too light or too slow, by Orgeron's estimation.

The Rebels' most impressive defensive end prospect was Dion Gales, a 6'6", 275-pounder from Mississippi Gulf Coast Community College. Only he was problematic: outstanding athleticism but shaky grades and attitude.

Before Orgeron could move on to the defensive backs, Saunders announced that one defensive end prospect he'd just talked to had gotten himself kicked out of school and would now have to get his GED. Orgeron responded by dropping the player's nameplate onto the shelf below the board, where it joined dozens of other onetime Ole Miss targets who'd fallen from grace.

"We can't bring guys like that in," Orgeron said. "We'll sink the ship."

The In-State Defensive Backs list was even thinner.

Two DBs had committed: Leroy Diggs, so long a shot to qualify academically that he was almost a lock to go to junior college first; and Jamison Hughes, a tall, fast safety—and son of Rebels CB coach Tony Hughes.

The latter connection triggered an awkward moment when someone mentioned the kid's penchant for taking plays off now and then. Others in the room showed discomfort at conducting this discussion in front of the elder Hughes.

"Don't worry about Tony," Orgeron said. "He knows this is a business and that we love his son." Hughes managed a tight smile, whereupon Orgeron whipped through the rest of the nameplates with a few perfunctory comments for each:

"A good athlete. Like him."

"Too small."

"No grades."

"Don't like his hips."

"Soft. Not worth it."

The nameplate of a safety listed at six feet, 180 pounds, with a plodding 4.84 speed elicited a somewhat more studied response.

"Are you shittin' me?" Orgeron snarled, his face scrunched up like he'd just bitten into a lemon. "Let's think about that." He grabbed the nameplate and flipped it into the center of the table. "When there's some crap on this board, just tell me. I want this thing moving."

The names on the board tended to fall into three basic categories: guys Ole Miss loved, guys they might have to take, and guys whose mere presence on the board got Orgeron very, very annoyed.

Then there was Darrius Young.

A shade under 6'1" and weighing in at 208 pounds, Young was a wide receiver from Shannon, Mississippi, about an hour south of

Oxford. An undersized high school power forward who'd played only a little organized football prior to his junior year, Young had made quite a splash, catching 25 passes for 680 yards and seven touchdowns as a junior. But he ran a tortoiselike 4.93 40-yard dash at a scouting combine in Oxford in May, which the Rebels hoped would scare off Alabama and Tennessee and anyone else who earlier had been interested.

Freeze went to watch Young in a spring practice game and called Orgeron an hour before kickoff to report that the kid didn't practice hard at all. Freeze was set to leave and told his boss, who had planned to join him, not to bother. But Orgeron persuaded Freeze to stay and said he would make it there as soon he could. Good thing he did, Freeze told the room: "It took me all of two plays to figure out that this kid is a player."

Orgeron got to the game in time to see Young grab three touchdown passes. "He was awesome," Orgeron said. "He's strong. He can jump. He's got big calves. He's an X guy you can throw the slant to. This is a damn good football player, but we gotta get him to our camp to see if he can run fast enough."

Receiver wasn't a top priority for the Rebels. In fact, they were planning to play four freshmen wideouts in the fall, though none was a big, physical receiver. At most, Orgeron wanted to sign two wideouts.

What the Rebels did need, he said, were "difference-makers." Ole Miss had tweeners: guys who weren't that big or explosive or all that special, at least not enough to make much of a difference.

Orgeron was at USC when the Trojans signed Mike Williams, a 6'5", 230-pound receiver from Tampa whom Miami, Florida, and FSU all wanted as a linebacker or a tight end. At USC, Williams blossomed into a superstar wideout, chewing up defenses in the red zone. Then, when Williams jumped to the NFL, the Trojans found a perfect replacement in 6'5" Dwayne Jarrett from New Jersey. The link between the two Trojans, aside from their height, was that both had amazing ball skills—coachspeak for a receiver's ability to maneuver his body in traffic and make tough catches in crowds.

But Orgeron saw an inherent risk in focusing exclusively on the big-and-tall path: "Everybody starts looking for the next Mike Williams and pretty soon you got yourself a bunch of slow-ass receivers."

The Rebels' top candidates at WR looked to be Roderick Davis, a dynamic 5'11", 185-pound speedster from Memphis, and A.J. Jackson, a 6'5", 225-pound junior college receiver.

Orgeron and his staff loved Davis. *Everybody* loved Davis. But Davis had a one-year-old daughter to whom he wanted to stay close. Fortunately for the Rebs, Oxford is only a little more than an hour from Memphis, while Knoxville and Norman are both six-hour drives. "His coach loves you," Freeze told Orgeron. "I really think we can get him."

Jackson, Brent Schaeffer's go-to guy at College of the Sequoias the previous season, might be the big target the Rebels wanted. Nielsen had been selling Orgeron hard on Jackson the past two weeks. The film he shot at a practice in the spring, which showed Jackson making a couple of acrobatic one-handed catches in one-on-one drills, was helping his cause. "If we want him," Nielsen told Orgeron, "he'll come here. I can get him."

Ideally, Ole Miss wanted junior college players who could get their associate degrees in December so that they could enroll at Ole Miss in January. That way, they could go through spring practice and learn the Rebels' system. Jackson, however, was at best a summer guy, meaning he'd join the team just as the Rebels began fall camp in 2007—assuming, of course, he was actually able to complete his junior college degree. That looked unlikely. He hadn't passed many courses, and most of the ones he had passed would have counted toward only a physical education major, which Ole Miss doesn't offer.

The In-State Offensive Line board was even thinner. Besides Sowell, there was Derek Sherrod, a 6'6", 305-pounder with outstanding grades from Caledonia. But Sherrod had ties to archrival Mississippi State, where his older brother, Dezmond, played tight end. His parents also hadn't forgotten that former Ole Miss coach David Cutcliffe had promised to call them back about Dez but never did. Orgeron felt like he and Hughes had won the Sherrods over, but beating Mississippi State for Sherrod, not to mention Notre Dame and whoever else had jumped into the picture, was going to be a big challenge.

The good news: The Rebels believed they had locked up the two best running backs in the state—Robert Elliott, from Okolona, and Johnny Brown, an all-purpose talent whom they projected as a possible safety.

The bad news: Jeramie Griffin, the state's top fullback and a teammate of Strong's at South Panola, was also committed to Ole Miss, but it looked like he too was going to be an academic casualty.

Orgeron had one hard, fast rule for the Out-of-State board: "Any red flags and we're outta there."

The bar for out-of-staters was higher. Orgeron had already seen enough instances where guys from faraway places got homesick or didn't have as much pride in playing for Ole Miss as the locals did. Maybe they got bored more easily. Certainly they required more work to land. The Ole Miss staff knew all this, and they knew they had to sell Orgeron harder on out-of-staters. His assistants praised their prospects to the sky, as if their own stock was on the line, which you soon realized it was. After all, the more guys an assistant brought into the program, the higher and faster he rose in the master recruiter's pecking order.

Frank Wilson, the Rebels' charismatic, 33-year-old running backs coach, wasted little time pronouncing Joe McKnight, a tailback/receiver/return man/cornerback from New Orleans, "the best player in the country."

Not only that, but Wilson was confident he could land the blue-chipper.

"Kent, you can laugh all you want," Wilson said, looking straight at his pal Kent McLeod, the boyish-looking coordinator of football operations, who had been teasing Wilson for months about having no real shot at McKnight. "But I think we're in the boat with him."

Orgeron: "You really think so, huh?"

Wilson: "Yes."

Orgeron: "Son, you're one helluva recruiter if you bring him in."

It revved Orgeron up to hear his assistants talk ballsy, because that was *exactly* what he was looking for in a recruiter. Orgeron and Wilson—one, a Cajun cult hero for his improbable coaching rise; the other, until recently the youngest director of athletics in the New Orleans public school system history—had proven to be a potent one-two recruiting punch in Louisiana. Together they'd signed 10 Louisiana players in two years.

Orgeron had learned about Wilson while recruiting for USC in Louisiana. J.T. Curtis, the legendary Louisiana high school coach at John Curtis Christian School in River Ridge (his latest star: Joe McKnight), had told Orgeron about this hot, young coach across the river in New Orleans whom he had to meet. When Orgeron heard the name Frank Wilson, he asked if that might be the same Frank Wilson who was a running back at Nicholls State, where he was a coach during the 1993 season.

It was.

After Orgeron interviewed for the Ole Miss job, Wilson was one of his first calls. By then, Wilson was just 16 months into his job in New Orleans. Orgeron had already reconnected with his former running back and told him he was going to hire him someday. A couple of days later, Orgeron called Wilson again to see if he was ready to make the move with him to Mississippi.

Wilson balked: "Man, Dennis Erickson is getting that job. It's all over ESPN."

"Lemme tell you something, you sonofabitch!" Orgeron yelled back into the phone. "It's fourth down, and this is Florida we're playing, and you better believe. So you gonna quit on me now?"

"No, sir," Wilson answered.

The next day, they were both heading to Oxford.

Coaches and players all over Louisiana loved Wilson. ("The mamas really love Frank too," Orgeron says.) Wilson was one of their own, a natural-born charmer who seemed to know everyone. Eric Held, a former teammate of Wilson's at Nicholls State who coaches at Baton Rouge's Redemptorist High, said that the sky was the limit for his old friend: "I really think Frank Wilson could be the mayor of New Orleans someday. He has such a magnetic personality. People are drawn to him."

As a wunderkind coach—he'd been named head coach at the age of 27—Wilson had transformed hardscrabble O. Perry Walker High's football program in New Orleans into one of the state's great success stories. He instituted mandatory study halls and pre-school breakfasts. Players had to wear dress shirts and ties every day. They had to sit in the front row of the classroom. Wilson arranged for an academic counselor, who got paid through a grant funded by the NFL's Play It Smart program. In one year, the team's GPA jumped from 1.5 to 2.5. The team also gave John Curtis Christian its first district loss in 25 years. By his third season, Wilson had the school playing in the state title game.

"Frank Wilson made all those kids believe that they could excel in football, the classroom, and as leaders," Louisiana state senator Francis Heitmeier said after Wilson's departure for Oxford. "It was just remarkable what he did."

In the fall of 2003, Wilson got a call from the Orleans Parish superintendent, who said that he loved Wilson's initiative and creativity. He asked if Wilson would consider becoming the athletic director for all of the city's schools. At 29, Wilson was ready for another challenge. Most of the high school coaches he would preside over, however, weren't ready for him.

"They were appalled," Wilson says. "I was overseeing people with 30 years of experience. I hadn't won 300 games or anything. They thought I was too young and came from the wrong place. My certification was in science, not PE."

Wilson's ability to find solutions quickly won over many of his critics. To help boost coaching quality, he solicited help from local college coaches and set up mandatory workshops where high school coaches could learn the finer points of swimming, tennis, and track—sports in which, in too many instances, they served at just slightly above the level of caretaker.

Wilson also persuaded the NFL to support a program to bring middle school football back to New Orleans, which had been cut 10 years earlier for budgetary reasons. The young AD believed that junior high was a point when many kids got involved in crime because at 3 p.m., when school let out, they had nothing to do. The problem was to find $500,000 for equipment. The NFL deal that Wilson forged enabled the New Orleans kids to use equipment furnished by Riddell, an NFL partner.

"Frank has always been so resourceful and persistent," says Tarence Davis, Wilson's former assistant AD. "People laughed at him, always told him, 'Slow down, you can't do that here.' But Frank always found a way."

Wilson discovered that he missed coaching, so when Orgeron contacted him about a job, he jumped at the opportunity.

With Wilson leading the recruiting charge, the Rebels were zeroing in on a half-dozen Louisiana kids for the 2007 class. For each of them, the Rebels realized, they'd have to beat out LSU, something they'd yet to do for a local kid the Tigers really wanted. The year before, Wilson thought he had a decent shot at snagging Keiland Williams, an all-everything tailback from Lafayette. But as much as Williams liked Orgeron and Wilson—he kept calling them throughout the wooing process—he ending up picking LSU over USC and Ole Miss.

No school in the country has a more powerful pull over kids from its own backyard than LSU. Some rival assistants say it's because there are many overzealous Tigers fans around the state who aren't shy about slipping cash to a player or befriending one of the kid's relatives and offering up a better job or car. Wilson refused to point fingers other than to say that the local community has such a passion for LSU that they make it "really, really hard" for a local kid to leave. Landing a ballyhooed recruit like Joe McKnight would certify Wilson as one of the top recruiters in the country.

And, of course, it would have every single LSU fan in the Bayou state accusing the Rebels of every single nefarious, back-room shenanigan under the southern sun.

Signing a tailback in the class of 2007 would be something of a luxury, since starter BenJarvus Green-Ellis would be a junior in the fall. Plus Orgeron thought he had the ideal replacement arriving in the summer in 235-pound Cordera Eason, a blue-chipper from the previous year's recruiting class.

Nonetheless, Ole Miss planned to sign at least one tailback this year, most likely Robert Elliott, a smooth, 195-pound, small-school star from the Tupelo area. Elliott had committed to Ole Miss in January but told an Internet site that Florida State had just offered him. Among the national names, only McKnight and Malcolm Smith from the LA area were paying the Rebels much attention.

The top name on the Rebels offensive line group was that of T-Bob

Hebert, the son of former New Orleans Saints QB Bobby Hebert, Orgeron's close childhood friend.

T-Bob's given name is Bobby Joseph Hebert III. The T stands for *petite*, a Cajun reference to the third generation. T-Bob wasn't huge as far as offensive line prospects go; only 6'2", 250. But after watching him at summer camp in 2005, Orgeron thought he would make a great center. For starters, he was tough. But more important, unlike most high school centers and even some college ones, he had the coordination and agility to snap and step—that is, he could make the snap and get out to the linebacker before he could start tracking the ballcarrier.

Oh, and one more thing—Orgeron thought he could land him: "T-Bob is really fired up about us."

Maybe so, but he was also getting recruited aggressively by LSU, which is where his grandfather went to college. Earlier in the morning, before his staff arrived, Orgeron said he expected a big battle for Hebert: "If we win this fall, he'll come. But if we don't win, I don't know about ol' T-Bob."

Reeling in Hebert would be one of several personal battles Orgeron would fight with LSU. Will Blackwell, a 295-pound defensive tackle from West Monroe, was another blue-chipper with family ties to Orgeron. Blackwell's grandfather, Jerry Arledge, had been Orgeron's college coach at Northwestern State. Arledge had told Orgeron he'd love to send his boy to Ole Miss, but this was another T-Bob deal: Both men know that if the Rebels didn't have a winning season, Blackwell would probably opt to become an LSU Tiger.

For now, Orgeron couldn't get bogged down with what if's.

In the five months since Orgeron had begun shaping his recruiting board for the class of 2007, there'd been a lot of movement. Among the nameplates dropped into the graveyard shelf beneath the board, a.k.a Guppyland: QB Mike Paulus (committed to North Carolina), LB Kevin Rouse (verbally committed to Iowa but eventually signed with Wisconsin), and S Harrison Smith, who had whittled his options down to Notre Dame and Tennessee.

Also gone was Karlin Brown, the diminutive linebacker from Tallahassee. During their last week on the road, Orgeron and Lubick eyeballed the 5'7" Brown in person and decided not to pursue him. Instead, the Rebels would end up facing Brown, who promptly committed to Mississippi State.

After devoting another 15 minutes to defensive players, Orgeron wrapped up the board report. There were other items on his yellow pad that he wanted to discuss, half of them punctuated with exclamation points. He wanted the names of all the high school sophomores (class of 2008) whom the staff had seen and liked. He wanted a detailed list of all the prospects who were coming to Oxford in June for the Rebels' football camp, and a list of their coaches. He wanted updates on all of the Rebels' incoming freshmen and academic reports on all the players already in the program. He also reminded his staff that on Wednesday they would have to be ready for the annual NCAA recruiting test—a 40-question multiple choice exam that coaches all over the country are required to pass.

"We gotta hustle," he said. "We can't fuck around now. Budget your time wisely. Only 10 days 'til summer camp starts."

The meeting ended at 11:50 a.m., but the recruiting work for the day wasn't done. For the next two weeks, seven hours of each nine-hour workday would be devoted to studying game tapes of the Memphis Tigers, the Rebels' first opponent that fall. But today, Orgeron's mandated 30 minutes of phone calls to high school coaches at 1:30 would be followed by a three-hour film session featuring the key recruits. Next there would be dinnertime text messages to recruits that would, with luck, elicit callbacks.

At 1:05 p.m., while Orgeron roamed the halls past each of his assistants' offices as they chatted up high school coaches over the phone, McLeod was back inside the war room, neatly organizing a stack of tapes by position for the next wave of evaluations.

McLeod smiled as he headed back to the film room to get another handful of tapes. A shaggy-haired six-footer weighing barely 150 pounds, McLeod may be the most physically unassuming member of any big-time football program in the country. He grew up a couple of hours south of Oxford in Ackerman (pop.: 1,700) and had never played much organized football, not because of any shortage of interest in the game, but because of a definite shortage of heft. Instead, he went to a junior college to play golf before transferring to Ole Miss, in 1996. "I thought I wanted to be an actuary," he says, "but then I met a woman who was an actuary, and she called it the most boring profession a person can have."

Luckily for him, McLeod had seen an ad for a part-time job in the Ole Miss athletic department, and he jumped at it. He became a $5.15-an-hour gofer under then-head coach Tommy Tuberville as the Rebels were trying to bounce back from probation. Over the years, McLeod had gone from stamping envelopes and sending out questionnaires to coordinating the academic evaluations of every prospect, which means deciphering the transcripts, determining what courses certain prospects needed to get into Ole Miss, and identifying prospects who had no shot.

McLeod was also responsible for putting together and organizing eval tapes. Although technically, by NCAA rules, he wasn't allowed to evaluate prospects, nothing pleased him more while cutting up game tape of a targeted player than spotting a guy on an opposing team who might just be an SEC talent as well. McLeod would then pull together all the information he could find and begin making an eval tape of the new find.

Over the course of the year, McLeod created about 300 of the 1,300 eval tapes in the Rebels' film library. The coaching staff generally agreed that about 50% of the players represented in the library were prospects, and that maybe 25% were surefire SEC-caliber players.

Eval tapes are different from highlight tapes, which are created by players or their high school coaches. Eval tapes are created by teams and are designed to give a more realistic picture of what kind of talent a prospect has. The process can be time-consuming—and mind-numbing: Get a game tape and the jersey numbers of a couple of supposed prospects, then watch and log whatever plays catch your eye. If you're looking at a linebacker, you can fast-forward through his team's offensive plays. Ditto if you're looking at a quarterback and the other team has the ball.

But often you'll be watching a couple of guys, rewinding tape to mark plays to be copied, studying carefully, and taking notes, all of which makes for long afternoons stuck in front of a monitor watching a high school football game whose outcome you don't care about.

It should come as no shock to learn that Orgeron believed, with every fiber of his being, that you can never, *never* watch too much game tape.

"Coach O always says, 'Don't make everybody look great,' " McLeod explained. It's not that Orgeron wanted to see an endless loop of some prospect failing, but if there was some flaw that the staff should know about, McLeod knew he wasn't to ignore it. Of course, sometimes that thoroughness ruffled Rebels assistants who were hoping to sell Orgeron on a recruit, not give him second thoughts. ("Me and Matt Lubick used to get into arguments all the time about that," McLeod admitted.)

McLeod's obvious knack for creating statistical breakdowns of recruiting trends and finding talent hotspots—in essence, a *Moneyball* approach in the gridiron world—quickly endeared him to Orgeron and earned him the nickname Kipe. That's Orgeron shorthand for Kiper, as in Mel Kiper Jr.

This particular week, McLeod's desktop was cluttered with lists and detailed charts and colored-coded maps that illustrated how, for instance, in the 2005 NFL draft, 47 draftees came from within a six-hour radius of Oxford. And of the 25 drafted players who were from Texas, 14 had played college ball out of state. And that only Louisiana produced more NFL players per capita than Mississippi.

What's it all add up to? In this last case, Don't be afraid to mess with Texas players, but never, ever forget to protect your own backyard.

McLeod coordinated all of the half-dozen recruiting services to which the Rebels subscribed. The film budget had been $20,000 when McLeod went to work in the football office back in 1997. In 2006 it was $30,000. McLeod would have liked it to be $40,000: "My whole thing is buy as many tapes as possible. The worst thing is if some coach says, 'Did you see so-and-so?' And my answer is 'Um, no.' That's not a good thing."

By National Signing Day 2006, the Ole Miss staff had already broken down 200 eval tapes for the 2007 class. Within another three months, the 2007 library would swell to 800 tapes of high school juniors, plus another 50 sophomore tapes. Since the 2007 recruiting season had cranked into high gear, McLeod and assistant athletic director Barney Farrar, a 20-year coaching veteran and the Rebels' film coordinator, had readied miles of video for review. They pared the incoming footage on each prospect down to a couple of minutes of action, then passed the file on to the assistant coach in charge of that area or position. After an initial screening—usually within 72 hours—the tapes would be passed on to Orgeron.

A typical workday for the head coach began at 6 a.m., alone in the staff room, an ever-present tall cup of black coffee by his side, his eyes glued to the video monitor, hoping to strike gold.

At the next recruiting meeting, which began at 10 sharp on Wednesday morning, May 24, more than half of the three dozen tapes the Rebels staff screened were of players Ole Miss had already offered. The rest was new tape of players who had just found their way onto the Ole Miss radar.

Nielsen, the Rebels' California recruiter, had just screened the tape of Chris Daniels, an unheralded tailback from the San Diego area whose name hadn't popped up on the Internet recruiting sites. Daniels' highlight tape had just appeared in McLeod's office a few weeks back. Two nights before, after watching Daniels make three zigzagging touchdown runs in the first three plays on the tape, Nielsen dialed up the kid's coach.

After two minutes of the Daniels tape, Orgeron and his staff were intrigued, especially by Daniels' acceleration out of cuts. The main concern was that he appeared to be small, which suggested he might make a better cornerback. It was an essentially positive assessment, but Nielsen looked dejected, as if he'd just been told that his own son wasn't good enough.

Orgeron had elevated the 27-year-old Nielsen to D-line coach after he fired Joe Cullen, who had been charged with public drunkenness four months after Orgeron's hiring. Nielsen had what some of the staff called "the double whammy": He was coaching not only for the man who had coached him in college (USC), but he was also coaching the specific position that the head coach used to oversee as an assistant.

More than any member of the Rebels staff, the intense Californian seemed driven to secure Orgeron's approval, both on the practice field and on the recruiting trail. Two years in, Orgeron was pleased by the strides his youngest full-time coach had made, especially on Signing Day 2006 when Nielsen landed four-star linebacker Jonathan Cornell from Southern California.

Daniels, Nielsen said, wanted to move closer to his dad, who lived in Florida. He added that Daniels's high school coach had told him that the kid was six feet, 175 pounds and that he had run a 10.83 in the 100m.

The merits of that 10.83 sparked the latest installment of what had become an almost daily debate: What is fast? More precisely, what is the best gauge of *football* speed?

Orgeron refused to buy reports of dazzling 40-yard times unless someone on his staff had been holding the stopwatch. He had seen too many instances where a 4.5 kid turned out to be a 4.9. Track times had more legitimacy, he said, although the difference between 100 meters and 40 yards produced its own set of questions. Shorter distances tend to favor guys with shorter legs; long striders who logged good times in the 100m might not have the kind of speed that produced the quick bursts required in football.

Orgeron's definition of fast was a 10.6 in the 100m. Wilson, McLeod, and Lubick believed that anything under 10.9 was moving. Perspective was a factor: Orgeron's standard was undoubtedly colored by what he'd witnessed at Miami and USC. Reggie Bush ran a 10.42 in 2002, the fastest high school time in California that year. The others noted that if Reggie Bush was your standard for fast, then just about every other football player on the planet was going to look slow.

The speed debate had turned into a running joke, with Lubick often taking the brunt of it for his habit of claiming that player he liked had won some obscure track title in Florida, his recruiting turf.

This morning, as the tape began to roll, Lubick introduced a receiver from Orlando named Marquis Rolle: "He's a legit 6'2". He won the Orlando City 100."

"What's he run the steeplechase in?" Kehoe asked.

The video showed close-ups of Rolle playing catch. He struggled to catch passes cleanly, bobbling a few easy catches. "Look at the way he attacks the ball," Orgeron said with a hint of disgust.

Rolle eventually did impress the Rebels staff by hauling in a long ball and sprinting down the right sideline, outracing four defenders. The film showed him to be a two-stepper, meaning he had the speed to cover a five-yard stretch in just two strides. Football coaches love two-steppers.

Still, judging by the mood of the room—or, more specifically, Orgeron's mood—it didn't seem to be a good day for viewing players. The next four up, two of whom the Rebels had already offered, all got picked apart. A four-star DL was suddenly deemed too stiff, while a highly touted DB was found to not break on the ball fast enough.

"You sure you wanna show your linebacker today, Ryan?" Orgeron asked Nielsen.

Before his colleague could answer, Wilson stood up, walked around the table, grabbed Joe McKnight's tape, and popped it in. Time to bring some sunshine to this parade.

"He's a fat 10.8," Wilson said as McKnight dazzled one and all with his speed, cuts, bursts, and all-around good looks.

"What exactly does that mean?" Kehoe asked.

"It means he's run an electronically timed 10.8," Wilson said before he turned to face Orgeron. "Now, you gonna try and tell me Joe McKnight isn't fast?"

On the screen, McKnight was gliding around the field as if he were on ice skates, with everyone else slogging around in overshoes. None of the defenders could get a hand on him. The film showed McKnight running back punts, kickoffs, and interceptions, as well as snagging deep passes. Each highlight elicited a *"God-damn!"* or a *"Fuuuuck!"* or some other technical coaching term from around the table. When the tape ended, you almost expected the Rebels coaches to applaud.

Orgeron: "You saying he's better than … "

He named two highly regarded tailbacks from Florida, but Wilson brushed them aside: "Who is better than this kid? *Who*? Now, go ahead and write it on the board, Kent! Go on, *write it!*"

McLeod, shaking his head and smiling, got up from his seat, grabbed a blue marker, and walked up to the dry erase board.

There, next to the Out-of-State Running Backs list, he scrawled five words and a date that could change the perception, and perhaps the entire direction, of Ole Miss football:

"Frank Wilson guarantees Joe McKnight—4/24/2006."

Chapter 8

SUMMER
CAMP

A LINE OF BURLY teenage boys, most with parents and/or high school coaches in tow, snaked around the perimeter of the cavernous Ole Miss Indoor Practice Facility. It was 8:05 a.m. on the first Friday in June, and already more than 200 hopeful linemen were assembled for the Rebels' O-line/D-line football camp. Some of the day campers had piled into minivans and SUVs and ridden seven hours or more just for the chance to compete for attention from the Ole Miss coaching staff.

The mood at the Rebels' first camp of five this summer was upbeat. Coaches and Ole Miss support people swarmed through the 150,000-square-foot complex like campaigning politicians, shaking hands and slapping backs. This was the first of several times over the next few weeks that the Rebels would get to show off what they had to offer while taking a hard, firsthand look at what several hundred high schoolers had to offer in return.

Just an hour earlier, Orgeron had delivered some disappointing news to his coaches assembled inside the war room: the university's compliance director had informed him that the Rebels could not videotape any of their summer camps.

The previous year, the tapes they'd made at the camps had been a huge help in the evaluation process. Orgeron had lobbied the Rebels' compliance officer, David Wells, to do it again but Wells insisted that the SEC office wasn't allowing it this year.

Another bit of bad news, at least from Orgeron's perspective: Because thunderstorms were forecast for the day, today's camp would have to be conducted indoors in the climate-controlled IPF. Although some of his assistant coaches didn't seem too broken up, he'd have liked to see how these big linemen responded to the sweltering Mississippi heat.

As the campers were ushered into the complex, they were greeted by a dozen smiling co-eds who handled the various registration duties of the camp. Several of the kids appeared so awestruck by the gorgeous young women that they fumbled the spelling of their own names. ("So, wait, that's Brandon with three n's and two d's?" one of the registrars asked a camper, who then sheepishly apologized three times after correcting her.)

After getting processed and fitted with a Rebels camp T-shirt, the players were quickly shuttled in groups of 30 from station to station inside the massive turf-covered structure. Each camper got ID'ed with a sticker on his shirt that showed his last name. Then their height and weight were measured and recorded. Now they were ready for three key tests.

TEST NO. 1: VERTICAL JUMP. The player stands on a slightly raised platform on what looks like a black doormat and is told to jump straight up. The device is rigged to a computer that calculates the height of the jump based on the time the player's feet are off the mat. Aaron Ausmus, the Ole Miss strength coach, and two assistant coaches watch to make sure no one bends his knees at the top of his jump to extend airtime. (Orgeron also used high school and junior college coaches from around the South to help work at the camp.)

TEST NO. 2: 40-YARD DASH. Four coaches man the starting line. Another six Ole Miss staffers wait at the finish line with stopwatches.

Every camper runs two sprints. Each camper inside the IPF knows these will be the most important 10 seconds of his day. "Run a great 40 and win a scholarship," or so everybody believes.

The need, the *necessity* to run faster than he's ever run before was imprinted on every young face in the house. One baby-faced camper began to hyperventilate as he counted down the bodies lined up in front of him waiting to run.

TEST NO. 3: SHUTTLE RUN. The shuttle is designed to gauge change of direction and quickness, two key football traits harder to measure than pure speed. It begins with a player standing in a half-crouch with his knees flexed in the middle of a 10-yard stretch of turf. Cued by a whistle, he scrambles first to his left and slaps his hand on the yard line, then back to the other side to slap the other line before hustling back to his starting point. Most of the campers end up sliding trying to make their first touch. Or they become too discombobulated to handle the second shift and wipe out in turn two. By the third wave of players, there has been so much skidding on the turf that a bubble has formed on the ground. More so than any other drill at the camp, the shuttle run is lineman unfriendly.

Orgeron, striding around like a lion on the prowl, didn't seem thrilled with what he was witnessing. He spied a couple of under-sized players struggling to finish the 40-yard sprint and winced. "Our program is all about *competin'*," he hollered in a voice that could be heard through the IPF. "You ran that first 40, now that second 40 better be better! Come on! Compete! *Com-pete!*"

Many of the campers looked terrified of all of the coaches—and especially of Orgeron—from the moment they set foot on the practice surface. A few sneaked peaks at him as he walked by, but most just stared wide-eyed at the ground.

They came to this camp to be noticed, but now they weren't sure they wanted to be noticed by *him*.

A mammoth kid with a small Afro and extremely long arms bouncing around near the start line at the 40 caught Oregon's attention. The coach sized him up for a minute and then hunkered down like an outfielder poised for the next pitch, his hands on his knees and his eyes locked on the big lineman.

"Let's go, big Johnson!" Orgeron yelled. "C'mon, big guy! C'mon, *ba-by!*"

The big guy was 6'4", 315-pound Rishaw Johnson, an unheralded prospect from Hammond, Louisiana. Johnson played his sophomore season at Frank Wilson's alma mater, St. Augustine High School in New Orleans, but he and his family were displaced after Hurricane Katrina destroyed their home. After bouncing to two high schools, he landed at Hammond, by which time most college programs had forgotten about him. The Rebels did too—at least until McLeod spotted Johnson's name in one of the combine reports he gets e-mailed to his computer from the Internet recruiting sites.

Johnson arrived in Oxford after a four-hour drive, with Frederick Jenkins, his stepfather, behind the wheel all the way, as he always was when the two went anywhere together. Unremarkable, until you consider the fact that Jenkins had lost both of his legs while saving Rishaw's life when the boy was seven years old.

Back in March 1996, Jenkins was standing with Rishaw and his 7-year-old foster brother near his 18-wheeler on the westbound shoulder of the Chef Menteur Highway by their home in New Orleans. A 6'9" former basketball player at Dillard University in New Orleans, Jenkins had gone out to check his load in the truck. Suddenly he heard a loud noise. He looked up and saw a car speeding toward them, swerving all over the road. Jenkins leaped toward his stepson, knocking him out of the way. Jenkins then turned and scooped up his foster son, but the car was coming too fast. It smashed into Jenkins and the boy. The impact sent Jenkins hurtling into the grass away from the shoulder. The first thing he heard was Rishaw crying out.

"My leg, Daddy! My leg!"

"Don't worry, son," Jenkins yelled from flat on his back. "Everything's gonna be alright. God's with us."

Jenkins called for help. Almost immediately, he heard a man's voice: "Don't look! Don't look!" Both Jenkins and Rishaw instinctively turned toward the voice. They couldn't help it. The voice was coming from a neighbor, who was standing in horror near the body of Rishaw's foster brother.

The little boy had been cut in half.

That sight was the last thing Jenkins remembered before he passed out—and one that Rishaw knows he will remember as long as he lives.

Jenkins had to have both his legs amputated. Rishaw, sent tumbling down a hill by his stepfather's lifesaving move, suffered a broken femur and spent the next three months in a wheelchair. Police subsequently determined that the driver of the car was drunk.

The accident sent Johnson into shock. "It took a long time for me to get over that," Johnson says now. "I didn't talk for three months." And when he did begin to speak a few words, they scared his mother to her core, because he'd say, over and over, that he wanted to go where his foster brother went.

"That really, really troubled me," his mother, Gaynell Jenkins, remembers with a shudder. For five months, Rishaw was in therapy, but he never opened up. According to his mother, it took more than two years before Rishaw got back to anything like normal. Even 10 years later, she is still pained by the knowledge that her little boy, now an imposing 300-pound man, suffers when asked to recall that tragedy or has nightmares about that March day in 1996.

At the time of the June camp, none of the Rebels staff knew anything of what Jenkins had endured. They only knew that he had a massive frame, quick feet, and a soft smile. Not to mention a big cheerleader on the sidelines in a wheelchair who rooted Rishaw on by screaming "Pick it up! Pick it up! Hustle! Hustle!" as his son tried to outwork everyone inside the IPF.

Rishaw wasted little time making the old man proud or getting Orgeron's attention. His 27-inch vertical leap was the second-best among linemen, and the kid who beat him with a 29-inch jump weighed almost 100 pounds less. Johnson's 5.25 40-yard dash time was by far the best of any 300-pounder at the camp. His 5.00 shuttle time also was tops among the camp's heavyweights.

The line drills wouldn't begin for another 45 minutes, at 9:30, but by then Orgeron and the Rebels were pretty sure they'd found themselves a lineman.

A few moments later, after Orgeron had moved away from the 40-yard dash setup, a stocky camper with a crew cut and a pencil-thin beard barreled his way toward the finish line with a possessed look. The kid ended the sprint in a tumbling heap, scraping his knees and palms on the track surface.

Say hello to Tyler McDermott, a 6'1", 269-pound center from Lake Worth, Florida, who popped up grinning, much to the delight of the coaches standing by. McDermott was even happier when he learned that he had shaved .02 seconds off his first 40 time of 5.19.

The 5.17 wouldn't qualify McDermott for his high school relay team, but it was respectable for an offensive lineman. More than half the 40-yard times by interior linemen at the camp were over 5.50. Only one camper, a 5'9", 201-pound guard, broke the 4.7 mark.

At 9:15 a.m., with the campers sitting around him on the practice surface, Orgeron delivered his introduction speech. Many of the kids were already drenched in sweat and looked exhausted.

"Everyone give me your eyes," he began, his voice booming throughout the IPF. "This is *not* a recruiting camp. You will be coached here just like an Ole Miss Rebel. Nobody talks back to a coach, and nobody's bending over or taking a knee on our fields. We do *not* show any signs of discomfort here. Got that?"

Ask any coach in college football: summer camp is the best mechanism that college programs have for finding players. Videotape is essential, but most coaches will tell you there's nothing that beats direct observation. Especially direct, *hands-on* observation.

Over the course of the next six hours the Ole Miss staff was able to see exactly what each kid had—athletically, intellectually, and emotionally. Just as college camps were doing all across the country, Orgeron and his staff got to put the campers through their personal coaching drills. They got to test them and see how they responded to hard coaching.

Orgeron had learned just how valuable summer camp could be in his USC days. In 2004, the Trojans signed Jeff Byers, a thick-necked blond from Colorado whom all the recruiting sites were touting as the best center prospect to come along in the last 10 years. USC never got Byers in camp, but still signed him only to learn after he arrived that his reputation had been built on mauling mediocre high school competition. In reality he had insufficient "pop" to blast a Division I noseguard away at the point of attack. Plagued by injuries, Byers had been unable to get off the Trojans bench.

The man who beat him out, Ryan Kalil, represented the flip side. Kalil grew up in Anaheim, an hour south of USC's campus. He showed up at one of the USC camps as a 6'1", 250-pound tackle without much fanfare. But within the first 20 minutes of drills, the Trojans staff learned two important things about Kalil: He was smart, and he was tough.

"We beat the shit out of him, and he kept coming back looking for more," recalled Orgeron. "His nose was sideways, and he goes 'What else you got for me?' God, we loved that kid."

The Trojans projected Kalil as a center, so they invited him back to their camp the following week and put him up against the kid touted as the top high school noseguard prospect in America. Kalil neutralized the guy and handled everyone else they put up against him as well. USC turned out to be Kalil's only scholarship offer. Based on his observation of Kalil's performance in the two Trojans camps, Orgeron said he wasn't surprised when Kalil developed into a two-time All-America.

Orgeron hoped to find his Ryan Kalil in one of his summer camps this year. In today's camp, the Rebels had roughly 50 kids who were on their radar, but only about two dozen of them were guys that Ole Miss labeled as prospects *possibly* worthy of a scholarship offer.

Tyler McDermott was one of those two dozen. Matt Lubick had returned from his spring evaluation travels promising Orgeron that he was going to love McDermott's tenacity when they got him in camp. Lubick knew well that the "intangible" his boss prized most was tenacity.

McDermott, an honor student with a 3.6 GPA, arrived in Oxford with his father. They would head to the University of Florida's camp on Sunday, then fly back for another Ole Miss football camp the following week, and then drive down to Auburn's camp a few days later.

Randy McDermott, a stockbroker, said his son had already been offered by Auburn and Florida International. But the Auburn offer turned out to be short-lived. Another center prospect, a kid from the top high school in Alabama, had committed to the Tigers, and now they weren't interested in Tyler any more.

The elder McDermott reported that the family was very interested in the Rebels—always had been—because of Art Kehoe. See, Tyler had been going to the Down & Dirty linemen camp in Florida for years, and Kehoe had worked at that camp and been its star speaker for almost a decade while he was at Miami.

"Tyler thinks the world of Art Kehoe," said Randy McDermott, who wandered around the IPF, following his son from station to station. "Since he was seven years old, he's wanted to play for him. He loves that aggressive style. Kehoe is just so tough. I think Tyler would have cut off his left foot to play for him at UM, and he'd love to play for him here."

Tyler McDermott was a scrapper cut from the Kehoe mold. Kehoe had been a 5'10"ish, 235-pound offensive guard who wrangled his way into the University of Miami from a California junior college in the late 1970s and started two years for the Canes, thanks primarily to a double load of grit.

Even though the battles at the camp were waged in shorts and T-shirts instead of in helmets and shoulder pads, there was enough violent contact to shake the rafters, with linemen barreling into one another and swatting arms and hands away to win the leverage tussle. Time after time in the morning drills, McDermott showed off his share of guts, always being the first off the ball, and never shy about getting in the last shot on an opposing lineman.

In a word? Feisty. The kind of player opposing teams would hate. The kind of player Art Kehoe would love to coach.

When Kehoe's O-line squared off against D-line coach Ryan Nielsen's guys in one-on-one pass-rushing drills, McDermott was always the first player to rush up to the line and grab the ball. The rules of the drill were simple. If a D-lineman beat his man and got to the tackling dummy (i.e., the quarterback) in four seconds, the defense won. If there was a stalemate, the offense won. The losing side, coaches included, had to do 10 push-ups for each lost battle.

On the first rep, Bradley Sowell, a 364-pound offensive lineman already committed to the Rebels, got his feet crossed up by DE Stanley Porter, another Ole Miss commit, who blew by him with an inside move. Sowell looked humiliated as Kehoe plopped to the turf to do 10.

On the second rep, an offensive guard got beaten by an outside move. Another 10 for Kehoe & Co.

Then McDermott was up. He snapped the ball, and his man, who outweighed him by least 50 pounds, bull-rushed him. McDermott blasted out before the other camper crossed the line, using first-strike leverage to maintain balance and knock his opponent off stride. McDermott then reset his feet and delivered another blow before the defender could recover. Score one for the OL, which promptly mobbed McDermott.

As it turned out, McDermott was the only offensive lineman to win a battle in the first two rounds of one-on-ones. Then, on his third round, McDermott drove his man into the turf after the player lost his footing trying to spin outside. The other camper threw an elbow, and the two players had to be separated on the ground.

McDermott didn't look the least bit rattled as he moved back among the rest of the offensive linemen. He knew he'd had a pretty doggone good morning.

On the opposite end of the IPF, away from all the yelling, six quarterbacks quietly threw passes to one another as Dan Werner stood behind them, arms folded, watching the warmup.

The understated passing camp hadn't been billed as an audition for Robert Marve, but that's what it had turned out to be. The muscular 6'1", 195-pound Tampa native was at the start of a chaotic six-week tour of college campuses where he hoped to elevate his recruiting stock while also getting a better sense of what each school was like.

A few weeks back, Werner had become intrigued with Marve after seeing him at the Nike camp in Gainesville during the evaluation period. Marve wasn't a ballyhooed Internet prospect, but that's probably because he'd been playing in the shadow of blue-chipper Stephen Garcia from across town.

In this setting, with Werner and his campers taking up less than a fifth of the practice field, Marve didn't have the opportunity of a 7-on-7 quarterback challenge to go against a defense. Even so, the Rebels coach seemed to like what he saw—and seemed to think he was seeing plenty.

A golf pro can recognize a scratch golfer just from watching a few swings on the driving range. A quarterbacks coach can size up a guy's arm without seeing him in game action. It's not the whole deal, but if the arm's not there, nothing else matters.

Among the QB group today, Marve clearly had a much stronger arm and far more developed skills. His throwing motion was fluid. The ball jumped out of his hand, and there were no "tail-draggers" or wounded-duck throws. All of his movements seemed assured. He demonstrated the cocksure body language of someone who knew he was acing his test.

A few feet away, his high school coach Robert Weiner beamed like a proud father. Weiner and Marve had spent weeks mapping out their summer schedule to showcase Robert. On the docket: trips to Alabama, Mississippi State, North Carolina, South Carolina, Duke, NC State, Purdue, Iowa, and Minnesota.

"This is the hardest-working human being I've ever seen," Weiner said of his protégé. "He comes in by 5:30 a.m. and he'll stay until 10 p.m. at night. He's smart, too. He got a 3.4 last semester. And he's a slave to the weight room."

Weiner estimated that the trips—most of them logged in his car— would cost Marve's family more than $2,500, "but they see it as an investment." Marve, who already held scholarship offers from UConn, Kansas and Buffalo, had been apprised by the Rebels of their tricky quarterback situation. He knew they were waiting to see what Garcia did before moving on to another quarterback.

But he and Weiner were hoping to force the Rebels' hand by showing them that he was just too damned good to pass up, which just might be the case. Later, Werner would admit that Marve's performance had given him a lot more to think about. But the Rebels didn't pull the trigger. Orgeron stuck to his guns about not being rushed into taking another quarterback.

Before Marve and Weiner left the IPF, the quarterback said he was pleased with the day. "I really like Ole Miss," Weiner said, adding quickly that there was still a bunch of other schools he planned to visit.

"Someone told me they have the most beautiful women in the world here," he said. "Too bad we didn't have enough time to look around."

The afternoon session for the linemen was another two-hour rotation featuring many of the same drills that the players had run through in the morning.

Aside from the one-on-one pass-rushing duels, the most important drill the Rebels coaches employed involved two giant hula hoops, each about 15 feet in diameter. The hoops were laid flat on the ground, almost in a figure 8 formation, but with enough room for the campers to run between them.

Ole Miss runs the Hoops drill with two players going at the same time. They start from a three-point stance, with one lineman set up just behind the outside foot of the other. Hoops is a chase drill designed to show who is stiff and who isn't. Players are urged to pull or push past the other, and the drill often gets physical. "There is no better agility drill than two big guys running the Hoops," Orgeron said. "You can really see their flexibility, because you can't cheat on the Hoops."

Seeing a huge guy like Rishaw Johnson gliding around the hoops without teetering off balance or making abnormally wide turns was quite a sight, especially after watching smaller linemen topple over or leave enough room for a Buick to cruise by on the inside. Johnson's stock rose on the Hoops. Another Louisiana offensive lineman already committed to the Rebels, Alex Williams, saw his sink. Williams' footwork was a mess, and compared with Johnson, his athleticism didn't seem so impressive either.

The one-day camp ended at 3:20 p.m. All of the campers were rounded up and gathered at midfield. Another 50 kids, many of them already at Ole Miss for the weekend's skill position camps, wandered in from the sidelines to see what was going on.

Orgeron decided to put on a show for them. He asked Kehoe to select his best offensive lineman. The OL coach called for Rishaw Johnson. Then Orgeron had Nielsen pick his best defensive lineman. He grabbed Bo Tillman, the 6'6", 300-pound younger brother of Rebels freshman Marcus Tillman. The younger Tillman was only going to be a junior that fall, but he'd been the one defender who'd dominated all of his one-on-ones during the day.

This would, Orgeron explained, be a One-on-One Off. Same rules. One rep. If Johnson won, all of the defensive linemen and defensive coaches had to do push-ups. If Tillman won, the offensive guys had to hit the turf.

Orgeron called the snap. Tillman tried a swim move to maneuver his big frame around Johnson, who uncoiled and knocked him back on his heels. Tillman tried to reset himself, but Johnson's base was too solid. He blasted Tillman again, knocking him back two steps. The whistle blew.

Score it OL 1, DL 0.

Coach Frank Wilson rushed in and jumped onto Johnson's back to congratulate his now-prized recruit. Before Johnson knew it, a dozen other offensive linemen were swarming him too.

On the sidelines, Frederick Jenkins couldn't stop smiling. His boy had just wrapped up a flawless day in Oxford.

In the year since T-Bob Hebert took part in the Rebels' 2005 summer camp, Bobby Hebert's boy had gone from being a curiosity as the son of a former NFL quarterback to being hailed by the Internet recruiting sites as the best center prospect in the country.

Bobby Hebert and Orgeron are third cousins, and the Ole Miss coach had been pleasantly surprised by his even more distant relation's performance at the Rebels' camp the previous summer. T-Bob was a bit on the small side, about 245 pounds, but he displayed great footwork and he was as technically sound as any high school center Orgeron had seen.

The elder Hebert credited that soundness to the tips T-Bob received as an 11-year-old sponge hanging on every word that Hebert's Atlanta Falcons teammates told him about the nuances of line play. "They showed him the proper steps and hand placement," said Bobby Hebert, "and they taught him how to get to the second level and get on linebackers."

The Rebels formally offered T-Bob a scholarship in January, the first school to do so. Three months later, LSU offered him. Hebert had gone to Baton Rouge for LSU's Junior Day when Tigers coach Les Miles broke the news. "It was a dream come true," T-Bob said of LSU offering him a scholarship. "That was such a great feeling."

Miles knew of the Orgeron-Hebert connection but offered T-Bob a counter to family ties: "You wanna be a champion, don't you?"

Even though T-Bob had spent most of his life in Atlanta, he'd always been an LSU fan and felt close to his family's roots in the Bayou. His e-mail address even ID'ed him as "LouisianaPunk."

"My dad's got him brainwashed pretty good," said Bobby Hebert. T-Bob's grandfather, who calls himself a "Go to Hell, Ole Miss" Tigers fan, had taken his grandson to his first LSU football game when the future prospect was just two years old. "My dad is such a die-hard LSU fan," Bobby said, "he'll watch a whole LSU women's basketball game, and I think he's even broken a couple of lamps watching them."

News of T-Bob's LSU scholarship offer, coupled with Hebert's strong performance at the Nike camp at Clemson, sent his stock soaring within the Internet recruiting community. Auburn and Georgia followed up with offers too.

Gauging by Internet hype, T-Bob was the highest-profile prospect to come to any of the Ole Miss summer camps. But now, on the Rebels practice field, Hebert wasn't looking all-world. In fact, he found more than he could handle in an unheralded junior nose guard from the Bayou named Joel Ross, a 6'1", 287-pounder, who kept throwing Hebert around like a laundry sack. On four successive matchups Ross dominated Hebert, clearly overpowering him. "I wanna go again, Coach," Hebert told Kehoe, who obliged. And again, Ross ripped past Hebert, leaving him flailing at air.

Hebert looked shaken, as though he'd never seen anything like this guy who was eating his lunch. Like most of the other campers and all of the Ole Miss coaches except one, Hebert had never heard of this Ross guy before.

Ross played for Vandebilt Catholic High in Houma, Louisiana. He came to the camp with his coach, a friend of Orgeron's dating back to their coaching days at Nicholls State.

After the practice session, the Rebels coaches tried to console Hebert, who looked like he'd been rode hard and put away wet. Whatever they told him didn't lessen the sting: T-Bob Hebert would never forget Joel Ross.

And neither would the Rebels. They'd been so impressed that they named Ross defensive MVP of the camp. He would make the six-hour drive back to Houma with a shiny trophy and his first college scholarship offer.

"It was pretty nice," Ross said later of his camping experience at Ole Miss. "I had never heard of T-Bob before that. I just knew I was a lot stronger than him and that he couldn't touch me."

The biggest disappointment the Rebels suffered in that first summer camp wasn't T-Bob Hebert; it was local wide receiver Darius Young. Ole Miss had blown hot and cold on Young, a soft-spoken,

209-pound wide receiver, for months. Despite running the 40 in times that normally would get his nameplate tossed right out of the war room, Young made enough plays in his spring game for the Rebels to remain intrigued. Orgeron figured that if Young lit up his summer camp, he'd take him.

At the Ole Miss camp, Young didn't look like someone playing for a scholarship. After a few impressive early catches, he became tentative. He looked distracted. Even though he was bigger than all of the defensive backs he was going up against, he looked uncomfortable with them getting physical. The Ole Miss coaches didn't know what to make of his sorry performance. Before the end of the morning session, Young took himself out, saying he was injured.

Young's father, Johnny, wasn't happy either. He left a note for Orgeron with his secretary: "Darius Young, WR, hurt during spec. camp (finger & knee). DBs too physical w/no equipment. Wants to talk to Coach O!!"

"Darius Young's daddy doesn't know what he did to his kid," Orgeron said later. "You say that the DBs were 'too physical with no equipment,' you might as well be telling me your son's not tough enough to play at Ole Miss."

The brightest development from summer camp, according to Orgeron's post-mortem during Monday's recruiting meeting, was that the Rebels had found some more linebackers.

The two fastest risers were Jerry Franklin, a 6'2", 210-pound kid from Arkansas, and Isaiah Smith, a 6'0", 225-pound, 3.7 student from Tennessee. Both were players Freeze had been targeting for months, and both locked up offers after they ran 4.6 40s on the Ole Miss practice field.

Franklin actually ran in the high 4.5s and had everything the Rebels were looking for in a weakside linebacker—toughness, instincts, the ability to change direction, and closing speed. To land him, Ole Miss would have to beat out the home-state Arkansas Razorbacks.

Freeze: "Arkansas hasn't been to his school in seven years."

Orgeron: "Then, let's go take him."

Smith was an unheralded prospect with so-so game film. But in camp, he caught the Rebels' eye with his athleticism and his smarts. "I love him," Orgeron said during the board report. "He's definitely a MIKE. He's got the head of a bastard rat."

(Translation: "MIKE" is coachspeak for middle linebacker; "bastard rat," judging from the ecstatic look on Orgeron's face, is the highest possible compliment one could pay a MIKE.)

Freeze: "Last night he called and said he likes us more than Alabama."

Orgeron: "That's awesome."

Freeze: "I think it was you wrestling with him that did it."

Orgeron: "Shit, that son of a bitch was strong. When he was pinching me under the arms, it was on."

The Rebels also believed they'd found another defensive tackle in Josh Chapman, a six-foot, 277-pounder from perennial Alabama prep powerhouse Hoover High in Hoover, Alabama. Chapman ran a 4.90 40 and was relentless in all of the drills. And he had not yet been offered by any other schools.

Kehoe: "I've never heard you push a kid so hard. I think he's a no-brainer."

Orgeron: "I know he's only 5'10", but he's one helluva player."

As Chapman's stock soared, the nameplate directly above his on the out-of-state defensive tackles column is about to get yanked down by Orgeron. "He keeps mentioning us on the Internet," interjected secondary coach Chris Rippon of the slightly undersized prospect. "And he's got offers from Auburn and Notre Dame."

Orgeron: "I don't give a shit. We didn't like him that much. Do you think Notre Dame knows more about coaching D-line than me?"

Rippon: "No, sir."

Orgeron: "Good answer."

The Rebels quickly shifted from the board report to watching game film of the kids they'd just had in camp. Alex Washington, an enormous 6'4", 348-pound offensive lineman from Monroe, Louisiana, was another prospect rising up the board. Washington ran a 5.39 40 despite being about 30 pounds heavier than what the Rebels would like. "He'll be a 5.1 when we get him in shape," Orgeron predicted.

Kehoe: "He's a sharp kid, too."

Orgeron: "Yeah, none of that dead-fish look you hate to see."

Washington was a mauler on film. He proved surprisingly agile, and he didn't quit on plays when the ballcarrier was beyond him. The staff did have some concerns about his flexibility, noticing that he didn't coil his massive frame and explode into a defender.

Orgeron flashed the red laser pointer on Washington's upright posture while engaging with another lineman: "I wanna see him dip and strike and get up in there."

Kehoe: "If he loses another 30 pounds, he could be a player."

Orgeron: "It looks like he plays high and doesn't know what he's doing, but he comes off the ball real good."

Washington, along with fellow Louisiana product Rishaw Johnson, emerged from the camp as the top offensive-line prospects. T-Bob Hebert, his struggles with Joel Ross aside, was also on the Rebels' keeper list. So was Bradley Sowell, Ole Miss's already-committed 364-pound prospect.

It was the next tier of O-line candidates that Orgeron challenged his staff to sort out.

Tyler McDermott fell into a cluster of second-level line prospects from camp that included Caleb Thomas, the 290-pound son of a former Ole Miss basketball player; Patrick Crump, a 285-pound teammate of Chapman's at Alabama's Hoover High; and Grant

Cook, a 305-pounder from Arkansas with a bushy full beard that made him look like he was 30.

All four had demonstrated in camp that they possessed plenty of grit, but Orgeron was concerned that none might have the athleticism he was looking for. "What we don't need is linemen with pudding in their drawers," Orgeron said.

McDermott's film wasn't anywhere near as impressive as Hebert's. McDermott did battle and wasn't afraid to throw his body around, but none of the Rebel coaches seemed inspired by what he showed on tape.

Orgeron: "He looks thin there. What I didn't like about him was his big belly."

Lubick: "He was probably trying to gain weight for the combines and camps."

Werner: "These guys all look about the same. We *know* T-Bob."

Orgeron: "T-Bob has a lot more upside. I think McDermott is tapped out. But T-Bob could go to LSU. And then what?"

By a show of hands around the war room table, the Rebels staff ranked the linemen they had just watched on film:

1. Alex Washington
2. Patrick Crump
3. Tyler McDermott
4. Caleb Thomas
5. Grant Cook

Orgeron didn't draw a line between No. 1 and the rest, but in his mind there was one.

Beyond Washington, the Rebels wouldn't chase the others.

Unless they had to.

"I want to talk to Jerry Franklin and Isaiah Smith *today*," Orgeron told Freeze as the staff began its post-lunch recruiting calls. He was referring to the two linebacker prospects who'd won

Ole Miss offers with their showing at summer camp, which just ended 24 hours earlier. But Orgeron was also driving home a point that he was adamant about: Ole Miss must build immediately and effectively on the connections it had made with its targets at camp.

The first callback to Ole Miss came from Jamariey Atterberry, a slender but exceptionally quick wide receiver/cornerback from Kosciusko, Mississippi, in the heart of Mississippi State country. Atterberry had in fact committed to the archrival Bulldogs a few months earlier, but he came to the Rebels camp nonetheless, and now Orgeron thought they had a shot at flipping him.

The Rebels began to warm to Atterberry after he ran a 4.47 40 and jumped 38 inches in the vertical at a combine on the Ole Miss campus earlier in the spring. His showing at camp got them only more excited. Atterberry liked Ole Miss too, particularly the look of the campus and the school's sports medicine program.

Before Rippon handed Orgeron the phone, he held it up so the staff could give Atterberry its primal Rebel yell.

"What do you think of that reception, Jamariey?" Orgeron asked. "Look, Son, I know you need to play cornerback for us *now*. The ball is in your court. Just take your time and call us every Monday. Okay, stud?"

A few moments of chitchat later, Orgeron passed the phone back to Rippon and pumped his fist in the air. "He is comin' *here*," Orgeron said, smacking the table for punctuation. "I can *feel* it!"

Soon half the coaches around the table were gabbing with recruits.

Freeze to DB prospect Harrison Smith: "Harrison, were your ears ringing today? Ole Miss was talking about you not two hours ago, saying how we need you to win a championship."

Rippon to another cornerback, Woodny Turenne from College of the Sequoias: "You know every time I watch one of our guys, I tell him Woodny Turenne is going to come to Oxford and take his job."

That was exactly the kind of vibe Orgeron wanted pulsing around the war room. Upbeat, positive, confident. In the back of his mind, of course, he knew how quickly things could go the other way.

Take Rishaw Johnson. Wilson had just heard from Johnson, who sounded like he truly loved Ole Miss. But Orgeron and his assistant couldn't help but be a little concerned. Like many of the top guys on their boards, Johnson still had a few more summer camps to attend. He was set to compete at Florida State's camp in early July and LSU's camp later in the month. Surely, after those schools saw what the big man could do, they'd fall all over themselves to get him. The other schools knew about Johnson, but they hadn't witnessed what the Rebels had seen.

Ole Miss' best-kept secret was sure to get out.

Chapter 9

THE
OKOLONA
KID

THE TATTERED SIGN on the two-lane road about 20 miles
south of Tupelo reads "Welcome to Okolona—The Little
City That Does Big Things!" In the patchy grass beneath
the sign are what appear to be the remnants of a dead skunk.

Okolona (pop. 3,200) is a hardscrabble old furniture factory
town in northern Mississippi whose biggest claims to fame include
producing Pulitzer-Prize winning columnist William Raspberry,
one member of the R&B group the Commodores, former Miami
Dolphin defensive tackle Tim Bowens, and veteran right-wing
politician Pat Buchanan's great-grandfather.

In the spring of 2006, a small army of football coaches found their
way down U.S. Highway 45 from Memphis past the dead skunk,
past the Todd's Superstore and the guns and pawn shop, and the
rusty shack with the sign offering fireworks. Their destination: the
home of a high school junior who was the consensus pick as the best
prep running back in the whole state of Mississippi.

Earlier in the winter, Ed Orgeron and his assistants at Ole Miss
had pegged Robert Elliott III as a small-town treasure tucked away
in a nowhere place, the kind of thoroughbred talent that eventually
becomes the stuff of legend if everything works according to plan.

The problem was that once Elliott accepted the Rebels' scholarship offer in January, he wasn't all that hidden any more. His name, picture, and highlights were all over the Internet. Alabama, Memphis, and Mississippi State started calling. Even the Florida State Seminoles called him. Said they loved his film. Told him they were so impressed that the man himself, Bobby Bowden, was gonna make the trip to Okolona and plunk himself down on Robert's mama's couch.

Imagine that—the winningest coach in college football history paying a courtesy call to Okolona!

Well, Bowden didn't make it to Okolona in the spring, but FSU did offer Bridgett Elliott's son a football scholarship. Quickly, just by virtue of an offer being made to an out-of-stater so early from a heavy hitter like Florida State, Elliott's stock started to soar in the eyes of Internet recruiting gurus at Rivals and Scout. FSU is a notorious latecomer on the recruiting scene, often waiting until the last few months to move on players. For the Noles to jump so fast, the recruiting world figured Elliott had to be something special.

Shortly after word got out about the Seminoles' offer, both the Rivals and Scout sites bestowed a "four-star" ranking on Elliott. Thus, thanks to the initial push from the Rebels' announcement, Elliott had surged to the status of big-name recruit. Based on word of mouth and some grainy videotape that pops up on a computer the size of a credit card, the kid from Okolona had emerged as the No. 1 prize in what was shaping up as another top 15 recruiting class for Ole Miss.

This was all mind-boggling stuff for Robert's mother. Before the start of Robert's junior season, she had asked him to write down a list of the colleges he was interested in. He dutifully sat down, jotted the names of three schools on a sheet of yellow paper and handed it back to her. His list:

Miami

Florida

Florida State

Bridgett, a supervisor at a Tupelo hospital, just shook her head. "Rob, be realistic!" she told him. "What chance do you think a school outside the state of Mississippi has of finding out about you?"

It's not that she doubted her son's talents. Not at all. Though shy, Robert had always been the best athlete around. And Lord knows Bridgett was never going question Robert's will or determination.

Take the time Robert set his mind on winning the state title in the 300-meter hurdles. His mother didn't have the nerve to tell him just how long a long shot he was. After all, Okolona High was too poor for the school to even afford hurdles for the track team to practice with. But Robert showed her, even if he scared her nearly to death in the process.

One night, she heard some noises coming from her front yard, and she peeked out the window. She spotted a male figure running from the neighborhood. Turns out, it was Robert training for the state track meet. He had lined up some plywood campaign signs he'd rounded up from other people's front lawns. He'd paced off his steps—15 between each sign—and was training for two hours every night in the dark. He eventually realized the signs weren't high enough, so he carried his mom's dining room chairs into the yard. Says Bridgett: "He broke two legs off my chairs."

The grassroots training methods enabled Robert to take third in the state meet. Not bad for a self-taught sophomore, but he was thinking a lot bigger. During his junior season, he ran for over 1,800 yards and 20 touchdowns. The Ole Miss coaches saw tape of Elliott gliding past defenders and accelerating into open space, and were sold. His mother said she was still worried that her son was making a mistake by talking to reporters about being open to visiting other schools after committing to Ole Miss, but he calmed her down by telling her he knew how the recruiting game was played.

Sitting on a couch at home on a hot spring day, Robert said he'd been shocked when Florida State offered him a scholarship. He said he was still loyal to Ole Miss because they were the first program to offer him. "I really like Coach Orgeron," he said, "and they have the best facilities in the state. I am definitely still committed to Ole Miss. I'd say there's about an 80% chance I go there."

But, Elliott added, he would be visiting the FSU campus and probably Alabama, too.

"I'm also trying to get a visit to Hawaii," he said, breaking into a sheepish grin. "I've never been to Hawaii, and I heard it's cool."

His mom, seated next to him, just shook her head.

The entire Elliott family had gathered in their living room: Robert, sister Brittanie (20), kid brother Devin (10), and their mother. Bridgett had obviously taught her children good manners. Robert began the answer to almost every question he was asked with a "Yes, sir" or a "No, sir." In fact, he even started answers that way to some questions that weren't yes/no questions.

As he began to explain where he thought he got his drive from, the young running back mentioned in passing that his father, who'd been a sprinter at Grambling, had died while Robert was in grade school. That detail hovered in the air for a few moments until the obvious question: How exactly had his father, Robert Elliott II, died?

"Car accident," Robert said, glancing away.

Bridgett looked at her son, shut her eyes for a few long seconds, took a breath, and then leaned forward on the edge of her sofa.

"No. Uh-uh," she said, shaking her head. "I shot him. Shot him with his own gun."

The killing of Robert Elliott II on August 22, 1996, stunned everybody in Okolona. According to Mississippi state police, Bridgett Elliott shot and killed her husband after a wild car chase and crash. She was arrested at the scene and subsequently charged with murder.

The case, which went to trial three times, was a combustible mix of sex, violence, and betrayal. All three trials ended in mistrials. Bridgett's attorney, Jimmy Doug Shelton, called it the most emotional case he'd ever handled.

According to accounts in the *Northeast Mississippi Daily Journal*, Donita Doss, the Elliott's next-door neighbor, testified in the third trial (as she had in the previous two) that she and Robert Elliott had been having an affair. Doss and Elliott had been out together the night Bridgett Elliott shot her husband.

Bridgett Elliott testified that she woke up the night of the shooting and remembered she had left her purse in the back of their green Cherokee. While at the car, she saw her husband getting in a blue Camry with Doss. Bridgett told the court she got in their Jeep and followed the Camry because she wanted to confront her husband.

A chase ensued. Doss testified that as the two vehicles raced along County Road 404, Elliott slammed the jeep into her car numerous times before finally knocking it across U.S. Highway 45 Alternate, causing it to spin out of control and slam into a tree.

Bridgett testified that her husband's gun slid out from under the driver's-side seat at some point, and that she picked it up after the crash because she was afraid. Bridgett said a close friend had previously told her that Doss had bought a gun with the intention of killing her. "She said she had a gun for me," Bridgett said on the stand. "I was afraid. I think I had a reason to be."

Bridgett testified that she was afraid of her husband as well. They had been dating since her sophomore year of high school, and they had been married eight years, but she said he had become abusive in the two years before his death. She testified that he'd broken her nose two months prior to the car crash and that he'd also bitten her on her arm and clawed her legs, leaving scratches.

She said she blamed her husband's personality changes on drug abuse. On the stand she presented a letter he had written her, saying he was addicted to crack cocaine and wanted help. "He asked me not to leave him," she said, crying. "His mother asked me not to leave him ... I wanted to stay with him, because I loved him and because we had three children, three babies."

Bridgett testified she knocked on the window with the barrel of the gun, causing it to go off accidentally. During cross examination, the district attorney asked Elliott if she at any time tried to help her husband after she realized she had shot him.

"No," she said. "I was just hysterical."

Bridgett's attorney called several witnesses for the defense. One was Robert III's second-grade teacher, who described Bridgett as a model mother. She said Bridgett regularly visited class, sometimes bringing candy for everyone.

On January 29, 1998, an eight-man, four-woman jury deliberated for 90 minutes before telling a circuit court judge that they were deadlocked. The judge declared another mistrial.

The D.A. told reporters he had no plans of retrying the case again. "I'm satisfied with the jury," said Jim Hood, who in 2005 became famous for prosecuting Edgar Ray Killen, the Klansman who had orchestrated the murder of three civil rights workers—Andrew Goodman, Michael Schwerner, and James Chaney—in Philadelphia, Mississippi, 40 years earlier. "It went as well as can be expected."

It was surreal to sit next to Bridgett Elliott on her sofa, just a few feet away from her three children, and listen to her calmly give the details of what had happened to her husband and of the aftermath of an incident that had left the whole town talking for years.

You might expect tears or other evidence of emotion. None. The incident had exacted a toll in pain and sorrow, but there was also something strangely uplifting that came in its wake. A father's death and a mother's trials could well have ripped the family apart, but Bridgett Elliott said that it made them all stronger, pushing her children to be better people. The hardest part was the two-year period during which the trials unfolded. Every step Bridgett Elliott took, she felt like she was being watched. Brittanie and Rob were old enough to feel that way too.

"A lot of people thought we'd move away from Okolona," Bridgett said. But most of the community rallied around her and her children. "They know what kind of kids I have, and everyone respected that. Even during the trials, people said, 'Hold your head up high, Bridgett!'"

To many in Okolona, the shooting of Robert Elliott II was justifiable homicide. "Around here," said Andrew Aldridge, Okolona High's head football coach, "if you mess with women and children, these people won't show much mercy."

Perhaps it was for that reason that the community closed ranks around Bridgett Elliott and her family. "It was such a shock," said Russell Brooks, a county supervisor and former classmate of Bridgett and Robert Elliott. "Nobody could believe it, but because of that, everybody wanted these kids to be something. We all know the family background about what good people they really are."

Brooks, the first African-American to hold elective office in Chickasaw County government, said Bridgett's son Rob had been a role model to the children of Okolona since he was a sixth-grader. Robert Elliott III became the face of Brooks' Okolona Raiders Pee Wee football program, which emerged as the salvation of the town's school system.

Brooks had created the program after taking part in studies in the state capital, Jackson, regarding how and when young men start to get caught up in criminal behavior. Brooks began looking for ways to reduce the dropout rate of African-American males in Okolona. "Something had to be done," he said.

His idea was to create a youth football team, with maintenance of a 2.0 GPA as a condition of participation. "Robert took a leadership role," said Brooks. "He was our model. He set the standard for all our kids to follow. In our first three years of the program, we went from 30 kids failing to just two. Now these kids idolize Rob."

The Elliotts' story was well known around Chickasaw County but not in recruiting circles. Hugh Freeze, the Ole Miss coach handling the recruitment of Robert Elliott, didn't know about the tragedy that had ripped through the running back's family or how it had affected the entire town. Neither did the Florida State coaches.

Members of the Rebels staff talked to Elliott and his family many times over the summer. They found Bridgett Elliott to be a strong woman, and they came to understand that she was clearly the key person in Robert's life. But Robert was a very tough kid to read. Maybe, they suspected, he was the kind of kid who was afraid to say no to anyone.

"I think we're in good with him," Freeze said at one point. "But I don't know. We might get surprised."

Like most top recruits, Elliott was a moving target. Even though he had said he grew up an Ole Miss fan and had been dutiful in his prompt responses to text messages, Elliott had made some comments online in the spring about how Florida State was one of the schools, along with Mississippi State, that could change his mind.

"I really didn't mean for it to sound like that," Elliott explained a few days later. "This reporter asked me, 'If there are two schools out there that could make you change your mind, which are they?' I guess I should've been more clear in how I said what I said about Florida State and Mississippi State."

Complicating matters were the constant message-board posts from Mississippi State fans talking about how Elliott was going to follow his sister over to Starkville. Brittanie had been a star athlete in her own right in Okolona, finishing second in the state in the 300-meter high hurdles. She also captained the cheerleading squad, was a standout basketball player, tutored area students at a local church, and was a member of the National Honor Society. Now she was at MSU on an academic scholarship.

Freeze said he doesn't bird-dog message boards. The former Memphis high school coach said he really couldn't worry about any of that stuff. Instead, he would take the Elliotts at their word.

In late August, just five days before Okolona's season kicked off, Robert Elliott said he planned to go on all his official visits and then make his decision on National Signing Day. For the time being, he said, he was more focused on leading the Chieftains, a 5–7 team in 2005, to a winning season and running for 2,000 yards.

Bridgett Elliott had much more basic goals for Okolona's 2006 season: "I'm just praying they don't run him too much and that he doesn't get injured."

On the eve of the season, Orgeron was praying too, but it was for his assistants to grind a little harder.

For all programs, juggling the rigors of recruiting against the demands of game-planning for upcoming opponents is a delicate balance. Chris Rippon, the Rebels' veteran secondary coach, who had spent much of his coaching career working for Orgeron's one-time boss Paul Pasqualoni, estimated Ole Miss devoted about 15% of its energy toward recruiting compared to the 5% or 10% they had back at Syracuse. He says it didn't mean that the Rebels were doing any less game-planning, but it did mean there was a whole lot more attention to detail when it came to all of the film evaluation as a staff and the organized Monday-night recruiting phone calls in the war room.

"We were dinosaurs," Rippon says of the Syracuse staff that got fired after the 2004 season. "If we'd done it this way we'd still be there. This is what Pete Carroll and USC did, and now everyone is trying to follow suit."

But was it enough for Coach O? The Ole Miss coaches had been spending 14 hours a day holed up in their respective offensive and defensive staff rooms breaking down tape of the Memphis Tigers, searching for tendencies and weak points to factor into their game plan. But Orgeron couldn't help himself from wondering whether they were making the most of the few hours a week he had cleared for them to focus on recruiting. Was the talent pool they had created deep enough?

That last question, especially, was driving him nuts.

Elliott was one of three top running backs committed to Ole Miss, but one, Johnny Brown, was expected to come in as a defensive back, and the other, 230-pounder Jeramie Griffin, figured to be a long shot to qualify. Should they expand their RB list? How solid was Elliott? Were they doing all they could to hold him steady?

It was almost 90 minutes before the start of the Rebels' weekly 8:00 a.m. Wednesday recruiting meeting. The season opener against Memphis was 10 days away. Orgeron sensed that the momentum of the Rebels' fast recruiting start in the spring—an SEC-leading 15 verbal commitments—was waning. Perhaps the carryover from summertime to two-a-days had fostered some complacency. Perhaps some assistants were getting too caught up in fretting over which recruits would get admitted to the school and which wouldn't. Perhaps the players they already coached had worn them down with shaky performances in the classroom.

Word had also gotten around that Ole Miss athletics director Pete Boone and compliance chief David Wells were leaning hard on

Orgeron, telling him that the staff couldn't mention to high school prospects the idea of going to Hargrave Military Academy, where they could get special tutoring and retake their tests a year later. The Ole Miss brass also had said that the Rebels coaches couldn't suggest to a kid what courses he should take. In one meeting with Boone, the coaches were told they shouldn't even be talking to high school academic counselors.

"It's more of a *mixed-up* message rather than simply a mixed message," one assistant would say later. "The people at this place have no clue. They are stuck in the 1960s."

Orgeron was concerned the staff had lost focus in terms of their recruiting goals. Their energy level, he explained, was not where it needed to be. He was frustrated. He felt like a big part of his recruiting board was "dead," or more specifically, bottom-loaded with names of players his coaches had stopped recruiting. He was about to establish a new rule: If he mentioned a player's name at a staff meeting and didn't hear anything from one of his coaches, he would yank the recruit's nameplate off the board.

"We can't have a dead board here," he explained. "When I was at Syracuse, we had so many names on the board it was ridiculous."

Orgeron then grabbed a can of Red Bull out of the minifridge behind his chair and popped it open. He took a big gulp and began scribbling notes on his yellow legal pad. On the top line he wrote "Recruiting—Junior College!" and proceeded to jot down the Rebels' updated need positions. His laundry list included all the positions he wanted his staff to target. He also wanted most of the recruits eligible to arrive in Oxford in time for spring football.

DEFENSE: two tackles, one end, two linebackers (one a middle LB), three or four cornerbacks.

OFFENSE: one center, two tackles, two wide receivers.

Before he had finished his first page of notes, Orgeron had downed the can of Red Bull. Matt Saunders, a 27-year-old Ole Miss graduate assistant, hustled into the war room and put two handfuls of videotapes in front of Orgeron. "I want that film room smokin'!" Orgeron told Saunders before he slipped out of the war room.

The second page of Orgeron's yellow pad began with the heading "Directions for Junior College Recruiting!" Beneath it were the six JC states Ole Miss wanted the staff to focus their attention on:

1. Mississippi
2. Kansas
3. Texas
4. Arizona
5. California
6. Pennsylvania

Beneath that list were three prep schools: Hargrave Military and Fork Union Military, both in Virginia, and Milford Academy in New Berlin, New York. Orgeron realized that most of the top talent at those schools had been directed there by major colleges. Part of the unwritten agreement is that prep school coaches protect players that colleges send their way—that is, they do their best to prevent other colleges' coaches from poaching them. Still, Orgeron was hopeful he might unearth a kid or two who fell through the cracks.

Under the prep schools section, Orgeron outlined exactly what he wanted each of his recruiters to do, step by step. The first directive: Call every junior college coach in your assigned territory. The second: Collect each prospect's cell phone number, game tape, transcript, counselor's name, and jersey number for the Rebels' files.

The third page of what was, literally, a rough schematic for rebuilding Ole Miss football was a 21-point must list for high school recruits. Most of the items were punctuated by exclamation points.

For example, NO. 2: INVITE PROSPECTS TO MEMPHIS GAME!

And, NO. 8: ALL PATRICK WILLIS ARTICLES SENT TO PROSPECTS! ("I wanna flood the market with Ole Miss articles," he said, obviously hoping to milk the star power of Willis, the Rebels' All-American middle linebacker.)

Only one item got both the exclamation point *and* an underline: No. 10: SENIOR TAPE! SENIOR TAPE! SENIOR TAPE! A MUST!

Orgeron had been telling his staff since Day One that the evaluation process was always, *always* ongoing, but even he sometimes forgot his own edict about not falling in love too fast or writing someone off too quickly. Players the staff loved—as well as ones they didn't—were always up for discussion.

That also included committed players like Elliott. Even though it was in Orgeron's nature to ride his initial reaction on a player, either good or bad, he knew he had to learn from past mistakes and go through the process as hard as he could, just like he preached.

"We need to crank this machine back up," he said before heading down the hall to grab a cup of coffee to top off the Red Bull.

The rest of the Ole Miss staff filed into the war room a few minutes before 8 a.m. for the Rebels' recruiting meeting. Orgeron reentered and circled around the table.

"I want these names to come *alive!*" he boomed, pointing to the recruiting boards. "We gotta re-recruit. They are out there, and we can get them. We got Brent Schaeffer here! We got Cordera Eason here! We got John Jerry! Those guys could've gone *anywhere*, but we got them to come *here*. This time last year, Marcus Tillman was committed to LSU, and he ended up coming here.

"We are just about ball now. Just ball and recruiting. Let's leave our shit at home. We can't worry about whether Jerrell Powe is here or not. Whatever happens, happens. It's all about ball. No more talking about David Wells. Nothing. Just ball."

Orgeron paused for a breath and a couple heartbeats, his words still hanging in the air as if afraid to leave the room. Then he wriggled his shoulders to shed some tension and brought his voice down a few decibels.

"I don't wanna be an asshole about this," he said. This was obviously the part of the top job he hadn't fully adjusted to, the part where he had to squeeze his buddies. "But please, *please* don't think your shit is so important you don't have to be out there recruiting. I'll take that as a dagger right here."

And he smashed his thumb into his heart with such force you half expected to see blood spurt out.

Yet this didn't qualify as a full-bore, gloves-off, let-'em-hear-you-in-Baton-Rouge Orgeron rant. His voice hadn't ascended to an indecipherable high-pitched shrill. His eyes had bulged out, but only slightly. His chin had stayed moored to his face.

Maybe Orgeron had toned his standard stump speech down a bit because the two former Miami assistants, Kehoe and Werner, and soft-spoken linebackers coach David Saunders were new to his system. Orgeron knew that Kehoe, a proud man who'd spent 27 years at Miami, was beloved by many of the high school coaches in the state of Florida and that he could do wonders for his young line on the practice field. But Orgeron also knew that the Canes didn't have to recruit very hard to stay on top. Blue-chippers sought *them* out. Orgeron didn't stare directly at Kehoe or at Saunders, the man who'd introduced him to his wife, but it became obvious these two guys were the principal targets of his "We Gotta Do More!" speech.

After the staff left the war room, Orgeron stood at the front, staring at his 2006 depth chart that was about to take on the SEC. What he saw scared him. Not only did he not have Powe, the all-world recruit, to anchor his defensive line, but Peria Jerry, a swift 285-pound lineman who actually ran a 4.78 40 and had been dominant in the spring, probably wouldn't be near 100% all season because of a foot injury. Another holdover, defensive end Chris Bowers, was hobbled as well.

Worse still, Hayward Howard, a 290-pound junior college transfer, had proven to be a headache for coaches, both on and off the
field, and no longer could be counted on. Orgeron was stewing about
the irony that he, a life-long D-line coach, just hadn't recruited
enough big people last year and now it was going to cost him. This
year, he knew, he couldn't afford to make that mistake again.

The head coach glanced over at the In-State Defense board that
was now less than half-filled with nameplates of recruits. The vast,
accusatory white space was a reflection of too few options, and
maybe too quick a gong. Whatever, Orgeron saw it as a by-product
of insufficient effort. "It's like a plant you didn't take care of and
so it dies," he said. "I ain't lettin' that happen here."

By 1:30 that same afternoon, Orgeron's edict had the Rebels office
complex buzzing, with all of the assistants at their posts calling high
school coaches. Orgeron, clutching his aluminum bat, stalked from
desk to desk, pumping his fists, grabbing phones to shout a quick
hello, making it good and damned clear to everybody on both ends
of the line that Ole Miss was on the recruiting trail.

A big grin came across his face when he heard receivers coach
Matt Lubick thank the answering machine of a high school coach
in Largo, Florida, for sending freshman receiver-return man Dexter
McCluster to Oxford. "We love him," Lubick said, his voice throb-
bing with sincerity. "He's gonna start for us."

Then tight ends coach Hugh Freeze approached with a cell phone.
Freeze was talking to the coach of Jerry Franklin, a speedy line-
backer from Arkansas whom the Rebels had loved in summer camp.
"Get him to come to the Memphis game," Orgeron whispered to
Freeze, who nodded in response.

The flurry of calls lasted a half hour before the assistants returned
to their respective staff rooms to get ready for practice. By 5:40 a.m.
the next morning, Orgeron was back in the war room looking to
restock his defensive-line board. Barney Farrar, an assistant athletic

director, already had a fresh pot of coffee ready. Farrar had spent much of the last 24 hours seated in a metal bridge chair in front of a stack of nine VCRs in the Rebels video room. The 46-year-old former assistant coach at Clemson and Rice had been in the office till 11:30 the previous night and back in by 5:15 in the morning. "I just wanna make sure everything is how he wants it," Farrar said in his syrupy drawl. "You don't wanna be pissin' Coach off."

Farrar and Orgeron have polar-opposite personalities. A 5'7" slow-talking Mississippi native, Farrar is a real-life *Dukes of Hazzard* character, more country than grape jelly on a sausage biscuit. He comes across as the lovable underling who usually gets the other coaches rolling when they catch him laughing hysterically at Orgeron's ancient one-liners. Farrar had been hired in January sight-unseen as an assistant athletic director for external football affairs, based on the recommendation of former Rice head coach Ken Hatfield, the onetime Arkansas coach who had given Orgeron his first break in the business.

"I used to think recruiting was August to January and then you go hard for a month in the spring," said Farrar, talking about his new boss' No. 1 obsession. "Not this guy. He's persistent, and it's all the time. He ain't takin' no for an answer. At Rice, we'd hear some kid say 'Texas A&M' and it'd be over, but I'd try anyway and end up getting laughed at. With him, people might laugh, but then he'll whip their ass for laughin' and out-recruit them."

Farrar said he knew that Orgeron had made him a better coach, and that he'd never met anyone who worked as hard or was so driven to succeed. Still, an awkward tension occasionally flared up between the two.

Farrar had taken on a bigger role in the film room a few weeks earlier after the Rebels' former video coordinator had quit. It wasn't Farrar's ideal job. He was desperate to get back to coaching on the field, but for now he would do anything to help the Ole Miss program, even if it meant spending hours in the film room splicing together eval tapes, a role few coaches with almost 20 years of Division I on-field experience could stomach.

But despite the sacrifice, the transition hadn't been smooth, though certainly not for any lack of effort on Farrar's part.

The first tape Orgeron popped in was impossible to follow, because the footage was too blurry. The video looked like it had been shot through a shower curtain. As the tape continued rolling, there was something you almost never experienced in Orgeron's presence—about 20 seconds of silence. Orgeron hates dead air. He feeds off energy.

As in, energy is enthusiasm … enthusiasm breeds confidence … and confidence leads to winning.

Silence, conversely, creates lulls, and lulls make people passive. And passivity? Absolutely, utterly forbidden in Ed Orgeron's world.

Finally, at 20 seconds going on 20 minutes, Orgeron broke the uncharacteristic silence: "So this is Barney-Cam, huh? We got ourselves in a new era. Barney's makin' tapes."

Farrar scratched at his coffee cup and kept staring ahead at the screen. Orgeron didn't have to tell Farrar that the blurry plays probably should never have been dubbed onto an eval tape, much less have made it into the war room.

You hoped, for Farrar's sake, that the next tape would be better, the way you pull for the kid flailing in the water in that shark movie.

Without displaying any obvious emotion, Farrar left the war room and walked down the hall to get another cup of coffee. Orgeron just rubbed his eyes and ejected the tape. "Okay, let's see what else we got," he said, grabbing the tape of a 6'4", 250-pound junior college defensive end.

Good move.

On the very first play, the player demonstrated the burst coming out of his stance that Orgeron especially covets. He also showed a natural pass-rusher's gift for turning the corner by buzzing under-neath the reach of an offensive tackle from an improbable body position. Think motocross rider hugging a curve.

Orgeron's reaction, as the end flattened the quarterback: "Wow!"

But the coach's enthusiasm was doused by one of his assistants: "His coach told me this kid is no good. And he has no grades."

Next, the highlight tape showed the same kid reversing field to chase down a tailback.

Orgeron's reaction: "Look at that change of direction! *Shee-it!*"

And then: "Maybe that coach was just having a bad day when you talked to him," establishing that not even recruiting geniuses are immune to snap judgments. Orgeron then giggled to let his assistants know he was just kidding.

The next tape showed off a 300-pound junior-college defensive tackle in Kansas rated as a four-star prospect by most of the Internet sites. Orgeron watched four plays and was incredulous: "Oh, my god! He's stiff as a board. Maybe he has an ankle problem or something. See how he waddles? I do *not* need anymore of that on our team. That's a nice turf field, though."

Orgeron watched four more linemen, none of whom stirred his blood. He then looked at a defensive back (No. 5, Tyree Burnett, 5'11", 175, Georgia Military College). The video showed two plays of Burnett in coverage before cutting to a shot of him fielding a punt and darting upfield. Orgeron came alive: "*Whooooo!* That's Jimmy Johnson right there! A cornerback returning punts. Son of a bitch, that's what you *wanna* see: ball skills! The only thing we've got to get are his high school track times. I'm not accepting anything else."

Burnett's tape kept rolling. On the next play, he flew into the screen and hammered a receiver. "Damn, is that him right there?" Orgeron asked, his eyes glued to the screen.

A few more plays seemed to show that No. 5 in red-and-black had somehow morphed into a guy about three inches taller and some 40 pounds heavier. Orgeron rewound the tape and watched again but couldn't seem to figure out whom exactly he was watching. Apparently, someone in the Rebels' film room had spliced together the wrong clips.

A little later, Kent McLeod, the Rebels' football operations man and admissions expert, delivered the scoop on the entire recruiting board's academic prospects and asked his colleagues to chime in.

Freeze offered up some good news: Robert Elliott made two A's and three B's on his last report card. But after that, the academic report on Ole Miss' RB targets didn't sound very rosy. Hughes told the group that Johnny Brown had "a ways to go" to get in. Joe McKnight, the do-everything back from New Orleans whom coach Frank Wilson called the best player in America, wouldn't have his transcript sorted out for a while because, like most Louisiana kids, it was stuck in post-Katrina red tape. McLeod said another big-name tailback from Florida was likely to have his ACT test thrown out because of a suspiciously big jump in score.

Even though the Rebels' Out-of-State running-back board was loaded with many of the highest profile recruits in the country, the day's academic update only made keeping Robert Elliott that much more of a priority.

Later, Wilson admitted he wasn't convinced that Elliott would have cracked the top 10 on their list if he were an out of state kid. His concern was that Elliott lacked the grit to be an SEC tailback.

"I think he's kinda soft," he said. "But maybe I'm wrong. I'll be seeing him play in two weeks. I'll know better then."

On game day in Okolona, you could smell the smoke from the huge barbecue pit next to the rusty old metal bleachers all the way down Route 32. The Chieftains were hosting rival Houston to open the season. An overflow crowd had already filed in a half hour before kickoff. A pair of toddlers scooted past, each wearing a T-shirt that said "You bring the aspirin" on the front and, on the back, "We bring the pain."

Robert Elliott's picture was on the cover of the game program. Like his big sister, he had become the pride of this town.

For all of the hype that had built up around Elliott, the Rebels coaching staff still was curious to see how he would handle the spotlight. Opposing defenses would be scheming to slow him down. Freeze said a great back at the high school level, especially playing at the small-school level that Okolona plays at, should still be able to overcome it all to get his yards.

Before the first snap, a couple of Okolona players heard one of the Houston guys predict that "Mr. All-American is in for a long night."

The kid was right. The Chieftains offensive line looked plodding against the aggressive Houston defense. Elliott struggled to find running room against a 10-man front. He got hit late by Houston tacklers on his first two carries and spent most of the first half running east and west rather than north and south. On the rare occasions when Elliott did find a seam or flashed enough speed to turn the corner, the play got nullified by an Okolona penalty. Half of his carries went for negative yardage. The Chieftains ended up committing 21 penalties and lost 38-6. Elliott managed just 43 yards on 14 carries.

Afterward, Elliott was the last player to exit the field. He apologized to his mother. It was her birthday, and he had wanted to do something special for her. He looked devastated. "We just couldn't get those guys blocked," he said with his head down.

The recap of the Houston-Okolona game on the Scout.com Ole Miss recruiting site was much more forgiving, in no small measure because Elliott reported to one of the Scout.com sites that he'd run for 121 yards on just 11 carries.

A bald-faced lie? You bet. Fact is, a prospect's lying to one or more of the Internet recruiting sites is common. Many boost their

GPAs, ACT scores, performances, and even the number of schools that have offered them, in hopes of increasing their stock among the online recruiting analysts and even the colleges themselves.

Elliott's lackluster performance didn't cause too much of a ripple inside the Ole Miss war room. The Rebels knew that high school stats were often deceiving, especially for just one game.

One week later, it was a similar story: a mediocre showing against Shannon High. But this time it caused a lot more concern. Wilson had driven down for the game, and he was disappointed by what he saw from the Rebels' top tailback recruit. Elliott ran for only 42 yards against what Wilson believed was weak competition. An SEC-caliber tailback should've had at least three times that much. Elliott didn't display the extra gear Wilson expected to see from a "speed" back. He also didn't run through tackles or finish off runs.

A big-time back finds a way to make something from nothing. Elliott offered little evidence that he was a big-time back.

Wilson was also bothered that Elliott didn't do anything else for his team. A true playmaker at the high school level should be returning kicks and punts and probably playing defense, too.

"For better or worse," said Wilson, not even trying to hide his disappointment, "Robert Elliott is ours. And if he's a problem, he's gonna have to be our problem."

Chapter 10

THE
JAILER

BY JANUARY OF his senior year, Jerrell Powe thought he had heard every recruiting pitch imaginable. The massive defensive tackle, deemed a "five-star" blue-chipper by the Internet recruiting gurus, had been sweet-talked, challenged, tempted, and flattered by droves of assistant coaches. He had been promised the moon, the stars, and the sky if he would just please-please-please come be the BMOC at their school.

But when Powe's phone rang at 4:30 p.m. on January 4, 2005, he heard something that caught him completely off guard.

"Jerrell, this is Ed Orgeron," the caller said in a Cajun accent so husky and rich that it seemed like the guy was talking with an entire po'boy stuffed in his mouth. "Do you know who I am?"

Before the pride of Wayne County High School in Waynesboro, Mississippi, could respond, the voice answered its own question: "I am the defensive line coach for the Southern California Trojans, and we're on our way from the hotel to the Orange Bowl, where we're going to kick some Oklahoma Sooners butt and win the national championship. Ain't that right, guys?"

As Powe listened to the howls of the USC team coming through his phone, he couldn't help but smile. The booming voice. The confidence. The energy. It was making the hair on Powe's arms stand up.

"Now listen, Jerrell," Orgeron continued, at a slightly more intimate decibel level. "I do want you to know I am on my way to win the national championship, but I am also thinking about *you*, and I just want to make sure you know that. Okay, stud?"

Powe didn't have a chance to explain that he was planning on following some former high school teammates over to Auburn or maybe go to LSU, but he was suddenly intrigued by another possibility. Powe had heard about Orgeron being named as the new head coach at Ole Miss, but he hadn't paid much attention. That afternoon Powe stayed riveted to his television as the Trojans, just like Orgeron said they would, kicked some Sooners butt, winning 55-19.

Impressed by how Orgeron's defensive line dominated the game, Powe said two years later that he really wanted to see what his caller actually looked like: "On the phone, he sounded like a real fat dude, but I got that feeling right away that this is somebody I wanted to coach me."

Jerrell Powe, in Ed Orgeron's eyes, was the kind of presence that could *guaran-damn-tee* the transformation of a struggling, downtrodden college football program.

The big kid had the raw power and heft to anchor any defense, but a lot of guys were big and strong. Powe had something else, something you couldn't teach and you rarely saw in a young man of his size and strength. He had the *first-step quickness* to ruin an offensive game plan.

Orgeron just knew that Powe would demand so much attention in the center of every play that even a good offense would come unstrung. He would dictate double-teams, in effect making plays without ever touching the ballcarrier. Sure, there would be times where Powe, an easy-going, borderline lazy sort, might not give much effort, but Orgeron believed that was as much a function of poor conditioning and a lack of motivation as anything else.

After all, he'd coached a kid like this before. When Orgeron was at Miami, the Canes had a similarly wired jolly giant named Cortez Kennedy, who'd been dubbed "Two-Play Tez" after his arrival at Miami from a junior college. Why? Because that was about all Kennedy ever delivered before taking the rest of his plays off.

Orgeron served as principle engineer of Kennedy's metamorphosis, pushing him to shed 25 pounds and riding him until he turned into an effort guy. Kennedy left Miami as the third pick overall in the 1990 NFL draft.

Powe was hardly an under-the-radar prospect. Every college program in the South had known about him since his 2002 sophomore season, when he led Wayne County High to a state championship. Powe made 11 sacks that season and created quite a buzz, but his transcript, loaded with D's and F's, had convinced most recruiters he'd have to be routed to a junior college first.

Powe's story, in many ways, epitomized the background of a lot of elite football prospects in the rural South. He'd been raised by a single mother in a tiny town (pop. 5,000) where everything revolved around two things: the timber industry and football.

Some core facts: Jerrell was the third of four children … his mother, Shirley Powe, was a shift supervisor at the local hospital … the family lived in a small brick house at the end of a country road … Jerrell didn't meet his biological father until he was 7 years old.

"My father was a rolling stone," Powe says. "I show him respect when I see him, but I'm mad at him because he didn't do what he was supposed to do."

Underneath his bed, Jerrell says, he keeps the only child support check his mom ever got from his father. It is made out for one dollar.

College never seemed even a remote possibility while Powe was growing up, at least until he *really* started growing and school linked up with football. Powe's D and F grades didn't seem to be much cause for alarm to anybody, not in a tiny, poor, blue-collar town like Waynesboro. The attitude went something like this: "Some kids do good in school. Some don't. Them that don't, let 'em quit and get a job." Powe was nonchalantly passed along through the Wayne County school system, all the D's and F's notwithstanding.

Jerrell's mother now says that she wishes she'd known what was happening—or *not* happening—in the classroom. But she says she was too busy working too many 12-hour shifts to put food on the table for her four kids to suspect there was anything wrong.

Powe never had any father figure in his life until he was in the 10th grade, when he met Joe Barnett, the father of his buddy, Wayne County punter Shane Barnett. Joe Barnett was a folksy real estate appraiser with a soft spot for underdogs. He was one of those parents who showed interest in what all his kids' friends were up to. Barnett did a spot-on imitation of everyone in town and never seemed to have any trouble making Powe laugh. "He is just a real funny dude," Powe says. "I felt comfortable with him right away."

It didn't matter to either of them that one was a black teenager and the other was a fiftysomething white guy. Powe went from coming over to the Barnett's house every three or four days, to every other day, to every day. Powe and the elder Barnett grew so tight that Jerrell took to calling him Pop.

Powe was overwhelmed by the recruiting process. The flood of phone calls from recruiters and Internet reporters became mind-numbing, and Powe and his mother asked Barnett for help. "There was so much pressure," Powe says. "Like 30 phone calls a night, and people just showing up at my house. It was wild. I wanted him to handle it, so I told everyone, 'I want you to talk to my pop.'"

Barnett, a Southern Mississippi grad, tried to bring structure to Powe's world. First, he asked Powe to whittle his college choices down to 10. Then, he had him whittle it to a final five: Nebraska, Texas A&M, Oklahoma State, LSU, and Auburn.

On New Year's Eve, 2004, Powe's options shrunk even further. Larry Porter, the assistant who'd been recruiting Powe for Oklahoma State, phoned Barnett to break some big news—Les Miles, the OSU head coach, was accepting the top job at LSU and Porter was going with him. "Just tell Jerrell," Porter told Barnett, "whatever he does, don't commit to Oklahoma State."

Auburn still seemed to have the inside track for Powe because some former Waynesboro players had gone there. Until Orgeron dialed up Powe the night of the Orange Bowl, Ole Miss wasn't even in the picture.

Orgeron told Barnett he wanted Powe to be the first recruit he visited. He arranged a meeting with the young hulk at Barnett's office in Waynesboro, and he told them he planned to devote the whole day to answering Jerrell's questions. Sure enough, Orgeron and then-Ole Miss recruiting coordinator Matt Luke arrived at Barnett's office at 9 a.m. sharp.

"I ain't here to blow smoke up your britches," Orgeron told Powe. "I've come here to tell you all of the things you can do for us."

Orgeron's pitch was about how Powe was a perfect fit with his vision for Ole Miss football. The *Parade* All-America would be his building block, his cornerstone. Other great players would follow Powe's lead. Before long, Powe and Orgeron were chest bumping.

Orgeron spent the morning bouncing around the office, talking about playing defensive line. At one point he shucked his sports coat, took Powe out to the gravel driveway outside Barnett's office, and showed Powe some pass-rushing moves. Minutes later, Barnett's phone rang. It was a friend who had been driving by and had seen the action: "Joe! There's a huge black man and a huge white man fightin' right in front of your office! You gotta call the cops!"

Barnett and Powe were both impressed by Orgeron's presentation. Not only did Orgeron demonstrate more energy and passion than the other recruiters they'd met, but he was also better prepared.

Orgeron even laid out an academic plan that he believed would give Jerrell a chance to become eligible at Ole Miss after he spent a year at Hargrave Military Academy in Virginia. Barnett balked at that and said other recruiters had told them that taking some summer courses would put Powe on the admissions track.

"No way," said Orgeron bluntly. "There's just too much distance for him to cover."

Part of Orgeron's plan included correspondence courses from Brigham Young University that Powe could take online with the help of a tutor. Orgeron explained that Powe would be able to replace his failing grades with new ones earned in the BYU courses. Several football programs around the country, including USC, had recruits taking classes through BYU. The correspondence courses were all within NCAA rules, but Powe needed to start them soon.

"Not many people know about the BYU program now," Orgeron told him, "but it's gonna get a lot more popular in a hurry."

For every question Barnett or Powe had relating to things on and off the field, Orgeron had a concrete answer. And, Powe's advisor said later, the Ole Miss coach didn't sugarcoat anything.

"It was incredible," said Barnett. "He treated Jerrell like it was a job interview more than just some recruiting pitch. And he talked straight to him."

After more than six hours, Orgeron and Luke said their goodbyes and left Barnett's office. As Orgeron drove away, Powe turned to Barnett and told him that was the man he wanted to play for.

"I knew I could become a better player if he coached me," Powe said. "He told me, no matter what, he would stick with me, and that's when I fell in love with him."

Two days after Orgeron's visit to Waynesboro, Barnett spoke with Wayne County High coach, Marcus Boyles, and Ginny Crager, a long-time teacher in the school. Crager, who was familiar with the BYU courses, checked out which courses Powe needed, and by the end of the week, Barnett called Orgeron to tell him that Powe's academic plan was in place.

Powe still hadn't committed to anybody, but it was around this time that he started losing interest in the team he'd been leaning toward, Auburn. He felt like they'd taken him for granted: "They got a little too comfortable. I wasn't looking for a two-hour phone call or anything, but when you say goodbye after a couple of minutes, it tells me you're not that interested."

Powe had told the organizers of the U.S. Army All-American Bowl in San Antonio on January 15 that he'd be willing to announce his college choice during the telecast. Unlike many of the dozen or so recruits who would be pulling hats out of a duffel bag for the NBC cameras that afternoon, Powe didn't figure to bring a lot of suspense to the deal. He'd actually scooped himself by tipping off an Auburn fan site before the game that he was picking the Tigers. But then, just before the start of the third quarter, Powe changed his mind. When his time came, he reached into a black bag, pulled out a purple hat, and said to the cameras, "It's LSU, baby!"

Then he smiled and added, "And I just want to say hey to every-body back in Mississippi."

Orgeron, along with thousands of Auburn fans, was stunned by Powe's announcement. Five minutes later, Orgeron was on the phone with Joe Barnett.

"Barnett, you just see that on TV?" Orgeron said. "What in the hell's happening?"

"Hey, everything is all right," Barnett assured Orgeron. "There've been several moves to get some pressure off of him, some I don't agree with, but it's his way of handling it. But don't worry. Trust me. All is well."

Powe's explanation of the LSU commitment after the game to the media illuminated the farcical side of the recruiting game perfectly, and to a much larger degree, his own bewilderment.

"I don't know why I committed to LSU," he said. "That isn't my final choice. It might change on Signing Day. It's just a commitment. My decision's subject to change. I might sign with LSU, Auburn, or Ole Miss. I've just got to do what's best for me."

Orgeron interpreted Powe's comment about doing what was best for himself as meaning he would sign with Ole Miss. But when Orgeron found out from online reports that Powe was visiting LSU's campus on the final recruiting weekend before signing day, the Rebels coach panicked. Orgeron called Barnett again.

Orgeron: "Joe, I'm worried about J.P. going on a visit to LSU."

Barnett: "Let him go. Everything is okay."

Orgeron: "I don't know, Joe. I'm worried."

Barnett: "Listen, you're gonna get him. I fuckin' guarantee it."

Orgeron: "Guarantee it? Whoa! I ain't heard that since Broadway Joe guaranteed the Jets were gonna beat the Colts in the Super Bowl."

Barnett: "Well, who won that goddamn game, you tell me?"

Barnett, or Broadway Joe as Orgeron began calling him, was right. After packing to go to Baton Rouge, Powe backed out on his visit to LSU, and after committing to Auburn and LSU, he made it official on February 2 by signing with the Ole Miss Rebels.

Now, after all that courting, all that back-and-forth, and all that last-minute anxiety, the real battle could begin: getting Powe academically eligible for admission to Ole Miss.

Powe never received a diploma from Wayne County High. Instead, at his school's graduation ceremony, he was handed a certificate of attendance. At the time, Powe was just relieved that he was being allowed to walk across the stage in his cap and gown along with the rest of the class of 2005.

He had been designated as a special education student—commonly referred to as "sped"—since the second grade. For almost 10 years, that added up to zero, educationally. According to Ginny Crager, Powe's tutor, he was dumped into the Wayne County special ed abyss and forgotten because doing so was too convenient for too many people. Not until midway through his senior year did he begin to get treated as a learning disabled student.

"In Mississippi, if you're sped, you get a 'crazy check,'" Crager explained, using a term used to refer to Supplemental Security Income checks. "That means your parents get a check because you're not smart enough to go out and do well in school and get a good job. And so if you're a single mother, like Jerrell's mother, and you have four kids, it's to your advantage to keep your children in sped and get those $600 checks."

(Shirley Powe denies there was any ulterior motive on her part to allow her son to get passed along through the Wayne County special education system despite not showing any academic progress: "I would never have done any of that.")

The federal money, or "crazy check," is intended for outside academic support for things like tutors. For years, education officials have complained that the availability of "free money" motivates parents to request that their children be evaluated for special ed classes in hope of making a financial score. A few skeptics even claim that some parents encourage their children to flounder so they can continue to draw the SSI checks. (An SSI payment is about five times what a parent draws from ordinary municipal welfare.)

Crager, who teaches gifted students, didn't know Powe very well before Barnett and Marcus Boyles, Powe's coach and the Wayne County athletic director, asked her to help. Her only previous

impression of the affable, quick-to-giggle Powe came from dou-
bling as the team's videographer. In Crager's 40 years as a high
school teacher, she had tutored a few special ed kids for no
charge, because she felt it was part of her responsibility as an
educator, and because the kids had been left in the margins by
an apathetic system.

Crager and Powe got off to a rocky start: For their first scheduled
session, he was a no-show.

She went down to the principal's office to find out where Powe
was. In class, she was told. "Well, he's not there," she replied. "I bet
he's in the gym." Crager went down to the school gym, and sure
enough, Powe was there shooting baskets.

"Jerrell Powe!" Crager screamed as loud as she could, *"You get
your black ass up to that classroom right now!"*

Powe shrugged his shoulders, dropped the basketball, and did
exactly as the 65-year-old said. It was the first time any teacher—
male or female, black or white—had spoken to him like that.
When he got to her room, he flopped down on one of the sofas in
the back.

"Get up!" Crager hollered. "You are going to sit in a straight-
back chair up here, and you are going to work."

Crager was furious. She'd been a teacher long enough to know
that Powe hadn't developed his manners and his attitude all on his
own. He'd been allowed to do nothing because it was just easier for
everyone involved. Crager had witnessed up close how the special ed
programs had been abused. She'd had to battle as a parent herself
when her youngest daughter, who is autistic, received no guidance
in the programs the school had placed her in—no progress reports,
no follow-up, and no adjustment of the basic special ed curriculum
to meet her daughter's specific needs.

Crager's conclusion: The special ed structure in Wayne County
had been allowed to rot from the inside.

From time to time, she'd confronted colleagues who complained about students not showing up and sleeping in their classrooms when they did. Crager always shot back, "If that was my classroom, they wouldn't be sleeping for long."

She says now that she'd ripped into Powe out of love: "For so long, people had let Jerrell get away with doing nothing and just passed him along because the easiest thing was to say, 'Jerrell, go to the field house.' I hate to say this, because I'm a Mississippi teacher, but a lot of Mississippi teachers just say, 'Let 'em go.'"

Less than an hour into their first tutoring session, Crager discovered Powe's situation was far worse than she anticipated.

Crager gently asked, "Jerrell, you can't read, can you, son?"

Powe looked up, said nothing, and dropped his head in shame.

She took a deep breath, walked over, put her arm around his enormous shoulders, and told him, "Jerrell, from this moment on, we have to do it my way."

Crager eventually concluded that Powe suffers from a mild form of dyslexia, and that he also has problems writing and processing information, especially when in a group setting. Powe was later reevaluated in Meridian, Mississippi, by a board-certified mental health counselor who, in an eight-page psychometric evaluation, confirmed Crager's diagnosis. Powe was also found to have Attention Deficit Hyperactivity Disorder (ADHD).

Barnett's lay description of Powe's condition: "Things go in the wrong drawers in his filing cabinet."

Crager, with the approval of the athletic director and the school administration, trashed Powe's meaningless curriculum and set up a new course of study. Every day, she and Powe met at 12:30 for work sessions that lasted three, four, sometimes five hours.

Crager had Powe seek out key words and then guide his eyes down the page with his two beefy fingers pressing against the paper, slowly moving from top to bottom. She had him underline key passages. She then quizzed him on everything he called out, giving him a vocabulary lesson along the way so he wouldn't just be a "word caller."

She also had to break through the defense mechanisms Powe had spent years developing to shield his pride. Sometimes he'd try to bluff his way out. Other times, if his teacher was a female, he'd try to charm her. "It was like with Pavlov's dog," Crager says. "He'd been so conditioned how to get around a woman and not do anything."

And, after being formally diagnosed with a learning disorder, Powe tried to use another crutch. "It's my ADHD, Mrs. Crager," he'd complain, more than once.

"You've got your medication, Jerrell," she'd fire back, making it clear that she wouldn't stand for any of that stuff. "Take it."

But for all of Powe's evasive antics, Crager said she couldn't help but be drawn to him. She knew how humiliating this all was for the teenager, a giant to the rest of the world, yet someone so fragile and vulnerable inside that every day was spent whistling through a graveyard. He made her laugh and cry. Kids like Powe were the reason why she'd wanted to become a teacher all those years ago. He was always respectful. He had never had a sip of alcohol, never smoked a cigarette, and always said "Yes, ma'am" and "No, ma'am." And he was a neat freak who was capable of paying great attention to detail.

"He's a great kid," Crager says. "He's so loveable and compassionate. I never had a son, but if I could choose one—and I'm white, he's black, who cares?—I'd choose someone just like Jerrell Powe. I just wish I'd gotten him as a freshman instead of as a senior."

Powe enrolled in 14 courses through BYU's online program between January 2005 and July 2006, including algebra, reading comprehension, and history. Each course was worth a half-credit.

Barnett says the pacing of the completion of the correspondence courses varied. Some courses Powe completed in a week after "he spent five or six hours a night at Mrs. Crager's home burning the candle." Other courses took him months.

"There was never any intent to deceive," Barnett says. "One course started June 30, but then he had to go to Hargrave Military Academy. He worked a little bit on it at Christmas, but he ran out of time. She had to get a one-week extension. That shows you the honesty and integrity involved on both sides. I mean, if we were going to cheat, she'd have just completed it for him and sent it in."

After a year of their sessions, Crager says, Powe went from a second-grade reading level to a fifth-grade level. As an LD student, he was also granted accommodations, such as getting twice as much time to take a test, or even unlimited time. He was entitled to a reader for his ACT. Without one, he had scored a 12 in the fall of his senior year; with the assistance, Powe jumped to an 18.

The difference in Powe's grades also was eye-popping. He received four A's; the only other A's he got in high school were in PE classes. And that was *before* the summer of 2005, when he headed up to Hargrave.

In the last decade, Hargrave Military Academy in Virginia has become a way station for gifted football prospects with spotty transcripts, low ACT scores, and learning disabilities. Says one Hargrave product: "When you try to enroll at most schools, they ask if you've got a transcript. At Hargrave, they just ask if you've got cleats."

The school is tucked away in the Virginia sticks, just north of the North Carolina border on Route 29 in a sleepy town called Chatham (pop.: 1,300). Over the past decade, nearly every major football program in the country has sent a scout to Hargrave to check out the Cadets' talent stash. One college coach who attended a Hargrave game projected that the Cadets had more future NFL first-rounders on their team than half the teams in the Top 25.

Among the members of the 54-man Hargrave roster Powe joined were two dozen players referred there by Division I programs in hopes of seeing the players "get qualified." Hargrave's head coach,

Robert Prunty, estimated that another two dozen would go on to sign with Division I schools. Over the previous three years, Hargrave had sent more than 120 players to Division I football, and the school touts having produced four first-round draft choices, including St. Louis Rams star wide receiver Torry Holt.

Despite the school's gaudy football résumé, Hargrave administrators insist they aren't running a football factory/diploma mill. And in fact, the daily work schedule is culture shock for most players. Reveille is at 6:00 a.m. Classes and chapel last until 3 p.m. Sports last until 5:30 p.m. A mandatory two-hour study hall follows dinner before lights out and taps at 10 p.m.

After two weeks at The Grave, Powe was struggling. He called Barnett: "Pop, I'm having it tough up here. It's more like being in a prison than being in a school."

Pop assured Powe that the year would move quickly, especially after he began making some friends and football season started. Barnett proved to be right. Powe, who'd been granted one of the school's dozen scholarships, soon became one of the most popular players on the team. "He's such a funny, likable guy to be around," said USC wide receiver Vidal Hazelton, a former Hargrave teammate. "J.P. could always make you laugh and smile."

Powe was a team captain, and when he and the other three Cadet captains went to midfield for the coin toss, the lone Hargrave player under 320 pounds was a 280-pound defensive end. It was an awesome sight to see that kind of beef meeting with the other team's captains. Still, Powe couldn't wait to get finished with The Grave.

"I just didn't like having to be there," Powe says. "But I knew I *had* to be there."

The Ole Miss staff believed—prayed— that Powe would be eligible for the 2006 season after having completed the BYU courses, along with others taken at Hargrave. He was one of three recruits the Rebels coaches were crossing their fingers for. The other two were junior college recruits: QB Brent Schaeffer and LB Rory Johnson. Both still had courses to complete, and their playing status wouldn't get resolved until fall camp.

Powe's case was different. Technically, he had done what he needed to do. He had a combined GPA of 2.54 from courses at Wayne County, Hargrave, and the correspondence offerings from BYU.

Powe had already dazzled his new Rebels teammates with his athleticism and drive during voluntary summer workouts. Few could've ever imagined that not only would he finish 16 110-yard sprints weighing in at 348 pounds, but that Powe actually was running past guys 100 pounds lighter in the process.

The big question was whether Powe could get past the NCAA Clearinghouse.

The Clearinghouse is an Iowa-based company that certifies the eligibility of all freshman NCAA athletes. By NCAA standards, a student-athlete needs at least a 2.5 GPA in 14 core classes, including English, math, and science, plus a score of 17 on the ACT college entrance exam. A sliding scale adjusts for lower or higher GPAs, along with lower or higher test scores. By definition, Powe was a qualifier. But to report for practice or enroll at Ole Miss he still needed formal authorization by the Clearinghouse.

On August 25, 2006, the NCAA reviewed Powe's case and ruled him academically ineligible, saying he would not be allowed to receive scholarship aid or play that season for the Rebels. Powe and Barnett say no reason was given.

Six days later, Powe applied for and was granted a temporary restraining order by a Lafayette County Chancery Court judge, allowing him to enroll in classes at Ole Miss. The TRO was granted on the eve of the deadline for students to be accepted into the University. The crux of the case, according to Powe's attorney, James

L. Carroll, was that the NCAA and Ole Miss were in violation of the American Disabilities Act, since Powe is learning disabled.

"A very fine young man was wronged by the NCAA," Carroll told *The Clarion-Ledger*. "The whole thing is, the NCAA was hoping nothing would be done, that the deadline would expire, and Jerrell would not be admitted to the University of Mississippi. They thought they could push him around, that they could take advantage of a poor, young black man, and nothing would happen."

NCAA spokesman Bob Williams told *The Clarion-Ledger* that Powe had been told why he was denied, because of "irregularities in Jerrell's high school course work and transcripts."

Carroll's response to Williams: "If the NCAA is suggesting irregularities in his high school transcripts constitutes some sort of fraud, then we will sue them over that. There is no issue about fraud in his transcripts. The issue is he didn't do good in school until he was finally diagnosed as dyslexic his senior year at Wayne County."

In court documents, Carroll wrote that if Powe were prohibited from practicing his "special talent of football," it would cause "irreparable damage and injury to his future potential for playing football on a professional level and for earning substantial income."

The court documents showed that Powe had failed nine classes at Wayne County and Hargrave, with a 2.18 GPA in his classes at those schools. He had, however, received 13 A's or B's in the BYU correspondence classes, which had given him his 2.54 cumulative GPA.

Included in the court documents were testimonials from Powe: "Without the help of Mrs. Crager I would not have succeeded. We worked on the Internet courses together. She read them to me, and I was able to answer the speedback lessons."

But it was Shirley Powe's statement that turned her son's case into a nationwide story: "I didn't know until he was almost done with high school that he wasn't getting the education he should have gotten. Coach Boyles and Mrs. Crager helped him get enough schooling to go to college. Jerrell really is a good child, but he just can't read. Please give him this chance to attend Ole Miss."

The words "just can't read" sparked a firestorm. "Why let a little thing like illiteracy keep a guy out of school?" wrote a columnist in the Memphis *Commercial Appeal*. "It's a farce, of course, an embarrassment to Ole Miss. But this isn't just about Ole Miss, and it certainly isn't new."

Overnight, Powe became the poster child for a corrupt system, a willing pawn in a shameless game.

"That really ticked me off," Powe says of the *Commercial Appeal* column. "It was a big lie. I can read."

Says Barnett: "The guy who wrote the book about the bell curve, well, he's basically right, whether it's with hunting dogs, athletes, or whatever. About 10% of people you can't help out, and they won't amount to shit, and then there are about 80%, which is the rest of us, and then the other 10%, who won't need any help whether it's education or financial. Well, that 20% of the people make 80% of the noise and bitch and gripe. This guy who wrote that article, he's in that upper 10% and he doesn't understand the rest of us."

Shirley Powe says her words were taken out of context: "I never said my child can't read."

Barnett says that her statement was taken too literally: "When I was in the military in 1968, I was the first person ever to fire a perfect record with an M-14 at Fort Knox. I got a trophy and a medal around here someplace. Well, they yanked me out of basic training, so all I ever did was go around and give demonstrations. I had perfect eyesight back then. I have lenses now, and so if someone asks, 'Do you wanna go bird hunting?' I'll say, 'No, man, I can't shoot anymore.' That doesn't mean I can't shoot. It just means I can't do it as well. That's exactly what Shirley meant. Jerrell couldn't read fast enough to keep up, but that whole thing got out there."

In hopes of doing a little damage control, Barnett allowed a reporter from *The Clarion-Ledger* into his office and had Powe log onto the Internet. Barnett asked the reporter to choose a story and then had Powe sit down and read it. "He read it just like you and I would've," Barnett said with pride. Barnett even asked the reporter to pick another story for Powe to read just so there would be no suspicion that Powe might've memorized something.

On September 17, after his advisors met with Ole Miss attorneys and compliance director David Wells, Powe dropped his lawsuit and withdrew his application for admission.

Said Barnett: "We didn't want Jerrell to be portrayed as some trouble-making black kid who decided to raise hell because he didn't get into school."

Over the past few years, the BYU courses that helped boost Powe's GPA have become the worst-kept secret in college sports. In Michael Lewis' best-selling book *The Blind Side*, about the life of another Ole Miss recruit, offensive tackle Michael Oher, the BYU correspondence courses were referred to as "the great Mormon grade-grab."

But the Utah school, according to a 2006 *Salt Lake Tribune* investigation, made changes to its Internet program in an effort to crack down on the cheating that had allegedly taken place by college athletes at a Kansas junior college, Nicholls State University, and at the University of Kansas.

Orgeron had learned about the BYU courses when he was at USC from Fred Stroock, the Trojans' former assistant AD for academic services. Stroock had been at USC for two decades and seemed to know every possible way to give a borderline student any hope of getting into school.

Orgeron, functioning as USC's recruiting coordinator, worked closely with Stroock. "He became an expert on NCAA rules,"

Stroock says of Orgeron. Stroock adds that the two years when the Trojans had their highest graduation rates both came during Orgeron's reign as recruiting coordinator: "People don't realize how much time and effort he spent getting their academic records and talking to teachers and staying on people. He really cared."

Stroock says he was opposed to the 2000 decision by the NCAA to change its core course definition to include approved Internet courses: "I thought it would open the door to abuse."

Still, so long as it was within NCAA rules, USC had no qualms about accepting courses from BYU. If a student-athlete was one course short, the Trojans used BYU as a last resort.

In the Rebels' 2006 recruiting class, 11 of 28 signees had Internet courses. "It's all legal," says Kent McLeod. "Lots of other students take them too. But if they tell us we can't take BYU courses, there are plenty of other places that we could use."

The attention of the Powe case, along with the NCAA's new APR regulations, had an impact on how Orgeron recruits: "Two years ago I could've brought in anybody I wanted. Now our review committee has put a limit on the correspondence courses, and there were some guys we've had to eliminate."

Orgeron maintains that there's a lot of ignorance when it comes to reactions to who is being helped in cases like Powe's. He cites the story of Mike Patterson, one of his favorite players, who became a first-round NFL draft choice and signed a $30 million contract. Patterson had always struggled in the classroom, but USC discovered that he suffered from a learning disability and worked to get him admitted to school and put in special academic programs.

"There's a difference between guys who don't go to class and are lazy, and guys who have a severe learning disability," Orgeron says. "If you identify a learning disability, and you have the proper departments to help these young people, it can get done. I saw it. Mike Patterson coming in could barely read, but he got an education because USC identified his disability, and he went to class and worked hard. What's the difference between that and having cancer? If you have cancer, you go get it treated. Too many young men, especially in the South, get written off as lazy or dumb. I think some of those people can be helped. Of course, each individual case is different, and it's gotta be legit all the way."

He went on: "How would you like to be a 6'3", 300-pound kid, and go into a classroom, and you can't read what the lady writes on the blackboard? And then, everybody says you're lazy. How terrible is that? But those are the challenges of recruiting. You gotta go to the guidance counselor and ask, is he on time? Does he come to class? Go talk to the coaches and see what type of person he is."

Then you decide.

Jerrell Powe thought about giving up on college football after being turned away by the NCAA and Ole Miss, but Barnett's motto of "Don't Quit" had taken hold.

On a sunny fall afternoon, as he and Barnett walked into the tiny Huff-n-Puff Smokehouse about a quarter-mile from Barnett's office, Powe, who literally shook the floor of the cramped rib joint, got sized up by the dozen or so lunch patrons.

"You need to go east," a white man in his late 20s said as the big lineman approached the register. "You need to be at Auburn, where you could get you some education, man."

"He needs to go west, is what he needs to do," said the 40-ish white woman waiting to take Powe's order.

"Where's west?" the Auburn fan countered.

"LSU," she said.

"Please. If he goes to LSU, he'll be just like that boy JaMarcus Russell," replied the Auburn fan. "That boy be dumb as rocks."

Powe just shook his head. He still planned on going to Ole Miss and playing for Orgeron. With Barnett's prodding, Powe would redo the BYU courses and send weekly updates to his lawyer, Jim Carroll, who would then send them, along with a report on how many hours were spent on a given class, to Ole Miss compliance director David Wells and to Lee Tyner, the university attorney.

"Jim said he was going to ask them to tell us if we're going too fast or too slow on anything," explained Barnett. "But he told 'em, 'You best tell us, and we'll readjust our schedule, whatever you want. Otherwise, silence is consent.'"

The new plan was to have Powe complete five credits by February 1, in time for Signing Day, or else Ole Miss wouldn't sign him again. And then he'd finish up the other half of his courses, according to Barnett's by mid-May.

To help his de facto ward fill his time, Barnett lined up work for Powe, an $8-an-hour job as an aide at the Wayne County jail. Powe's main responsibility as a jailer was feeding the prisoners, which meant he watched a lot of TV. The worst part of his part-time gig was the day he had to put on rubber gloves and scrub the caked-on feces off an inmate who'd become unresponsive and been tasered by one of the guards.

"I have to close my eyes every time I think about it," he said later. "We had to strip him down because there was crap all over him. It had even dried up and caked on his manhood."

Barnett hoped being around the inmates would reinforce the importance of making good decisions to Powe. Just to make sure, Barnett said he had plenty of spies in the local police force watching over Powe so he didn't get caught with the wrong crowd.

A few days after Powe returned from Oxford in August, he was talking to some friends who were in a rough neighborhood around Waynesboro. Powe's cell rang.

"Jerrell, you get your ass out of MLK!" Barnett told him, referring to Waynesboro's roughest area, a strip along Martin Luther King Jr. Avenue.

"How'd you know I'm down here?" Powe replied.

"That's all right, I know," said Barnett, who claims he has sources in every arm of law enforcement in the 601 area code. "Just get your big ass out of there. They may be selling drugs down there."

Barnett said that despite the NCAA rules people and "certain people" at Ole Miss (read: David Wells) who were trying to block Powe's admission, he wouldn't let Jerrell Powe be cast aside. Barnett made clear that he still had big plans for Powe. In his benefactor's estimation, Powe would get a good signing bonus when he eventually got to the NFL, and then have eight good years of pro football.

But before Powe got his crack at the NFL, Barnett said, there were many lessons to be learned, and not just the ones from Mrs. Crager: "I tell him all the time to watch how he presents himself. I'll say 'Jerrell, you need to think white and talk white. Be more like Tiki Barber,' and he'll go, 'I got ya.'"

Orgeron wished he'd had Powe on his team in 2006. He was exactly what the Rebels D was missing, an unblockable lineman. But Orgeron knew it was going to be a long shot to get him in the class of 2007, regardless of what Broadway Joe said.

Either way, Jerrell Powe was going to cause some havoc.

Orgeron just hoped it would be on the field.

Not in the newspapers or in the courts.

Chapter 11 ▶

FACE
TIME

THERE IS A grace period that all new head coaches get when they take over a rebuilding job. It varies depending on the school, the circumstances, and the coach. In Orgeron's case, that grace period appeared to be ending just one month into his second season. The talk-radio circuit was already buzzing, and so were most of the local columnists. Perhaps most telling of all was that his bosses had felt the need to come publicly to his defense. For a guy trying to sell his program in competition with the Floridas and LSUs of the world, it was not a good sign.

The 2006 season had got off to a promising enough beginning, with the Rebels beating Memphis 28-25 in their opener. But in Week 2, the Rebels went to Missouri and got blown out, 34-7. Next, they were routed 31-14 by Kentucky, the only SEC team they had beaten in 2005. Ole Miss then returned home, only to be destroyed by Wake Forest, 27-3. The wheels appeared to have come off the wagon.

At 1–3 on the season and 4–11 overall since taking over, Orgeron was getting ripped at every turn. Even former Ole Miss coach Billy Brewer, host of the *Hotty Toddy Hotline* post-game radio show, which runs on a dozen stations across the state, got in some shots in an interview in the *Chattanooga Times Free Press*: "If you see the facilities and things and what they've done to this campus and the money they've spent, there should be no way that anybody—I don't care if he's out of kindergarten—shouldn't win at least five or six ball games here."

All of the carping prompted the Ole Miss administration to jump to Orgeron's defense. Athletics director Pete Boone said that many of the Rebels' problems could be attributed to the recruiting efforts of former coach David Cutcliffe. Chancellor Robert Khayat echoed the point, confirming to *The Atlanta Journal-Constitution* that recruiting was the main reason he decided to make the coaching change: "The No. 1 thing was recruiting. The teams that are the most successful have the really good athletes, and they keep replenishing them. We felt that we needed to recruit better, and I think that Coach Orgeron has shown that he will be able to do that on a consistent basis. We didn't get into this situation in one year, and we won't get out in one year."

Still, the Rebels' nightmarish start underscored a cold reality that Orgeron's manic energy had—to some extent—partially been able to gloss over. Ole Miss, no matter how much Orgeron spun it in chest-out style, was still Ole Miss. And unless the Rebels started winning games, they weren't going to be able to compete on the recruiting trail with LSU, Tennessee, Florida—and certainly not USC.

The big question was just how much would the actual losing sting? By the initial reactions from the recruits who had been receiving Ole Miss text messages, the answer was pretty clear: quite a bit. The Rebels out-of-state boards were a telling benchmark as many of the big-name recruits started to fade away.

So did Stephen Garcia, the top name on the Rebels quarterback board. The Tampa native and his father had been saying for most of the off-season that Ole Miss was right there in the race, along-side South Carolina. But then the Rebels' losing streak hit, and

Werner reported to Orgeron in early fall that the Garcias weren't returning his text messages.

More bad news: T-Bob Hebert, the top-rated center prospect on the Rebels board also stopped returning text messages. "His daddy told me he's worried that if he comes here, and then I get fired, he's stuck here," Orgeron said. "I understand where he's coming from."

Things appeared bleak with the 10th-ranked Georgia Bulldogs coming to Oxford for a nationally televised night game on September 30. The Bulldogs were a rugged team that figured to maul the young, undermanned Rebels, who already were starting a pair of true freshmen defensive linemen and were missing their two best big men, Jeremy Garrett and Peria Jerry.

Making matters worse, he was benching starting DT Hayward Howard for skipping a class. Another true freshmen, 255-pound Marcus Tillman, would have to shift inside and start at DT against the Bulldogs. Orgeron knew an ESPN audience could be a great recruiting opportunity. But he also knew that if the Rebels got humiliated, it could be devastating to his class of 2007.

"If we get beat 51-3 on ESPN," said one Ole Miss assistant going into the Georgia game, "a third of the kids we're trying to recruit will probably drop us."

But Orgeron had challenged his players all week, and this time they responded. His team was more physical than the bigger Bulldogs, which was quite a statement given that Georgia had the luxury of rotating nine different defensive linemen, while the Rebels played only 13 different defensive players in the entire game. It was a testament to just how little depth Ole Miss had.

The Rebels played loose and took chances. They blocked a punt. Actually, they blocked two. The first one came late in the first quarter and gave the Rebels the ball at Georgia's 5-yard line. But the play was called back when an Ole Miss player was flagged for holding.

Georgia came back in the second half to win, 14-9, but the Rebels had acquitted themselves well in the national spotlight. In the stands to see it firsthand were several Ole Miss recruits, including junior college blue-chipper A.J. Jackson, quarterback Brent Schaeffer's former go-to receiver, who came to Oxford on an official visit. The 6'5", 228-pound Jackson said after the game that if he had been out there playing for the Rebels, the score would've been different.

Yet, despite the respectable showing, the Rebels dropped to 1–4. Lowly Vanderbilt was up next. It was Homecoming. Orgeron couldn't stomach what losing this game against the Commodores might mean to his program's future. No doubt more rumors would swirl that the Ole Miss brass might be thinking about pulling the plug on him. And how do you persuade recruits to sign on with a regime that might not be there when they show up?

Orgeron was also getting pounded all over the Internet in a popular parody song created by a Memphis radio host. The song, *Colonel Reb Is Crying*, was a play off the retired old Rebels mascot, the infamous tale about Orgeron's tearing off his shirt to fire up his team, and the coach's husky Cajun drawl:

> Colonel Reb is crying in his Confederate handkerchief,
>
> Colonel Reb is crying, he needs some real relief.
>
> He asks Coach Orgeron, Can you save us from this dread?
>
> Coach O rips his shirt off, and this is what he says:
>
> Yaw, Yaw, Yaw, Yaw!
>
> Yaaaaaw, Yaaaaaw, Yaaaaaw, Yaaaaaw!
>
> *Foot-baw!*

A few days after it popped up on the web, the song was set to video, complete with menacing photos of an enraged Orgeron on the sidelines, and circulated via YouTube. A few staffers got a chuckle out of the song, but cringed at the thought of Orgeron's hearing them download it on their computers. However, during a meeting of the team's freshmen, a few of the young Rebels goaded Shay Hodge, one of the receivers, into singing the Coach O song for Orgeron, who, to the relief of everyone in the room, seemed to get a kick out of it.

One assistant says moments like this are what makes Orgeron such a paradox. He is a fiercely proud, extremely competitive man who has the shortest fuse of perhaps any head coach in the country. Yet Orgeron had no problem at all reading a parodied speech taken from an Alabama fansite that skewered him to the other defensive coaches to break up the monotony of a postspring meeting.

Orgeron said he learned a long time ago from Jimmy Johnson never to pay attention to what was written in the newspaper or get caught up in what outsiders thought. Besides, he had more important things to think about, like the Rebels' dwindling numbers on the practice field. Many of his younger players, some of whom hadn't had the chances to get rested because there were no viable backups, were breaking down.

At times, the stress did appear to be getting to Orgeron. His emotional roller-coaster ride in the course of a given 18-hour workday jerked from upbeat cheerleader to irate drill sergeant, from chatty jokester to dejected captain of a ship that has taken on water, to manic survivalist just trying to stay alive. All the while, he stoked his furnace with vats of coffee, Diet Coke, and Red Bull.

In his first season at Ole Miss, Orgeron rode his team so hard that many of the upperclassmen quit on him. A few others rebelled. The team lost its final four games of the year, each a blowout, culminating with a humiliating 35-14 loss to archrival Mississippi State, which had entered the game 2–8.

Orgeron later admitted he lost the team in 2005, but that he had learned from it, particularly about when to push and when not to push too hard. Sitting in the war room, the Wednesday morning before the Vanderbilt game, he conceded he just hoped the Ole Miss administration gave him a decent shot to see this plan through. "It's comin'," he said as he leaned forward in his chair. "I can feel it. That place was rockin' the other night against Georgia. I really believe in what we are doing here. Is it gonna work out? I don't know, but I'm going for it."

"Going for it" in Orgeron's lexicon meant doing it his way. No pussyfooting around. If he flopped, as many were predicting, he knew he'd have little trouble landing a good job somewhere else coaching D-line and recruiting his ass off. And hell, yeah, he'd be happy doing it too. But running the whole show had been his dream for as long as he could remember. It may not have always looked like it, he said, but he was having the time of his life.

Of course, there were also those days when he joked that he'd retire to Southern California and just pump iron on Muscle Beach and get huge.

The dismal first month of the 2006 season convinced Orgeron that he *had to* identify more defensive linemen and linebackers.

Even though the Rebels had five D-linemen already committed to the class of 2007—three tackles (Ted Laurent, Drake Nevis, Jerrell Powe) and two ends (Stanley Porter, junior college transfer Dion Gales)—none of the five was a sure thing to make it to Oxford in the fall of 2007. Laurent, Porter, and Gales were borderline students. Nevis was a decent student, but as a Louisiana kid, Orgeron feared he might be tempted to de-commit if the home-state LSU Tigers made a move. And Powe's situation, given his history with the NCAA Clearinghouse, could only be categorized as a long shot.

As it stood in 2006, Orgeron had to move two freshmen tight ends to defensive end and flip a freshman guard to nose tackle in fall camp just to be able to put a D-line on the field.

Vandy weekend would give the Rebels a chance to woo one of the players on the top third of their out-of-state defensive tackles board, Ian Williams, a 300-pounder from the Orlando area. The weekend visit by Williams was one of the five official campus visits allowed recruits by NCAA regulations. The Rebels were excited by the prospect of hosting him.

The Internet recruiting websites had Williams listed as a "four-star" prospect, which seemed a bit generous to Orgeron & Co. The Rebels staff didn't think Williams had the explosive power or quickness of Laurent and Powe. But they ranked his talent level close to that of Nevis, and Williams was a solid student who wouldn't have any trouble getting admitted. A few weeks back, he took an official visit to Notre Dame and hadn't come away raving, if Internet reports were to be believed.

Matt Lubick reported that Williams was leaning to Florida. (And, in fact, Williams later acknowledged that he'd given the Gators his commitment the preceding spring.) The Rebels had their doubts whether the Gators would save a scholarship for Williams once some more highly regarded prospects showed interest. In addition to Florida and Notre Dame, Williams was also considering Clemson and Auburn. He had told the Internet reporters that he would make his announcement on November 3 before his high school's Homecoming Game.

"We're fourth right now for him," Orgeron said Friday morning, about eight hours before Williams was scheduled to arrive on campus. "But after this weekend, we'll probably be second."

Kent McLeod, Ole Miss' coordinator of football operations and the person who orchestrates the itinerary for the official visits of all recruits, later said the Rebels had a lot of distance to close: "His mom's not coming with him. That's usually not a good sign."

Since schools are not allowed by NCAA rules to pay for the travel or hotel room for a recruit's family, it's not uncommon for a prospect to come alone on a visit. (The schools are allowed to pay for the player's meals, travel to the campus, and hotel room.) McLeod said if an out-of-state kid was seriously considering committing, someone in his family usually came along to check things out. But given Williams's abbreviated time frame before his announcement, it didn't look too good for the Rebels.

Williams was the second recruit the Rebels had hosted on an official visit this season. Jackson, the big junior college receiver, was the first. In accord with NCAA rules, schools are allowed to host 56 prospects on official visits, which usually begin Friday afternoon and end Sunday morning. As is the case with every other football weekend, the Rebels game against Vanderbilt was scripted right down to the minute.

At 1:15 p.m. Friday afternoon, Orgeron assembled the staff in the war room for a quick meeting. He went over every facet of the upcoming weekend, ranging from what time the Rebels would have their Friday walk-through to what time dinner would be served in the team's banquet room. Then, at 1:58, he put in Williams's eval tape so his coaches could get reacquainted with their visiting recruit.

The staff watched four plays without comment. "I remember at first we didn't like him much till we saw more film," Orgeron said. It didn't help Williams's cause that he played for a bad team (0–6 at the time) and that he'd been asked to play most of the season at offensive guard. The Rebels had tape only from his junior season.

Williams made a few plays in which he impressed more with effort than athleticism. The staff was hardly wowed. "He's got good feet," Lubick offered. "Nice explosiveness, huh?" No one bit. Another minute passed, and then, finally, Williams darted inside to smother the quarterback. *That* got Orgeron fired up. The next clip showed Williams bull rushing over an undersized lineman. The next one showed a bit more explosion off the ball into the backfield.

"That's pretty good right there," Orgeron said.

A replaying of the tape distanced Williams's stock from Laurent's, but Ole Miss wasn't in a position to be all that choosy. "He could probably help us right now," Orgeron observed, and then turned to Lubick. "Anything special with him, Lube?"

"He went to Notre Dame already and didn't really like it," responded Lubick. "I guess he felt like he didn't really fit in."

"Okay, then," Orgeron said. "We are going to shock him."

Before the staff left the war room, Orgeron had one final message: "Let's not talk about how we should've won games. I don't wanna hear that. No, it should be, 'We're about winning championships, and you're going to be a part of it.'"

The schedule for Williams's weekend in Oxford was almost as detailed as the team's. He arrived at the Memphis Airport on Northwest Airlines flight No. 943 at 5:02 p.m. After McLeod got Williams checked in at his hotel, the Downtown Inn, he drove the young man back to the Ole Miss football offices so he could sit in on the Rebels' defensive meeting, which was scheduled to begin at 7:15 sharp.

But first, at 6:45, there was a half-hour meeting just for the coaches and the players involved in special teams. Each of the Rebels' four assistant coaches involved in an aspect of special teams addressed the room to hammer home the week's big strategic points, stressing Vanderbilt's tendencies and going over their own possible trick plays. Each coach also took the opportunity to give his own mini pep talk.

The meeting was heavy on call and response, with clapping in unison any time one of the coaches called out *"Rebels, Ready-Ready?"* Players responded to each prompt with battalion-worthy precision. It was hard to imagine that a 1–4 team could sound so unified and sure.

At 7:15 p.m. the Rebels formed into offensive and defensive units with their own coaches. As the players scurried to their respective halves of the team room, all of the coaches except Orgeron formed an assembly line and began sliding floor-to-ceiling panels around a track system to divide the room.

The separate meetings featured more of the same revved-up vibe. The team looked as if it were primed to take the field. In Orgeron's address, he emphasized how the Rebels took it to the Georgia Bulldogs for four quarters. He called out the names of the players who stepped up, which only seemed to get the other players fired up.

"And Greg Hardy, you kept on knockin' the shit out of that offensive tackle," Orgeron yelled as his body literally started shaking. "You were knockin' his head off! He didn't want no more! Are you gonna get after it like that tomorrow?"

This was Orgeron's way not only to begin to raise the Rebels' spirits for tomorrow's kickoff but also to bolster the confidence of the other players in the room that Ole Miss had a few more playmakers than just All-America middle linebacker Patrick Willis. For Williams, seated in the back row of the small auditorium, the team meeting was a window to get a read on the pulse of the team.

"It was very intense," Williams said later. "I loved it. Charlie Weis was more of a sit-down-and-lecture guy. Coach O is more of a player's coach."

At 7:45 p.m., Williams left the Rebels football complex to get dinner with his host for the night, junior defensive tackle Jeremy Garrett. An honor student and one of the team's leaders, Garrett wouldn't be playing in the Vanderbilt game because of a leg injury, so he didn't ride down to Tupelo to stay with the team, which always spent the night before a home game outside of Oxford to minimize distractions.

"Jeremy is a great kid," said McLeod. "He's a very clean-cut, mature guy." For his hosting duties, Garrett gets paid the NCAA-allowed $30 by McLeod.

As Williams headed out to eat dinner with Garrett and Lubick, the Rebels boarded three buses to make the 45-minute drive to Tupelo. The team, as always, would bunk at a weathered old motel called the Summit.

At 9:00 p.m., in a vacant banquet room, assistant AD Barney Farrar had already set up the Rebels' film projector so Orgeron and the staff could spend an hour studying more prospects. Maurice Harris, another Ole Miss assistant AD, arrived toting a gallon of milk and two boxes of fresh-baked chocolate-chip cookies from a nearby grocery store.

The first player the Rebels watched was Rolando Melancon, a defensive tackle from Lutcher, Louisiana, just down the road from LSU. Dressed in the Tigers purple and gold, Melancon (pronounced Meh-LAHN-so) looked so much like an LSU lineman that Orgeron couldn't help but hum the Tigers battle cry: "Duh-*da*-duh-*dah!*" as in "Hold That Ti-Guh!"

Orgeron had seen tape of Melancon many times over the past two years. He loved him. Melancon wasn't a huge inside player, but he looked unblockable as he smashed a guard into a running back, toppling both of them. "*Gaaawd!*" Orgeron howled.

Melancon had been a dominant presence in southern Louisiana high school football since his freshman season, when as a 245-pounder, he led Lutcher to the Class 3A state title and was named district defensive player of the year.

"This is the quickest kid we're recruiting," Orgeron told the room. "He says he's 6'3", but he's only about 6'1", and it don't matter. He's Mike Patterson."

Melancon's tape had eyes popping. He burst past centers before they could get out of their stances. "You gotta work your magic on this kid, Frank," Orgeron said to Frank Wilson, the Rebels' recruiter in Louisiana.

"He says he likes Michigan," Wilson replied.

"Michigan? What are his grades, Frank?" Orgeron asked.

"Not good," Wilson said. "It's gonna be close for him to make it."

"Okay," said Orgeron, shaking his head. "Michigan, huh?"

Farrar changed tapes, and the Rebels watched two more defensive players. One was a junior college defensive end from Georgia Military College, Jarius Wynn, whom the staff liked. ("He's really fast-twitch," said Werner.) The other was an outside linebacker who got canned after five plays. ("He's alligator fast," Orgeron said, the terminology for a player with good straight-line speed, but without the ability to go side to side.)

They then watched a half-dozen offensive linemen who failed to grab anyone's interest. The only energy in the room came from the cell phone of tight ends coach Hugh Freeze, who was getting calls from junior recruits about every three minutes.

Every kid was "Big" to Freeze, as in "What's up, Big Donte so-and-so?" Orgeron was thrilled that Freeze was setting the tempo for the rest of the staff in junior recruiting. The bad news was that one of the calls Freeze received was from Kenneth Davis, a junior tailback already committed to Ole Miss. Davis was calling to say he thought he tore his MCL that night.

"Show us something, Barney," Orgeron said, hoping to rejuvenate the room. Farrar put in tape of Joe McKnight, the New Orleans-area tailback whom Wilson had proclaimed in the spring to be the best recruit in the country, then guaranteed getting him on May 24.

The Rebels had marveled at McKnight on the various tapes they'd seen. His eval tape had footage from McKnight's first national TV appearance, when his school (John Curtis Christian) played the nation's top-ranked team (Alabama's Hoover High of MTV's *Two-a-Days* fame). The Patriots fell behind 14-0. Then, McKnight took over, catching three passes for 134 yards and two touchdowns and making the game-sealing INT as Curtis won 28-14.

McKnight was the first recruit Wilson offered a scholarship to after he joined Orgeron's staff in 2005. McKnight was a sophomore back then. At the time, McKnight's coach, J.T. Curtis, a Louisiana high school legend, kept trying to sell Wilson on his seniors.

"Yeah, all right, J.T., but how can I get Joe?" Wilson persisted. "I wanna start recruiting Joe."

Wilson realized then and there that if the Rebels had any shot at landing McKnight, they had no time to spare. Orgeron, too, had brainstormed about a plan to get McKnight to Oxford. Going head-to-head with LSU for a player whom the Rebels staff believed to be the best back from New Orleans since Marshall Faulk certainly sounded like a long shot, but Orgeron suspected adding another heavy hitter into the chase could change that.

USC, which had already gotten commitments from blue-chip tailbacks Marc Tyler and Broderick Green, knew about McKnight, but the Trojans were recruiting him as a cornerback. USC linebackers coach Ken Norton had even told one of Curtis High's assistants that he thought if McKnight went to USC, he'd start three years at cornerback and go right to the NFL as a first-rounder.

Before USC coaches went out on the road for their spring evaluations last May, Orgeron dialed up old pal Pete Carroll and told him Joe McKnight would be their next Reggie Bush and was better than any back in the country. "I wanna help Pete," Orgeron later said, "but it doesn't hurt to get Joe away from LSU."

To Orgeron, USC was the perfect diversion. Sure, USC could open the kid's eyes to things far beyond Tiger country. But USC was also a four-hour plane ride away. Orgeron figured if there were some confusion in McKnight's mind, it might give Ole Miss a chance. Ole Miss might become a viable alternative for a kid who was conflicted, especially since Orgeron felt that if anyone could win McKnight's trust, it was Frank Wilson.

"If he goes to USC, he's gonna win the Heisman," Orgeron said. "His tape is better than Reggie's high school tape. If he comes to Oxford, we'll change the bricks on Manning Way to McKnight Way."

Melancon and McKnight weren't the only Louisiana prospects high on the Rebels' wish list. "Wait 'til y'all see the Breaux brothers," Wilson drawled.

As the staff watched both tapes, Wilson didn't indicate which brother he thought was the better prospect. Delvin, a 6'1", 190-pound defensive back, made two big hits and appeared more physical. Lionel, a 6'0", 190-pound wide receiver/return man, flashed more speed. On two separate plays he snagged bouncing kicks and effortlessly fielded them before bursting upfield. "I love that right there," whooped Werner. "I'd take 'em both."

Wilson then explained that Delvin had already committed to LSU. The Tigers offered him a scholarship even though he broke his leg in the first half of the first game of his junior season and missed the rest of the year. Lionel, Wilson added, was the state 400-meter indoor champ. His speed was startling. On one play Lionel caught an underthrown ball that forced him to slow down, letting two defensive backs catch up to him, but he was able to crank up to top speed in four steps and still outrun the defense.

"Whoa, that don't look right," Kehoe interjected from the front of the room. "Look at how fast the cheerleaders on the sidelines are jumping up and down. The tape got sped up."

Farrar rewound the tape and, sure enough, Breaux—along with everyone else on the field—indeed seemed to be moving 20% faster. That curious detail notwithstanding, everyone in the room was sold on Lionel Breaux.

"Is he okay with being a cornerback?" Orgeron asked.

"He wants to play receiver," Wilson said.

"All right, if he can run like that and catch the ball, we can use a receiver like that," Orgeron said. Of course, it wasn't a stretch to think that if Breaux didn't shine as a receiver, Orgeron might play him at cornerback.

Farrar grabbed the tape of another Louisiana product, Rishaw Johnson, the 6'4", 315-pound offensive lineman Orgeron and his coaches had loved in their summer camp. Johnson committed to the Rebels in June. At the time, he was an unknown commodity to the Internet recruiting services. However, after he committed to Ole Miss, he visited Florida State's camp and was offered a scholarship by the Seminoles.

"That was a great job by Frank getting this kid to camp," Orgeron told the group. "If he's not in camp, he doesn't commit."

Johnson's tape showed everything the Rebels were looking for in an offensive lineman. He was quick off the ball, and he demonstrated that he knew how to play with leverage: "Look at him dip his hips and strike!" gushed Freeze.

Just as important, Johnson was flexible. Two coaches noted that all of Johnson's cleats were into the ground when he went down into his stance—a sign of good ankle flexion, a key trait for linemen. Johnson also showed his athleticism when he lined up at defensive tackle and made a couple of plays crushing ballcarriers.

"*Whooo!* That fires me up right there!" Orgeron roared. "Way to go, Frank!"

The mood of the room sank when the next tape came on. It was J.T. Beasley, a lightly heralded 6'2", 250-pound lineman from Dyersburg, Tennessee. Freeze, who handles Tennessee for Ole Miss, reminded Orgeron that Beasley was a prospect they'd watched as a junior but decided was too small. But now, with T-Bob Hebert drifting off the radar, the Rebels needed to find more candidates they could bring in as possible centers.

"I think T.J. could possibly play for us," Freeze told the room as the tape showed Beasley locking on defenders and driving them back. Another clip showed Beasley tracking a middle linebacker eight yards downfield before flattening the guy. Freeze added, "I like how he has a flat back and the way he sets down."

Kehoe scrunched up his nose, but didn't say anything.

"We need to know," Orgeron said. "What do you think Arthur?"

"I don't know," said Kehoe.

"He wrote me a letter and sent us three tapes," Freeze said, his tone shifting to salesman mode.

"When you're huntin' rabbits, be careful the ones that jump right in front of your gun," replied Orgeron. "Just keep evaluating him."

While most of the room was still trying to make sense of the rabbits line, Orgeron asked for a show of hands. He wanted to do a little drafting: Rolando Melancon vs. Joe McKnight. The Rebels, with their dearth of defensive linemen, opted by almost a 2-1 count for Melancon.

"Hmmm," said Orgeron, an amused look on his face. "Just like the Texans' taking Mario Williams over Reggie Bush."

Ian Williams' wake-up call on Game Day came at 8:15 a.m. By that time, the Grove, the sprawling, 10-acre lot graced by husky oaks, elms, and magnolias, was already teeming with Rebels revelers sprucing up their red-and-blue party tents.

Game Day in the Grove is an Ole Miss tradition that's like no other tailgate setting in college football. It's equal parts cocktail party, alumni reunion, and frat-house bash. Men, teenagers and up, wear white button-down shirts and blue-and-red ties to go with their khakis. Women deck themselves out in low-cut dresses, pearls, and spiked heels. The ratio of men to knockouts in Oxford on Game Day is about 1:3.

"I came down to visit and saw all those great women and went, 'Fuck it. I'll fake a Southern accent for four or five years,'" said an Ole Miss sophomore from New York. "God bless the Grove!"

Everywhere you turned, booze was flowing like water. Sharing was obviously the rule, not an exception. The motto in the Grove: "We may not win all the games, but we've never lost a party."

Two weeks ago, most of these folks braved a torrential downpour and gobs of mud for the Rebels' 27-3 loss to Wake Forest. Today's weather was perfect. The sun hovered above the treetops, and it was balmy enough so that none of the women in the Grove had to cover up in jackets.

The stunning pregame party scene would be one of the main stops for Williams on his campus visit. Williams had a breakfast meeting with the Ole Miss academic staff at 9:00 and then a separate academic meeting focusing on the Rebels' programs in Business and Broadcast Journalism, two fields he'd voiced an interest in. At 10 a.m. he would be given a tour of the equipment room and then get a weight room demonstration by Aaron Ausmus, the team's strength coach and a former All-America shot-putter who had worked with Orgeron at USC. All of the show and tells would take place inside the Rebels' shiny new Indoor Practice Facility.

In addition to Williams, the Rebels had about 80 other prospects on hand for "unofficial" visits. Most of them would never be offered scholarships, but Orgeron thought it was always a good idea to have area high school programs represented. No player who asked to come was turned away. Half of the high schoolers milling around the IPF were from Patrick Willis's hometown, Bruceton, Tennessee.

For the prospects, this was a great chance to check out the facilities, score a ticket for the game, and get a little face time with the Ole Miss coaches, who circulated inside the IPF for a few minutes before going into the locker room to get ready for kickoff. Many of the recruits had their high school coaches and/or parents in tow.

They were all greeted and signed in by a dozen beautiful coeds decked out in snug dresses and stilettos. The "scenery" at Ole Miss is, was, and always will be a selling point, even if it's not mentioned in any of the literature. The old joke—"At Ole Miss, they redshirt Miss Americas"—still seemed to be operative in Oxford.

One of the coeds helping at the IPF was Sarah Mokry, a pharmacy major and the reigning "Ole Miss Most Beautiful." Observed Ms. Mokry about the school's reputation for eye candy: "Around here, the real head turners are the ugly ones."

One parent was so taken aback by another of the Rebels' student volunteers that he accidentally stepped on his boy's foot, tripping him. "I've never seen nothin' like this," said the parent. "Sign me up right damn now. I still got four years of eligibility left."

Ian Williams looked to be enjoying himself as well. At 10:40 a.m., a few minutes before the Rebels' buses arrived from Tupelo, he began a tour of the Ole Miss campus with one of the school's Ambassadors, Jaklyn Wrigley, a more voluptuous version of Renée Zellweger in a gray cocktail dress and matching 3-inch heels.

The Rebels, like other college football programs, relied on their school's "Ambassador Program" to provide guided tours for recruits. Before 2004, most programs used their own hosting groups, which typically enlisted some of the hottest coeds on campus as volunteers in such outfits as the Texas Angels (the University of Texas), the Carolina Classics (University of South Carolina), and the Bulldog Belles (at Mississippi State). The hostesses even had their own team picture in the football media guide.

Some former hostesses have told stories about how coaches often urged them to do "whatever it takes" to make sure a recruit had a good time on his visit. But in the wake of a scandal at the University of Colorado, which was investigated for, among other things, using sex and alcohol in football recruiting, the NCAA banned the use of hostesses in the recruitment of athletes. Now only current athletes or students who give campus tours to prospective students in general can play host to recruits.

At Ole Miss, students need at least a 3.0 GPA to be considered for the Ambassador Program. In 2006, around 40 Ambassadors were chosen among 130 applicants. Pretty-stiff competition for a job that pays nothing.

A junior Spanish major with a 3.5 GPA, Wrigley said that she planned on going to law school and that she was thinking about becoming a sports agent. She said she enjoyed giving the recruits tours: "I like to think I'm personable enough to communicate with even the shyest people."

McLeod said that Wrigley's chatty nature ("Jacky will talk for hours without ever shutting up") made her an ideal Ambassador. Of course, her stop-traffic looks didn't hurt either.

Unlike everyone else milling around the Grove, Wrigley was not raised as an Ole Miss fan. She grew up on the Mississippi coast in tiny Ocean Springs, almost six hours away. "I despised Ole Miss," she said. "I really wanted to get out of the South." But Wrigley, the first person in her immediate family to attend college, won some scholarships to pay for Ole Miss and became a diehard Rebels fan.

The original drill was that before she was introduced to a recruit, the corresponding position coach met with her and gave her the detailed scoop on the kid. She said it often started with something like, "We gotta have him, Jacky. He's awesome. He's the best player in the state." After a while she figured out she'd rather not hear too much background before they were introduced: "That way, there's a lot more to explore with him."

The campus tours are fairly simple. If the recruit has a specific interest in a program, she'll show him that department and point out various buildings on campus before leading him to the Grove and the "Walk of Champions," the route the Rebels take through the Ole Miss fans before going to the locker room.

"I just try and focus on the Grove and point out some key things," she said. "Most players don't care that much where the math department is."

Wrigley said that no one on the coaching staff had ever asked or even so much as hinted that she behave in a suggestive manner around any recruit. She also said she has a personal policy against getting involved with athletes.

Nonetheless, she said, there had been a few awkward moments.

In her first year as an Ambassador, she was watching a game with a recruit who had been perfectly polite and proper the whole day, when out of the blue, he asked her if she wanted to take a shower with him. (She said she laughed it off.)

Another time a recruit tried to put his arm around her. That was a little trickier to handle. "You recross your legs the other way or shift around," she said. "You try and keep it light and funny, because you don't want him leaving Ole Miss here saying, 'The girls there are all bitches.'"

Williams offered no such hassles. He was a perfect gentleman, Wrigley reported: "Ian is so polite and sweet. He's probably one of my top five favorite recruits I've met."

The Vanderbilt game got off to a nightmarish start for the Rebels.

Freshman Dexter McCluster, their lone big-play threat and most reliable receiver, was drilled returning the opening kickoff. Helped off the field by the trainers, McCluster wouldn't play another down the rest of the season as a result of a severe shoulder stinger.

Without McCluster, the Rebels offense dropped from mediocre to nonexistent. Quarterback Brent Schaeffer passed for a season-low 31 yards, completing just three of eight throws, and was intercepted

twice. The homecoming crowd showered him with boos when he trot-
ted back onto the field in the fourth quarter.

But the Rebels D came through, forcing six turnovers. Vanderbilt
pitched in by missing a pair of field goals, fumbling a punt, and
failing to get a punt off, the latter setting up an Ole Miss touchdown. It wasn't pretty, but the Rebels snapped their four-game losing streak with a 17-10 victory.

"Our team competed," Orgeron told the media afterward. "We
hung in there and made the play when we had to."

Orgeron sounded more buoyant when he addressed his team after
they entered the locker room and gathered around him. In
postgame press conferences, he's often curt, typically showing little
interest in postmortems or even being chummy. After the
Homecoming win, however, he did take the opportunity late in
the press conference to wax a little philosophical, and in the
process, send out a message to A.J. Jackson or any other blue-chip
receiving prospect eager to make an instant impact in the SEC.

"How do we fix our passing game?" Orgeron said in response
to a reporter's query. "Well, we get us a big, tall receiver, and we
get him to run down the field, and we throw him the ball over
everybody else's head. We're missing the 6'4", 6'5" receiver who
can beat one-on-one coverage. I know we have to get that
in recruiting. I don't think we're where we need to be at the
receiving position, we're not where we need to be in protection,
and we're not where we need to be in the passing game. It's a
combination of all three."

Williams, along with all of the prospects on their unofficial visits,
jammed into the Rebels locker room after the game. The mood of
the team was more one of relief than of joy. But a win's a win, so it
was a good place to be.

On the way out of the IPF, Williams spied a TV showing the LSU-
Florida game and stopped dead in his tracks. Orgeron and his staff

were aware that he was strongly attracted to Florida; now that affinity for the Gators became palpable. Said Lubick ruefully: "You could see how jacked up he was to watch it."

By 7:00 p.m. Williams was off to have dinner at Doe's, an upscale steak house just off the Square, Oxford's quaint downtown area. He was joined there by Orgeron and his wife, Kelly, a few other Rebel coaches, and Williams' host for the night, fullback Jason Cook. McLeod had prearranged with the restaurant to make sure that his boss's meal was served in clockwork order, with no intervals between courses. "Coach O hates waiting," explained McLeod. "If he has to wait for a while, he gets mad."

The dinner conversation was more social than football. Williams's maturity shined as he discussed the silliness of the MySpace community that he sheepishly admitted to being a part of.

Orgeron saved his X's and O's spiel for his one-on-one visit with Williams on Sunday morning. It's in this half-hour sit-down, Orgeron said, that he always looks for clues to the prospect's character and makeup. He was curious what kind of reaction Williams had to the Ole Miss campus, the coaching staff, and the team.

Above all, Orgeron wanted to find out how much Williams loved football. Orgeron said later that he'd seen too many kids he'd liked on film turn out not to have the will to work hard every day. A few times at USC, Orgeron saw Carroll veto blue-chippers who he believed had coasted by on ability and little else.

What Orgeron wanted to find without directly asking: Is Ian Williams passionate? Does he play with a chip on his shoulder? Is he sharp enough to take hard, in-your-face coaching?

Williams had already made a good impression on Ryan Nielsen, who had 40 minutes with the defensive lineman right before Orgeron. Nielsen's session focused on how the Rebels coach their defensive linemen and what is expected of them. In Williams,

Nielsen saw another Jeremy Garrett—that is, a solid, disciplined, high-character kid with what it took to be a leader.

As Williams departed Oxford with McLeod at 11:05 a.m. on Sunday morning, Orgeron told the staff that the young lineman had made a good impression. "He's a bright-eyed, good kid," he said. "I really liked him. And I really think he liked it here and liked us. I just don't know if he's coming."

Orgeron's read was dead on. Williams confirmed later that he had liked Ole Miss more than Notre Dame. "There was a lot more to do there than at Notre Dame," he said. "I loved the Grove and their coaching staff. I really had a great time."

Williams' self-imposed November 3 deadline was fast approaching. He sent another text message to Florida defensive coordinator Charlie Strong: "Am I still one of your prospects?" According to Williams, Strong called back to say that they were getting too full of commitments and that they were holding off taking on any more recruits for the time being. But a couple of days later, Williams read that another defensive lineman from California had committed to the Gators.

The 18-year-old was crushed. For six months, he'd been telling people that he was leaning toward Florida. Now, Florida was telling him—and indirectly telling the whole country—that he wasn't good enough to be a Gator.

Williams' gut response: set up an official visit to Auburn, the team that had just beaten Florida, 27-17.

The Rebels coaches didn't realize it, but at the moment their biggest obstacle in landing Ian Williams wasn't Florida, or Notre Dame, or Auburn, or anybody else in the SEC.

It was the bruised psyche of a teenager.

Chapter 12

PLAN B

B
Y HIS OWN admission, Barney Farrar was a coaching jour-
neyman. The Rebels assistant AD for football affairs had
spent eight seasons (1986-93) at Clemson as the Tigers
tried to rebound from a stiff NCAA probation. At one time or
another, he'd coached every position on the defense for the Tigers.
He'd spent another dozen years at Rice, from 1993-2005, coaching outside linebackers and cornerbacks as the Owls feebly tried to
stay relevant after getting booted from the big-time when the old
SWC went under.

Farrar hadn't been much of a player himself at Mississippi's
Delta State, and he'd once got himself booted out of college as a
consequence of his penchant for a second interest, bar fighting.

But through all that, there had been one constant: Farrar just loved
being around football. And in his 25-plus years in the business,
Farrar thought he'd seen just about everything the game could throw
at him. (Key words: "just about.")

After he took the Ole Miss job but before he showed up in Oxford
in 2006, some of his buddies in the coaching profession warned him
about Ed Orgeron's temper. "You'd better get ready for this guy"
was the consensus recommendation. Farrar just laughed them off.

Hey, he'd been around the block. He'd seen more than his share of oversize personalities.

Maybe so, but all the dustups and breakdowns and explosions he'd witnessed before couldn't possibly have prepared him for the raging bull he encountered on the night of October 19, 2006.

Earlier in the evening, Farrar had received a telephone call from Steve Bramlett, the Oxford Police Chief. Bramlett told Farrar that there was a problem. He explained that he'd had to write a citation for disturbing the peace at the Sterling University Terrace apartment inhabited by some Rebels football players. Bramlett said the police had responded to a noise complaint at the off-campus apartment of LaMark Armour, a defensive end, and Robert Russell, a middle line-backer. When the police arrived, they'd smelled marijuana. Several people, all Rebels players, tried to run from the apartment, but they'd been detained by police.

The officers searched the apartment but couldn't find any marijuana or determine who'd been smoking it. No one was arrested, but Bramlett said he was going hold the players at the apartment until Farrar and Kehoe arrived.

Fifteen minutes later, the two Ole Miss assistants ordered the players, some of whom had been in the Rebels' doghouse, to go directly to the football complex: Orgeron would be waiting for them.

His blood had hit the boiling point even before he could pull out of his driveway.

Lord help him. No, Lord help *them*. How could they *possibly* do this to him? How dare they put his program through this? Put his family—his wife and three young boys—in jeopardy like this? How dare they?

How fuckin' dare they?

The 10 players marched into the team room at the IPF and sat down in the front row. Coach O was already there, stalking around the room like the proverbial caged lion. Many of the players would say later that they thought they'd seen Orgeron mad before, but that this was different. *Real* different. This was flat-out scary.

The man looked like he was about to explode. His eyes bugged out. The big vein in his neck bulged and throbbed. And then, as he walked up and down the line, he got so close to their scared faces that his chin, jutting out with almost unbridled hostility, was practically spearing them.

You've embarrassed this university!
You've embarrassed your teammates!
You've embarrassed your parents!
You've embarrassed me!

His voice boomed throughout the IPF. Somehow, window panes remained intact. The tension escalated in pace with his blood pressure. Barrel-chested, muscular young men with thick-rope dreadlocks and buzz cuts—men who came from places where even the appearance of soft was a mortal sin—literally cowered amid this torrent of rage. No one said anything. No one even dared. No one even flinched, for fear of fanning the flames of his ire.

Do you understand me?
Do you <u>understand</u> me?
<u>*Do*</u> *... <u>you</u> ... <u>fuckin'</u> ... <u>understand</u> ... <u>me?</u>*

Even the most soft-spoken, folksy football coaches have their drill-sergeant moments. They almost always take place behind closed doors. Orgeron is no different. This was for the 10 people in front of him, not a larger audience.

But this particular Orgeronian rant may well have set a new gold standard in college football for "ass-chewing." It sputtered into another zone, another dimension, and came across as something so raw, so primal, so uncontrolled that Farrar feared his boss' head might explode.

Then Orgeron, positively radiating with anger, kicked it up a notch. Suddenly his husky, scratchy Cajun voice morphed into a nearly indiscernible, high-pitched screech, as if he'd gone Pentecostal:

"You will not bring down my program!

"You will <u>not</u> bring down my program!

"<u>You</u> ... <u>will</u> ... <u>not</u> ... <u>bring</u> ... <u>down</u> ... <u>my</u> ... <u>program!</u>"

Farrar said that he was afraid Orgeron would have a heart attack. Lord help this man, he thought. And Lord help these boys, too.

"It was scary, but at the same time, it was almost funny," Farrar said later. "Those guys didn't move an inch. Not one inch. And you know what? He was right about everything he said. I guess maybe they knew it."

Orgeron let the players go home at 2:00 a.m. and ordered them back to the IPF by 5. All of the players involved were then given a drug test and marched outside to do a nauseating mix of sprints, bear crawls, up-downs, and field rolls. (Aptly named: a player lies down on the ground and rolls the width of the field and back until the coaches are satisfied). With Orgeron and five of his assistants glaring, the punishment lasted more than an hour in the chilly morning air.

Thirty-six hours after the incident, the Rebels, who the previous week had lost in overtime at Alabama, took the field at Arkansas. Aided by blown assignments by two of the players involved in Thursday night's incident, the Razorbacks returned the opening kickoff for a touchdown. One of the Rebels players, starting line-backer Garry Pack, was benched midway through the first quarter in favor of freshman Jonathan Cornell.

The Razorbacks coasted to a 38-3 win.

The Ole Miss record dropped to 2–6.

Two days later, with the drug-test results in, Ole Miss announced that Pack had been dismissed from the team for a "violation of team rules," while Armour, Russell, Hayward Howard and LeRon King had been suspended indefinitely. Quentin Taylor, a former starter at linebacker, who had tested positive for marijuana, quit the team. All except Pack were sophomores.

Just like that, the Rebels were down four linebackers and two defensive linemen.

Linebacker, which hadn't been one of the Rebels' top five recruiting priorities back in January, suddenly sat atop Orgeron's shopping list for 2007.

Just to finish the season, he converted starting strong safety Jamarca Sanford (5'9", 200 pounds) and freshman safety Allen Walker (6'0", 200 pounds) to linebacker. The suspensions left the Rebels incredibly thin, but it turned out to be a blessing—addition by subtraction. Gone were a half-dozen headaches on the practice field and in the locker room.

"You could tell right away that it helped get our guys more focused," said one of the assistants. "I wasn't sure at first because of our numbers, but it turned out to be a good thing for the program."

Orgeron admitted he hates booting players from his program, especially ones he recruited himself. He'd been in their family's homes and told their parents how he'd take care of their babies. He'd promised to watch over them, see to it that they got a good education and do whatever he could to help them grow into men.

But there were limits. A few weeks earlier, Howard—who'd racked up $900 in parking tickets in the spring and was benched for the Georgia game for skipping a class—had quit the team in midweek before the Vanderbilt game because he couldn't seem to stay out of Orgeron's doghouse. The next day Howard's mom drove up from New Orleans and pleaded with Orgeron to take him back. She said her boy would not be anymore trouble. He'd be early for meetings. He'd never miss another study hall. No more attitude, either.

This time, Orgeron yielded to a mother's plea—and two weeks later regretted it.

Orgeron walked over to one of the orange name plates on his In-State Defense recruiting board and ran his index finger across it. The orange color signified a committed player. The name on the plate belonged to a 6'6", 275-pound defensive end who, everybody who'd seen his eval tapes agreed, looked and moved just like an NFL defensive end. The Internet recruiting sites had him listed as a five-star recruit. From an athletic standpoint, that might be an understatement. But from a character standpoint, the kid might be exactly what Orgeron had just booted off the team.

Orgeron paused, looking over the rest of his recruiting board. "The person I really feel bad for is Frank Wilson," he said after a long breath. "I know it's hard on him, because he brought in a lot of those kids we had to get rid of."

Wilson later responded: "Yeah, it hurts me a lot. You do take it personal, because you feel like you didn't do a good job of identifying the young man as a person. But I try to learn from it."

In the wake of the house cleaning, Orgeron decided to have his staff create a list of "character questions" that would give them a clearer picture of exactly what kind of people they were recruiting. Trying to find the warning signs they might have spotted while sizing up the recent castoffs, Orgeron and his staff brainstormed for a list at their Wednesday morning meeting. This is what they came up with:

How hard does he work?

Does he have a good class-attendance record?

Is he a leader off the field?

Has he ever been arrested?

What are his parents like?

Does he have any children?

Is he football-smart?

How would you rate his toughness?

"How does the NFL ask these questions? We have to be careful how we ask the questions," Orgeron said as he finished going down the list at the end of the meeting. "If we ask, 'How does he take hard coaching?' it might scare some people off. They'll ask, 'Well, exactly how *hard* is the coaching?'"

They were all criteria Orgeron believed revealed character, but he didn't want the probing to spook coaches or, more important, potential recruits who might not be character risks but who might misinterpret the emphasis of the questions.

The new, heightened focus on character was followed by a discussion of an updated outline of academic requirements for recruits, explained by David Wells, the school's compliance director. Among the new rules: a cap on the number of correspondence courses at six in a calendar year, which the school hoped would curtail the perception of shady doings. Like the rest of the SEC, Ole Miss formed an athletic-admissions review committee that would look for things that might spark the NCAA Clearinghouse's attention. Among the yellow flags: too many correspondence courses, a suspiciously high jump in ACT score, a prospect's transferring to another school in the middle of the academic year (often for the purpose of loading up on credits from a diploma factory).

As his staff digested the updates, Orgeron went over the night's travel plans. Orgeron had decided to disperse half his staff to scout the Mississippi junior college games as teams wrapped up their regular seasons. To maximize their time, while not sacrificing practice time for the Rebels' upcoming game against Auburn in just 72 hours, he had chartered a plane. The plane would depart Oxford at 8 p.m., with running backs coach Frank Wilson, receivers coach Matt Lubick and linebackers coach David Saunders, heading to Jackson. Recruiting coordinator Hugh Freeze, defensive line coach Ryan Nielsen and offensive line coach Art Kehoe all would be driving to scout their games. The trips would last no more than 18 hours, just enough time to see a few prospects in person and then get back to Oxford for Thursday night practice.

For two months Orgeron had been adamant about finding junior college talent, particularly players who could enroll at Ole Miss in the winter, so they could play spring ball. The Rebels had more than a dozen JC prospects on their board, a few who'd already committed to them. In almost all cases, grades were a big issue. But so, in the aftermath of the Sterling Terrace 10, was character.

The staff had already known character would be an issue with some of the junior college prospects; now, after the fallout from last week's incident, it was paramount.

Identifying talent was no longer the prime focus of a junior college scouting trip. That was the easy part. Identifying talent that could cut the mustard academically, now *that* was tough.

Orgeron had stressed more times than he could count that each assistant who visited a junior college campus must come back with prospects' transcripts. Sounds simple enough, right? Unfortunately, it's often not.

"It's not like high school," said Kent McLeod, who processes all the recruits' transcripts and does the academic workups. "With junior colleges, the only way you can actually get the kid's transcript is if the kid goes and gets it himself. And they're JC kids, so even if they tell the coach, 'Yeah, I'll get it,' they almost never do."

Deciphering a junior college prospect's academic profile—once you had his transcript—could be even more vexing. Four-year schools require that after two years at a junior college a student must have completed at least 40% of the credits toward his major to qualify for admission. If a student has been there for three years, he must have completed 60%. "Most junior college coaches are just worried about keeping their guys eligible," explained McLeod, adding that often JC players load up on electives and classes that won't help them transfer. "And many four-year college coaches don't understand the rules about what a JC kid has to have."

McLeod, 29, is the staff's soft-spoken clearinghouse for such information. At first glance, the Ole Miss graduate with a degree in mathematics seems miscast in this world of aggression and brute force. He doesn't smoke, raise his voice, or curse, and he's never had a sip of alcohol in his life.

His office, down the hall from the war room, is usually littered with transcripts, VCR tapes, highlight DVDs and copies of newspaper stories on all-league teams from half the counties in the South. On the floor behind his desk is a 2-foot x 3-foot map of Mississippi with color-coded pins targeting each high school in the state by class size. His cell phone doesn't seem to go five minutes without someone on the staff calling. The ringer is set to play "Hava Nagila," the Jewish celebration song. (McLeod had no idea what the song was. He said he just liked the melody.)

McLeod is one of those behind-the-scenes guys who keeps a big-time college program ticking. Among other tasks, he coordinates all of the coaches' travel, updates the recruiting boards, handles every detail of the recruits' official visits, and analyzes transcripts to determine whether prospects have a prayer of getting into Ole Miss—and what they could do to improve their chances.

"We couldn't operate without him," says Wilson, the former athletic director for the New Orleans public school system. "Many high school ADs and counselors know what an athlete needs to graduate, but they don't realize that what the NCAA requires for a student-athlete to become eligible is something totally different. Kent has such in-depth knowledge that he can tell you exactly what a student must do to get eligible. I think he's head and shoulders above what everyone else has."

Despite not having any on-field coaching experience, McLeod has a keen eye for talent. He explains that's because he's spent more than his share of time "studying the people who study tape." It also helps that he's worked with three different coaching regimes at Ole

Miss, picking up pointers from each of them. When he first broke into the business, as a student worker, he tried to learn on his own. He pulled the eval tapes of the big-name players and watched what he thought made them special. The Rebels defensive line coach Rick Petri noticed McLeod's zeal to learn the evaluation process and offered to let him sit with him as he watched recruiting tape. "Coach Petri would tell me all the things he'd be looking for," McLeod said. "It helped get me hooked."

McLeod said that he looks at tape differently than most coaches: "A lot of the time, they'll look at a player and notice something like 'His technique is bad' or 'I don't like the way he tackles.' They're conditioned to pick up on that stuff. When I turn on the tape, the first thing I look at is a kid's athletic ability, because I know if he can't run and he can't bend, then he can't play for us."

McLeod said he realized in Orgeron's first recruiting meeting that the new head coach had a different perspective on scouting than other college coaches did. Orgeron wanted to see the eval tapes of all the kids committed to Ole Miss. Midway through the first tape, one of the Rebels assistants was ready to nix a player: "I don't like that right there, the way he took that angle." Orgeron stopped him: "Hey, don't ever get turned off a kid because of a technique deal," he told the staff. "You gotta feel like you can correct that."

Unlike his predecessor at Ole Miss, Orgeron relished being the first one in the water for a recruit. "A lot of coaches don't want to be the first to offer a kid," McLeod explained. "They go, 'What if he can't play and then we're stuck with him?' Ninety percent of coaches are like that. Not Coach O. He loves being the first to offer. He has a lot of confidence in himself and what he sees."

McLeod said his dream was to get an NFL scouting job some day. As the Rebels coordinator of football operations, he's the point person for all the NFL scouts who come through Oxford to watch tape and get a better read on the Rebels' pro hopefuls. Thanks to

All-American middle linebacker Patrick Willis, the NFL scouts have flocked to the Ole Miss campus over the last year and a half.

A few years back Petri set McLeod up for a three-day visit with the Cleveland Browns scouting staff. McLeod didn't know what to expect. But after sitting in on every meeting and getting a feel for how NFL teams handle their evaluations, he was convinced it was for him: "If you told me to go get every top player in college football and rank them, I could do it all day."

Mike McIntyre, another former Ole Miss coach who was on Bill Parcells' staff in Dallas, tried to get McLeod an entry-level job last year with the Cowboys, where they'd teach him how to be a college scout. It would've paid only $20,000—about half of what McLeod makes at Ole Miss, and no benefits—but McLeod said he would've jumped at it. Fortunately for Ole Miss, the Cowboys opted to go with someone else.

McLeod has been contacted a few times by Internet recruiting sites interested in hiring someone to scout parts of the South for them, but he didn't think the timing was right. His other escape route would be to go teach high school math and coach golf.

"I'd make the same money, and I'd have summers off," he said. "But I'd miss the recruiting. There is something about finding that guy that nobody knows about yet. It's such a huge challenge."

As a lifelong Mississippi resident and someone who followed junior college football in the state, McLeod wasn't too optimistic about what the Rebels coaches were going to turn up when they asked their character questions.

He told the story of a former blue-chip high school defensive back now at one of the Mississippi junior colleges. The player had committed to another SEC program out of high school but had been telling coaches he was back on the market. Freeze called his cell phone and got a voice message delivered as a decidedly smart-ass taunt: "If you're not my mom or a hot girl or tryin' to give me money, don't even bother leavin' a message."

That was all Freeze needed to hear to know this kid would never set foot in the Ole Miss locker room.

Judging by what Orgeron learned in his assistants' reports of their trips the next time they convened for a staff meeting, McLeod's instincts appeared to have been spot-on. Freeze began the roundup by saying that of the three prospects the Rebels had targeted at Northwest Mississippi Community College up the road in Senatobia, only one seemed to have a chance to qualify academically. And only that particular prospect, Curtis Steele, passed the character test.

"But," Freeze said, "I don't think he's more than 5'10", tops."

The Rebels had hoped that Steele, a tailback listed on his eval tape as 6'1", 185, might make a good cornerback. He looked shifty on tape, an indicator that he might have the swift hips needed to play the corner, and he displayed a good burst of speed, another virtue for cover men. But Steele said he'd never been a cornerback and didn't plan on trying to become one, thank you very much.

Steele's teammate, fullback Eric Nicks, was already committed to the Rebels. On film, Nicks ran like a freight train, flattening everything that got in his path. Textbooks gave him a lot more trouble. He was, at best, a long shot to make it into Ole Miss. Said Orgeron: "I'd rather have to fight for a defensive tackle than a fullback."

Cornerbacks coach Tony Hughes reported that he hadn't met anyone who passed the Rebels' character test on his trip. But Hughes mentioned that he had seen two freshmen defensive ends he thought the Rebels needed to monitor.

Wilson, back from visiting Gulf Coast Community College, home of all-everything DE recruit Dion Gales, began his turn by breaking into a sheepish grin. Gales, like Wilson, was originally from New Orleans. In 2003, he was voted New Orleans Player of the Year after recording 65 tackles and 16 sacks. Former Rebels coach David Cutcliffe signed Gales even though he wouldn't qualify. He was placed at Gulf Coast, where he dominated—whenever he felt so inclined. Gales was the quintessential man-among-boys, the kind of prospect a scout offers after watching one play on the eval tape.

But, of course, it wasn't that simple.

Since Gales would have been in junior college for six semesters, he would need to have gotten 60% of the credits needed for his major to be eligible for admission at Ole Miss. That would be a stretch, to say the least. "It may go all the way 'til July," Wilson said. On the bright side, Gales had cut his dreadlocks. On the dark side, Wilson added, "He does walk around with a pack of Kools."

Orgeron smirked and shook his head. Nielsen, the D-line coach, winced. "Dion is *ridiculous*," said Nielsen, using his favorite term for describing a special talent. "If he doesn't get into trouble, he'll be a first-round draft pick. Guaranteed. I wish we could take him."

Wilson glanced back at his notes and brought up another impressive defensive-line specimen he saw. "The guy is a legit 6'4", 240," Wilson said, excitement surging back into his voice. "Pregame—*Wooooo!*—he was the shit, boy. He looked as good as any of our guys." Wilson paused, and then delivered the punch line: "But then the game started, and I don't think he made a single play. This big, good-looking boy got himself pancaked all night long."

Next up: receivers coach Matt Lubick, son of Sonny Lubick, the longtime head coach at Colorado State. Orgeron and Lubick's father had coached together at Miami. The elder Lubick was one of the first people to visit Orgeron when Orgeron's life began to spiral out of control.

Lubick is 35, but with his slight frame and baby face, he could pass for 25. His dietary staples—protein bars and Subway sandwiches—and aversion to fried foods and pretty much every other aspect of the Southern lifestyle make him an easy target for his buddies' digs. So does his penchant for hyperbole. Everyone is "the best" or "the worst" in his eyes.

Orgeron often ribs him for the number of Ole Miss recruits from Florida who curiously end up considering Colorado State, but no one jokes about Lubick's dogged work on the recruiting trail. In the late 1990s, he was the recruiting coordinator under Dennis Erickson when Oregon State went from doormat to Fiesta Bowl champs. Lubick also was the one who found diminutive Dexter McCluster, the Rebels' top big-play man, in Largo, Florida.

Lubick's scouting trip had taken him to Pearl River Community College, the top JC program in the state. The Rebels were interested in three Pearl River players, none of them in good shape academically. The prize: Demetrius Byrd, a 6'2", 200-pounder from Miami, listed third on the Rebels' In-State Receivers board.

Wilson's story about the defensive line prospect who'd spent most of a football game on his back had drawn laughs, but the real comedy for the day came from Lubick, who possesses wonderful comedic timing and probably would make a great straight man in a sitcom.

"He's a great-looking kid," Lubick began his report on Byrd. "He's big and fast, and he's exactly what we don't have right now. He's real undisciplined." Then, without missing a beat and still with a straight face: "I think he could help us. He had to call a timeout because he was so tired, which actually didn't make any sense because he was loafing the whole game."

Perhaps the day's best news on the junior college front came from Illinois, of all places. An outside linebacker named Chris Patterson had flashed across the Rebels' radar. Hughes had seen Patterson's name on a prospect list the Rebels got from one of the recruiting services they subscribe to and had spoken with Patterson's coach at Joliet Junior College.

At Hughes' request, McLeod got some game film and made an eval tape. He was stunned by Patterson's speed and ability to chase plays down from behind. He Googled Patterson's name and discovered that the linebacker was a former five-star, all-everything high school recruit. Nicknamed The Freak by Chicago-area recruiting analysts because of his blazing speed, Patterson had signed with Oklahoma, along with ballyhooed tailback prospect Adrian Peterson, as part of the Sooners' heralded 2004 recruiting class. He failed to meet eligibility standards, so OU placed him at Northeast Oklahoma A&M, a nearby junior college. But that's where Patterson's story petered out.

Hughes eventually got Patterson on the phone. Patterson said he hated it in Oklahoma and that his relationship with the Sooners had soured. He said he'd been put into the wrong classes and, subsequently, had been told he was two classes short of being a full qualifier. "They said they weren't going to have a scholarship for me," Patterson told Hughes. "They treated me like a walk-on."

After two years in Oklahoma—he played only one season for NEO— Patterson was frustrated and homesick. He ended up at Joliet Junior College in Illinois. To get the word out that he was available, Patterson called the recruiting writer who had tagged him The Freak. The writer goes by Edgy Tim (real name: Tim O'Halloran); he's a Chicago-based analyst for Rivals.com.

Patterson was small for a linebacker: 6'2", 215 pounds. But the Rebels loved the way he ran. On film, he made plays few linebackers could pull off. In addition to Ole Miss, Patterson had said he was interested in Minnesota, Wisconsin, and Iowa State. According to McLeod, that boded well for the Rebels, since Patterson had some classes on his transcript that the Big Ten schools couldn't accept because D grades weren't transferable.

Hughes had been talking to Patterson at least once a week for a month. The Rebels made sure Patterson knew what their depth chart would look like going into next season. They also let him know that one of their own, Patrick Willis, was the front runner for the Butkus Award, given to the nation's top linebacker.

Patterson liked what Ole Miss was selling. "I just want to go somewhere where there's an opportunity. They seem like a good young team, and I know they play in a great conference," he said. "Besides, the distance, the school's prestige, and all that other stuff doesn't matter any more. This is all about business for me now."

There was, however, one potential snag: the SEC has a rule requiring junior college transfers to have been at the same JC for the previous three semesters. It was put in place a few years back to block schools from having borderline students transfer their last semester to a dubious junior college to load up on easy credits.

The Rebels were hopeful the SEC would give Patterson a waiver, because his case didn't violate the spirit of the rule.

"He went to NEO because Oklahoma sent him there, and then when they weren't gonna take him, he transferred closer to home," McLeod explained. "He isn't going to Joliet just to get eligible. He should be able to get a waiver."

A victory over seventh-ranked Auburn Saturday would go a long way towards resparking the Rebels' sales pitch, if only by shifting focus—at least for a weekend—from current realities.

Ole Miss was 2–6, and it wasn't a pretty 2–6.

Quarterback Brent Schaeffer, named by Orgeron as the team's starter seven months before he even set foot in Oxford, had foundered. The Rebels ranked dead last in the SEC in scoring offense (13 points per game), passing offense (127 yards per game), and third-down conversions (27%).

Stephen Garcia, the top QB prospect on their board, appeared to be a lock to sign with South Carolina. Even so, Orgeron had been adamant that he wouldn't sign another quarterback just to sign one. But he was starting to believe that maybe, just maybe, he might have found the Rebels' quarterback of the future smack-dab inside his own program.

The candidate? A 21-year-old former minor league pitcher-turned-walk-on whom Orgeron had nicknamed Talladega Nights.

Cliff Davis, a 6'4", 225-pound native of tiny Eupora, Mississippi, just an hour from Oxford, had the kind of arm strength that evokes barroom debates and the toughness that usually settles them.

"He's a quick-tempered guy who never has been a real good loser," said Kenny McCain, a family friend of Davis's, who used to announce Eupora's games. "Cliff was the type that you might get him on the field, but he might find you after the game and show you who really is boss."

Davis grew up an Ole Miss fan, but said former Rebels coach David Cutcliffe never offered him a scholarship. Instead, he signed with Alabama. But his 96 mph fastball was drawing a dozen scouts to all his baseball games. The Houston Astros selected him in the sixth round of the 2003 draft. A self-described country boy, he was offered a six-figure contract and jumped on it.

But Davis had a Nuke LaLouch-like existence in the minors, always struggling with his control. "I was more brawn than brains in the minors," he reflected after he hung up his spikes. "I guess you can get away with that a little bit more in football."

During his second year in the minors, Davis unleashed a curve-ball and heard a "pop!" He wasn't hurt, but the sound haunted him. Davis could never bring himself to throw another one again: "Subconsciously, I just couldn't release it."

In three seasons, Davis topped out in the New York-Penn League's Class-A Short Season for the Tri-City ValleyCats of Troy, New York.

Two days after getting waived, Davis picked up a football. His cousin, an Ole Miss grad, contacted the Rebels' football office for him. He was told he first had to get a release from Alabama. Davis didn't expect that would be hard, given that he had signed on with the Mike Price regime, which was two coaches ago for the Crimson Tide. But one of the Alabama assistants tried to get him to come to Tuscaloosa, saying their quarterback situation "isn't good."

"What are you talking about?" Davis replied. "You have a starter who's only going to be a sophomore, and you have two new blue-chip freshmen coming in."

Three weeks later, Davis got his release.

The Rebels weren't expecting much. When two-a-days started in August, Davis came across as one of those characters out of a goofy Hollywood football movie. On his biceps was a tattoo of a half-naked woman dressed in the Rebel flag. His understanding of the nuances of football were sketchy at best. Every pass he attempted, from screen passes to fade routes, was a blazing fastball. He even broke a finger of tailback Cordera Eason on one throw.

Orgeron called him Talladega Nights after the Will Ferrell movie. "I'm not sure why he started calling me that," Davis says. "I guess because I signed with Alabama, and Talladega is in Alabama. But it just stuck, and I actually don't mind it."

Two weeks into camp, the Rebels thought Davis was having second thoughts about his second career. He didn't show up for the Rebels' first scrimmage, and he missed a meeting the following day. He met with Orgeron, who explained he had had a similar situation when he first got to LSU, and that he had bailed. Davis said he didn't want to. He would be willing to be fifth-string and share reps on the scout team with freshman Michael Herrick.

"I liked how they cared about me," he says. "These guys are real down-to-earth guys, and you can talk to them about your problems. I realized I still have a lot to learn. I need to improve my footwork and to do better on the mind portion of the game. That stuff is way out there for me."

Davis' next month was rocky as he began to learn how to read coverages and study film. "I came from 2-A football in Mississippi, man," he said with a grin, as if that explained everything.

But midway through the season, the Rebels defensive staff said that Davis was nothing to snicker about when he worked against the first team in practices. Orgeron watched some of the throws Davis made—deep outs, seam passes through tight windows between defenders—and couldn't help but think that Talladega Nights might someday be his starting quarterback.

Dave Corrao, the Rebels defensive graduate assistant who ran the scout team, said he'd even take Talladega Nights over Stephen Garcia. "He can throw the dig route and fit it into a three-foot window, and he can do it against college players," Corrao said. "Stephen Garcia hasn't proven that yet. Cliff's got the best arm of any quarterback we've faced. That freshman at Georgia, Matt Stafford, who was supposed to have the best arm of any quarterback in his class? He doesn't throw it as well as Cliff does."

Corrao said it was too early to know whether Davis would develop the savvy to manage the offense or read the middle of the defense. "But I do know this," he said. "There aren't many other quarterbacks who can do what we've seen him do. He can do things you just can't teach."

The viewpoint in the offensive staff room, however, was more restrained. Werner just smiled politely when asked about the rising expectations regarding Talladega Nights. Werner was, after all, the one who'd been quizzing the ex-pitcher about the kind of defenses he was trying to beat and where he needed to be looking to throw.

"I don't know about him yet," was as far as Werner was prepared to go. "I'd still like to get Stephen Garcia in here."

Chapter 13

SECOND
SEASON

N O MATTER WHAT the *College GameDay* guys were saying, the 2006 Egg Bowl between Ole Miss and Mississippi State on November 25 was a monumental battle.

Okay, so the rest of the country had no interest in watching a pair of 3–8 programs at the bottom of the SEC West duke it out, but this was absolutely the biggest game of the year in Oxford.

See, the Rebels were battling the Bulldogs for a half-dozen senior prospects, and Orgeron knew the game probably carried even more weight in the eyes of the class of 2008 kids. It was also a "can't lose" game for him and third-year MSU head coach Sylvester Croom since both were teetering on hot-seat status.

And, just in case Orgeron's players hadn't figured out on their own how significant the Egg Bowl was, Ole Miss Chancellor Robert Khayat left notes on the locker of every Rebels player urging him to whip the man in front of him. Khayat wanted payback for 2005, when—in Orgeron's Egg Bowl debut—State hammered Ole Miss 35-14. Orgeron said afterward he had underestimated how big a deal the Egg Bowl is in Mississippi. He vowed he would never make that mistake again.

The Rebels, he promised, would never lose the Egg Bowl again as long as he was coaching in Oxford.

The Rebels were still reeling from a devastating OT loss at ninth-ranked LSU, a 27-point favorite. Tiger Stadium had been jammed with over 92,000 fans. Orgeron was so charged up for his return home to Louisiana that he was bouncing around in the tunnel like he wanted to get on the field and knock heads. "He was jacked-up even by Ed's standards," said one of the Rebels assistants. "I wish we could've suited him up."

Orgeron's game plan against a team that had outscored its opponents at home by a shocking 108-7 in first quarters was to beat the Tigers to the punch—at everything. He even had his team run out of the tunnel at precisely the same time as LSU did to throw the home team off-balance, and to let his players hear the cheers of the crowd roll over them.

For almost 60 minutes, almost everything worked. Two fake punts, an onside kick, numerous blitzes, and assorted fourth-down tricks helped the Rebels carry a 20-7 lead into the fourth quarter. Then, after forcing a fumble, they had a chance to seal the upset, as Ole Miss defensive tackle Brandon Jenkins and linebacker Rory Johnson closed in on the loose ball. A pack of Rebels followed, along with a single LSU player. Jenkins was too lost in the moment to "scoop and score," something Orgeron always harped on every-day at practice. The ball squirted loose and bounced right to the lone Tiger in the scrum.

LSU stormed back, capping its rally by connecting on a fourth-and-goal pass from JaMarcus Russell to Dwayne Bowe with 14 seconds remaining to tie the game 20-20. The Rebels, though, had one more big play left in them. John Jerry, a 6'6", 350-pound offensive guard not normally on the kicking team, swarmed through the line and blocked the extra point to send the game into overtime. Shortly thereafter, the Tigers forced Brent Schaeffer to fumble and, six plays later, kicked the game-winning field goal.

"We showed an improvement in the program from the way LSU

manhandled us last year," Orgeron said in his postgame press conference. "But there's no way we're going to be satisfied."

As crazy as it may sound, the Rebels—losers of four of their previous five games—had some momentum. They lost to Georgia by five points, to Auburn by six, and in overtime on the road against both Alabama and LSU. They should've beaten Georgia and LSU, and they had their chances against the Tigers and the Crimson Tide. Then again, they probably should've lost to Vanderbilt.

Orgeron had some Rebels fans starting to believe that Ole Miss was on the brink of turning the proverbial corner. Recruits were a bit more skeptical. Many of the blue-chippers Orgeron targeted early—notably QB Stephen Garcia, center T Bob Hebert, line backer Chris Donald, and defensive back Golden Tate—had already committed elsewhere or were about to do so.

Orgeron said he couldn't imagine what life around his program would be like if the Rebels lost at home to Mississippi State. When the Ole Miss coaches gathered in the banquet hall at the run-down Summit Motel in Tupelo for their Friday night, home-game tradition of watching recruiting tape, the next weekend's guests were a hot topic. Orgeron had assistant AD Barney Farrar bring all of the eval tapes of the recruits expected to be coming.

The Rebels begin by watching tape of D'Angelo McCray, a 6'4", 290-pound defensive lineman from Jacksonville, who (per the Internet recruiting sites) was the highest ranked among the prospects headed to Oxford the following week. Two of his former teammates, safety Jamal Harvey and wide receiver Mike Hicks, already played for the Rebels.

McCray had committed to Florida in April but then de-committed during the summer. Many people assumed he would still end up at Florida, but McCray had soured on the Gators after Marcus Thomas, a standout defensive lineman at UF, also a Jacksonville product, told him some very unflattering things about coach Urban Meyer.

McCray said he liked Ole Miss a lot. Asked who the best defensive line coach in the country was, his reply was immediate and definitive: Ed Orgeron. At the moment, McCray said, he also liked Florida State and Illinois. The Fighting Illini, who had an assistant from McCray's high school, were touting instant playing time and the chance to be part of a turnaround. Plus, like the Rebels, they had a frenetic, charismatic head coach, Ron Zook.

But word was that FSU was the team to beat. Lubick had heard that McCray had a girlfriend at a Tallahassee community college. (McCray later downplayed the significance of the romance angle: "Yeah, I got a girlfriend in Tallahassee. I got one in Jacksonville, too. And if I go to Illinois, I'm pretty sure I'll have one there, too.")

For all the hype, McCray's eval tape didn't bowl over the Ole Miss staff. Because McCray had torn his ACL early in the season, many of his plays showed him blocking at tight end. He was a fluid big man who ran like he weighed 230 pounds, not 290. True, McCray's rep was built off a dominant performance in a spring football scrimmage and at the Nike combine in Gainesville the previous May. Still, Orgeron knew that reeling in McCray would make a big splash in recruiting circles.

Next up were two recruits—junior college outside linebacker Chris Patterson and Louisiana offensive lineman Rishaw Johnson—whom Orgeron called high-priority guys. Patterson he called a flyer, maybe the fastest junior college linebacker in the country. Johnson, he said, was a mauler with nimble feet. Orgeron became more fired up with each play on their respective tapes. His excitement carried over to the third prospect, Alex Washington.

Like Johnson, Washington was an offensive lineman from Louisiana who had been committed to the Rebels for months. But the Ole Miss coaches saw Washington as more of a project. When he came to camp, he turned heads by running a 5.39 40 at a whop-

ping 363 pounds. Orgeron said he'd love to see what the 6'4"
Washington could do if he shed 40 pounds.

Coming off the viewing of Patterson's and Johnson's film, the
spirit in the cavernous room was exuberant. However, a few plays
into Washington's tape, Orgeron noticed something. He went back
to a play where Washington pulled around to meet a smaller linebacker, but was unable to knock the player back upon impact.
Their bodies rose up and came down together as if they are engaged
in a ballroom dancing maneuver.

"I don't like that," Orgeron said. "See that? He catches that guy!
He don't knock him back! He's running straight up! I don't wanna
spoil the party, but that concerns me."

In dispute was Washington's flexibility. Ideally, the Rebels wanted
to see a lineman dip his hips and strike, exploding out with force.
The play had Orgeron wishing he had that summer camp footage
that the Ole Miss compliance people said he couldn't shoot. Maybe
a refresher viewing from camp would ease his concerns.

"Do you remember seeing him squatting with his heels on the
ground?" Orgeron asked Kehoe.

"Yeah," Kehoe said, "he got in his stance pretty good."

Orgeron seemed satisfied by Kehoe's response, although just like
that, from one suspect play, his mood had clearly soured.

The next prospect on the screen was another mammoth offensive
lineman bound for Oxford the following week: Mark Jean-Louis, a
6'2", 360-pound guard from Cerritos College in California. Jean-
Louis, originally from Florida, was another high priority, although
that had as much to do with his availability as his athleticism. Jean-
Louis was one of the rare JCs who had actually been a full academic
qualifier coming out of high school, which meant he was eligible to
sign in December and enroll at Ole Miss in January. He had opted
to go to junior college to get noticed and would have three seasons
of eligibility with the Rebels. When the staff first watched Jean-

Louis, his tape didn't blow the coaches away, but they saw enough to offer him. They told him he could compete right away for the soon-to-be vacant left guard spot after senior Andrew Wicker, the team's most reliable lineman, finished up his career.

Two weeks earlier, during the Rebels' open week, most of the staff went out to California to scout JC games. Dan Werner watched Jean-Louis. "I thought his feet were good," Werner said as the tape continued. "He was aggressive and had decent athletic ability."

The Rebels main competition for Jean-Louis was Kentucky, but Werner said he believed Ole Miss had the inside track. Jean-Louis had been telling people he wanted to play for Kehoe. Landing Jean-Louis would make the California trip, which already had proved to be fruitful for the Rebels, that much sweeter. Orgeron got two commitments himself from his trip to Compton College, where he found a linebacker (Lamar Brumfield) and a defensive lineman (Larry Dennis), who said they wanted to play for him.

Brumfield was actually a prospect Orgeron had seen when he was at USC. At the time, Brumfield was at Carson High in the Los Angeles area. The Trojans were intrigued by Brumfield, but had other linebackers ranked above him, so he committed to Washington State. But after Brumfield red-shirted at Washington State, he got homesick and left for Compton. Brumfield was stunned when Orgeron showed up to watch him play and told him how badly his program needed linebackers.

Rebels defensive line coach Ryan Nielsen thought that he too had found a JC linebacker in California. A coaching buddy of Nielsen's at West LA Community College called him about a player they thought could start in the SEC right away. Said the kid had NFL tools. But the linebacker had some baggage, too.

His name was Willie Williams.

Three years ago, Williams became perhaps the most infamous college football recruit in the sport's history after the University of

Miami admitted him in 2004 despite a rap sheet that included 11 arrests for everything from burglary to hugging a woman without her permission. By the time Williams signed with Miami, his record was so well-known that when he tried to transfer in the summer of 2006, he sent every college coach (and even a few junior college coaches) running for the hills.

But for all his off-field troubles, Williams was an excellent student who had scored almost 1200 on his SATs. He had been hailed as the top linebacker in the class of 2004, but he couldn't crack the starting line-up at Miami and left after the 2005 season.

A chiseled 6'3", 235-pounder, Williams reportedly had 50 tackles and nine sacks in his first four games for West LA. ("Reportedly" because JC stats are often a little wobbly.) "I don't know if he's better than Rory Johnson," said Nielsen, referring to the Rebels outside linebacker. "I do know he's bigger, stronger, and faster. But Art Kehoe has to stand on the table for the kid."

Yet despite Nielsen's optimism, Kehoe wasn't going to make any plea for Williams. And even if he had, Orgeron wasn't interested: "We can't take a kid like that here." Case closed.

On the same California trip, the Rebels yanked another high-profile JC kid down off their board, cornerback Woodny Turenne. A 6'1", 190-pound track standout, Turenne had been rated by the Internet recruiting sites the No. 1 JC player in the country. He had won the 2006 national junior college title in the 100 meters. On paper, Turenne was exactly what Orgeron wanted: a tall corner with blazing speed. The Rebels felt like they had a shot, too, because Turenne had been a teammate of Schaeffer's and wide receiver recruit A.J. Jackson at College of the Sequoias.

Just one little problem: when Nielsen watched him play, Turenne was getting kicked all over the field. "He couldn't play," Nielsen reported back. "They were picking on him the whole game."

It would be hard for the Rebels to bypass a "five-star" recruit. Most coaches say they don't pay attention to what kind of rankings recruits get, but Orgeron admits that he does. He wants to sign high-profile prospects. He believes they increase the attractiveness of his program and help entice other blue-chippers to look at Ole Miss. And he knows his bosses pay attention to that stuff as well.

Even so, Orgeron knows better than to get caught up in the star system. He knows that many players deemed two- or three-star prospects miraculously blossom into four-star guys when a Florida or LSU enters. And he knows that it cuts the other way, as well.

Just in the past month, the Rebels staff had noticed a couple such examples. Florida stopped chasing DT Ian Williams, and he went from four stars to three stars on the Internet sites almost overnight. A little later, LSU jumped in on Ole Miss defensive tackle commit Drake Nevis, and he went from a three-star prospect to a four-star sure thing.

One defensive tackle prospect the Rebels really liked was a two-star player from Alabama named Justin Sanders. Neither Alabama nor Auburn had offered the 6'4", 278-pound Sanders, but Ole Miss, Louisville, and South Carolina had. On film, Sanders looked strong at the point of attack, used his hands well, and played hard. The Rebels need more tough guys, and that's what they thought Sanders was—a blue-collar, stick-his-face-in-the-mud scrapper.

Initially, Orgeron had projected Sanders as an offensive lineman in the mold of Andrew Wicker, another gritty country boy who actually had been buried on the defensive line depth chart before blossoming into a solid offense guard. But Sanders' eval tape, along with the fact that the Rebels were painfully short-handed on the defensive front, had changed Orgeron's mind. Regardless of what the big boys in Alabama or the Internet gurus might think, Sanders was the kind of defensive tackle the Rebels now needed to chase.

He was a sure thing to be academically qualified, which was some-thing Orgeron couldn't say about for certain about the embattled Jerrell Powe and Ted Laurent.

"I really think Big Justin would help us," Orgeron said. "I know at Syracuse, we would've killed for this guy."

If Orgeron didn't slide to the edge of his seat as he had when he watched Rishaw Johnson and Chris Patterson, his mood perked back up when he saw the name Rolando Melancon pop up on the screen. The more the staff watched tape of the defensive tackle from Luther, Louisiana, the more Orgeron loved him: "You got five stars? Put this sumbitch at 10! *Whooooo!*"

All of Melancon's plays on the tape were eye-popping. He elicited more calls of "Jeee-*zuz!*" than a Southern Baptist church on Sunday morning.

"It's up to you Frank," Orgeron said, turning to Frank Wilson, his recruiter in Louisiana. "C'mon, Frank, guarantee him."

Wilson just grinned and tipped his chair back: "We'll see. I got a three-hour visit with him on Sunday."

With Orgeron's spirit back up again, Hugh Freeze then had Farrar put the tapes of a couple of prospects he wanted Orgeron to see. Several other assistants also had players they'd like to show, but Freeze's decision to sit right behind the projector had paid off. Also, despite being the smallest and least physically intimidating guy on the staff, Freeze was always adept at getting his way.

His first player was A.J. Greene, a defensive end from Tennessee.

Greene's tape didn't appear to do much for the staff. It ran for a minute without any comment. If Greene weren't a certified decent prospect, the staff would've gonged his tape sooner. Of course, he had a hard act to follow.

"After you watch Rolando Melancon," said Orgeron, "it's kinda tough to watch anybody else."

Orgeron clearly wished he had a Rolando Melancon right now. The Rebels' pass rush—last in the SEC in sacks—has been so pitiful that Orgeron had come up with the "Cheetah" package to spice things up for the Egg Bowl. In the Cheetah alignment, the Rebels deployed linebackers Patrick Willis and Rory Johnson as defensive ends wired to fly up-field, hopefully beating State's plodding tackles before they could even get out of their stances.

The look was just one of a couple new wrinkles Orgeron had come up with for Mississippi State. Another twist was the decision to use freshman DE Greg Hardy, a 6'5" 250-pounder who also plays basketball for Ole Miss, at wide receiver in red zone situations.

The Hardy-to-WR move proved a whopping success within the first five minutes when the erstwhile defensive end out-jumped a helpless Bulldog defensive back to reel in a fade pass into the corner of the end zone. The touchdown gave the Rebels a 7-0 lead. Later, again near the MSU goal line, Hardy was inserted to the Ole Miss offense and drew a pass interference penalty.

The Cheetah package paid off, too, with Willis and Johnson harassing the Bulldog quarterback for much of the game.

The Rebels clung to a 20-17 lead with 47 seconds remaining. They had the ball on fourth-and-inches at the State 37-yard-line. Rather than punt the ball, Orgeron sent out his offense. Werner had called for a quarterback sneak by Seth Adams, the Rebels' back-up QB who replaced Schaffer after he struggled. But the Bulldogs stuffed Adams at the line. No first down. Down in the pile, Wicker got tangled up with an MSU defender and threw a punch. Flags were thrown. Ole Miss was penalized 15 yards. State's ball—on the Ole Miss 48. The Bulldogs advanced the ball to the 34, but then, with Willis and Johnson applying the pressure, their drive stalled. With six seconds left, Croom sent his kicker in to try to tie the game with a 51-yard kick. Orgeron, with his hands on his knees, watched as the kick sailed toward the goal post.

Enough distance, but wide left. The Rebels win. Barely.

His team celebrated like a band of crazy men at midfield and then in the locker room, but Orgeron spent little time dwelling on the victory at his press conference. Mostly, he talked big picture. The goal of the program, he explained, was to win the Sugar Bowl.

"It's definitely a big victory to win the Egg Bowl," Orgeron said, "but lemme say this to you—a *big* victory, to me, is winning the Sugar Bowl. We're not going to settle for anything less."

Some 12 hours later, at precisely 3:59 on Sunday morning, November 26, Orgeron was on a treadmill in the Ole Miss weight room inside the IPF.

He was getting fired up about the new season that in his mind had already officially begun. He played out the Rebels' 2007 schedule, and he pictured the Rebels winning at least eight games—maybe more with a little luck.

By 9 a.m., when the rest of the staff assembled in the war room, Orgeron's yellow legal pad was filled with eight pages of notes. He had downed two cups of coffee and a Diet Coke. Two chilled cans of Red Bull sat on the table waiting for him. At least one thing was damned sure: He wasn't going to be short of caffeine.

Orgeron knew it had been a long season, but it was over. He was aware that many coaches give their staffs a day or two to catch their breath before jumping into full-time recruiting. That would *not* be the case at Ole Miss. With startling quantities of sodium and caffeine coursing through his system, he was determined to reset a high-energy tempo for the staff to kick off the sprint portion of the recruiting race.

Today was the first day of the NCAA's two designated "contact" periods. Over the next three weeks, coaches would be allowed to meet with each prospect and their families once a week. Orgeron could be on the road too, although head coaches were allowed only one visit with each prospect through Signing Day.

For many other schools, the contact period falls at an inconvenient time. Practices for late games and bowls cut into recruiting time. Then again, it's a lot easier to sell a bowl-bound team than one that just lost eight games. But Orgeron believed the Rebels now had some momentum.

Presentation, he said, would be everything.

In a few hours, Orgeron would hit the road himself, heading to see junior college DT Jessie Bowman for an afternoon home visit. Six other assistants would soon depart Oxford on their own trips.

The morning staff meeting was short. No philosophical Sunday morning sermon. No season wrap-up. Orgeron spoke in bullet points. No misunderstandings. No mixed messages. The Rebels were, as the football cliché goes, on the clock.

"Stick to the plan," Orgeron began, pounding the table. "Be persistent. I expect you out of the hotel by 7:00. No sleeping in 'til 9:00. I wanna hear, 'That coach told me he was going to be here at 8 o'clock and he was here at 7:50.' That means a lot to me."

The No. 1 thing was attitude toward work, he said, but you got the impression that it was Nos. 2-10 as well: "We're rockin' and rollin' now! Be organized! Stick to the plan!"

Orgeron knew all too well, of course, how many unpredictable factors lurked to torpedo the best-laid plan. A blue-chipper's parent might call at the last minute to say his kid couldn't be there for a home visit. What did that mean? The kid had to go visit a sick grandmother? Another school was horning in on Orgeron's turf? The kid was just plain irresponsible and couldn't be relied on?

Orgeron had seen and heard it all. Didn't matter. The plan was the plan: "I'm not changing nothin'. I am the head coach. Coach Freeze is second in charge when it comes to recruiting. No bitching. No nothing. I ain't takin' no shit. It's rock and roll time now."

And while you're rockin' and rollin', keep a few things in mind:

BE CHOOSEY. The Rebels may have just finished the season at 4–8, Orgeron warned, but do not ever, *ever* think like a 4–8 team.

GET TRANSCRIPTS. Be absolutely current on each recruit's academic standing. "'I don't know' is not acceptable," Orgeron emphasized. "Go to the counselor and find out."

DO *NOT* BREAK RULES. "You're gonna be tempted, guys," Orgeron said, his voice softening. "Don't do it. Period."

CALL YOUR PLAYERS EVERY DAY. You may be on the road recruiting, but first and foremost you're a *coach*. Each position coach *must* stay in touch with his players. Team chemistry requires it.

KNOW YOUR JUNIORS. The Rebels had gotten off to a faster start than many other teams in scouting high school juniors in 2006, but Orgeron now sensed that the other programs were catching up. He told his people he wanted to target and evaluate more 2008 prospects while locking up the 2007 recruiting class. He set December 18 as Junior Offer Day, when the staff would present their cases for HS juniors who should get scholarship offer letters. (But be careful out there: The NCAA rule that coaches trample on most often is the one prohibiting contact with juniors while visiting a high school. Do not yield unto temptation.)

NO BAD ACTORS. Tough, but absolutely critical. Orgeron was definitely of the single-rotten-apple school, especially when it came to drugs: "Find out if they are on drugs," he pounded the table. "I don't want no sonofabitch drug user around here."

SHOW THE OLE MISS FLAG. Each coach was to wear Ole Miss gear—golf shirts, hats, Ole Miss belts—while on the road. "Sell the program," he yelled. "Sell it! Sell it! Sell it!" A key part of the sales pitch? Dropping by high schools to "talk ball" with the coaches, building bonds and relationships all over the football world.

MAKE FRIENDS. "When you go inside the home," Orgeron said in his best schoolmarmish style, "it's no 'Hi, howya doing?' bullshit.

Address the parents by their first names 'Hello, Mary' and 'Good to see you, Dan.' Don't try to just float by with 'Ma'am' and 'Sir.' Get a personal relationship going. And when you're on a home visit, call me. I'd love to talk to them."

BE THOROUGH. "The best compliment I can get," Orgeron closed with, "is 'Coach O, your assistant coach already covered that.'"

Orgeron believed the Rebels could make up a lot of ground for their 4–8 record with the right preparation and attention to detail.

For each player on his visit list, each assistant received a blue folder containing printouts detailing every conceivable Ole Miss selling point. The folder contained information about the university's history, campus life, and academic programs of interest to the recruit. Perhaps most important, each assistant would be armed with a personalized academic plan that McLeod had worked up for all recruits who might struggle getting qualified by the NCAA. Orgeron wanted it spelled out, step-by-step, to the recruit and his family.

"The most impressive thing you can do," he told the staff, "is to walk into the home with an academic plan that will get their baby boy a college degree. Nobody else is going to have this."

Orgeron's schedule for the next three weeks, like those of his assistants, was tighter than an OL on fourth-and-goal from the 1. In between trips to high schools to scout juniors, he was slated to have home visits with Jessie Bowman, Robert Elliott, Chris Strong, Johnny Brown, Stanley Porter, Bradley Sowell, and Oxford High products Johnathon Frink and Jamison Hughes, the eldest son of Rebels assistant Tony Hughes—*all* in the first week.

Week 2 called for more home visits and more junior recruiting, plus side trips to Charlotte and Orlando for stops on the college football awards circuit with Willis, his star linebacker.

Week 3? More of the same.

"It's all Red Bulls and Slim Jims from here on in," said Coach O, and you sensed that he couldn't have been happier at the prospect.

Orgeron exited the war room at 10:51 a.m. wearing an ear-to-ear grin. A private plane was waiting for him. Before leaving the war room, he had one parting message for his staff yet to hit the road: "Just remember, you can tell a trapper by his furs."

The hunt was on.

Jessie Ahmad Rashad Bowman was going to be a tough sell.

The six-foot, 305-pounder had signed with Mississippi State out of high school. Mississippi State promptly parked Bowman at Copiah-Lincoln Community College in Wesson, Mississippi.

To a large extent, Bowman got lost in the hype surrounding another big nose tackle in his area, Jerrell Powe. But his junior college coaches had assured the Rebels that Bowman was a player. The quick take: long arms, plays hard, mean streak.

The Rebels saw Bowman as a "midyear" guy, meaning if he could pass the right combination of courses, he would be able to enroll at a four-year school in time for spring football. They also had heard reports that Bowman was up to 330 pounds, but Orgeron was pleased to find that he was only 305 and "looked great."

But what about State? If Bowman was still firmly committed to the Bulldogs, he wasn't tipping his hand to Orgeron. He explained that MSU recruiting coordinator Shane Beamer called from time to time, but never came to see him. "I guess he always has something else to do," Bowman told Orgeron. Inside, Orgeron was thinking, "Always stick to the plan. It shows the recruits your intent."

Orgeron presented Bowman the academic blueprint McLeod had devised for him to graduate as an education major from Ole Miss. The Rebels also had figured out that if Bowman could pass two correspondence courses—McLeod suggested a lab science course and a humanities course, both offered from Adams State College—he could qualify to enroll for the start of the spring semester. In addition, the plan listed the classes he could take over each semester in his junior and senior years in Oxford. Bowman's eyes lit up.

Orgeron realized, of course, that Bowman could use their plan and still sign with the archrival: "Hey, that's the chance you take."

The meeting with Bowman's family went well, although his cousin did bring up Ole Miss' sordid racial history and the environment for blacks on campus. Orgeron heard her out and then responded: "I heard about that when I first got here. But it's just not that way any more. It's not. One of my coaches, Tony Hughes, is an African-American, and he doesn't feel that way. If he did, he wouldn't be sending his son to Ole Miss. The number of African-American students on our campus has gone from 5% to 16% in the past 11 years. That stuff you're talking about really is from the 1970s, and people really need to move past that old image."

Before Orgeron left, he thanked the Bowmans for seeing him and reminded them that during his entire 90-minute visit, all he talked about was his school, and didn't try to bash anyone else.

"It was a good visit," Bowman said later. "I liked that I was his first visit. That really says a lot. Coach O is really down to earth. He's someone who could make the hard work seem like fun. But I don't know. State's got the biggest hole. They're losing three D-linemen and Ole Miss has all them freshmen."

Whether he turned Bowman or not, Orgeron believed the Rebels had a great first day of the new recruiting season. He felt good about Bowman and even better after he got a call from Nielsen. The young coach reported that he'd had a rough start to the day in Atlanta. He waited three hours for defensive tackle Cameron Heyward, the son of the late former NFL star Ironhead Heyward. (Heyward's best friend, the team's quarterback, already had committed to play basketball for the Rebels and had been telling them he could sway his buddy.) But Heyward's mom felt the Rebels didn't recruit her boy hard enough and refused to let Nielsen in the house.

On a positive note, Nielsen reported that he'd had a terrific visit with Ted Laurent, the powerful defensive tackle who'd been committed to Ole Miss since spring. Laurent's originally from Canada; his mother speaks no English. Over the course of the year, Orgeron had scored points with her by speaking to her in French. The Rebels had feared that LSU and Auburn were going to try and turn Laurent, but Nielsen said the kid was 100% a Rebel. "Those guys don't have a shot in hell of getting Ted," Nielsen said, adding that seeing Laurent had "turned a shitty day into a great day."

Orgeron hoped Nielsen's assessment was right. He was back in the war room by 5:35 the next morning. He had more notes to make for the Rebels' 7 a.m. team meeting.

The final Rebels' team meeting of the year struck a similar tone to Orgeron's Sunday morning recruiting speech to the staff, only this time he was a bit more congratulatory. Orgeron opened by thanking the seniors. He told them that the staff already had been out on the road, and the feeling around the state was that the program was turning. He took a long pause and scanned the room. Several of the players' heads nodded. He had their attention. Orgeron then echoed some of the things he'd stressed earlier with his coaches, reminding the team that 2007 already started: "The way we act over these next three weeks is going to help us win next year."

Then Orgeron called over to the team's star linebacker, who was seated in the second row of the team room: "When did you start seeing yourself get stronger?"

Patrick Willis answered that his biggest gains in the weight room happened exactly at this time last year. Willis was the most respected man inside the program, and Orgeron was praying that his players follow that example.

Satisfied that his message had been received, Orgeron then turned back to recruiting. "You all know this is the lifeblood of our program," he says. "We need your help."

Then Orgeron enlisted current players to become de facto members of the recruiting team: "We need the guys who are hosts to keep doing a great job, and that's important because when these recruits talk about what they really liked about Ole Miss, and when we talk to the parents, they keep saying how they love the team chemistry. That's *you* guys. And that's important, because we've got some guys to replace. We need to get us some players."

Next Orgeron cautioned his team about not trying *too* hard to show the prospects a good time, an indirect reference to the wild stories about prospects being taken to strip clubs or set up with hookers. "Don't forget our rules," he said. "One a.m. curfew. No drugs. No alcohol. No sex. All of that stuff is out the window."

Before dismissing the team and giving his juniors a separate pep talk, Orgeron hammered home one final point: *"Protect the team! You busted your ass to change the momentum, and we've had a big-time swing. Now let's rock and roll!"*

Back inside the war room, a few of his assistants swapped stories from the road. Ten minutes later, Chris Rippon, the Rebels' Alabama recruiter, told Orgeron of the two great home visits he'd had the day before with DT prospects Justin Sanders and Josh Chapman.

"You're gonna love Justin Sanders when he gets here," Rippon said. "He's a big, strong, tough kid. His daddy's a big ol' boy too. I got the impression Big Tim is pretty tough too. He told me he raises gamecocks. He showed me the cages in the backyard."

Orgeron smiled at hearing Rippon, a New York City native, talk about recruiting in the Deep South. He would love to hear more, but Orgeron didn't have a moment to spare right now.

"I got to get outta here," he said. "I need to see some juniors, because right now we're hot as a firecracker in the state of Mississippi!"

Chapter 14

ROAD
SHOW

JOE McKNIGHT HADN'T seen the Egg Bowl. He didn't even know what an Egg Bowl was. But even if he had known and cared, the all-world tailback from John Curtis Christian School near New Orleans couldn't have traveled to Oxford to watch it because he was too busy with his high school's run in the Louisiana state playoffs.

That's the way coach J.T. Curtis liked it. The 66-year-old veteran had sent dozens of players off to college with football scholarships over the years. He was Louisiana's all-time leader in wins with 441, the most recent coming on December 8, 2006, when his Patriots—led by McKnight—won their 21st state title. And he'd always had a policy of discouraging his players from getting too involved in recruiting until the season was over.

You had to think those three facts are related.

J.T. Curtis wasn't a man given to gushing. Even though the Scouts Inc. recruiting analysts for ESPN had anointed McKnight the nation's No. 1 prospect—something Rebels coach Frank Wilson had done a year before—Curtis wasn't about to load all that hyperbole onto the shoulders of his star running back. Instead, he was relatively restrained: "Joe has the ability to be an outstanding player in college, and if he can stay healthy, he could become an outstanding professional player."

Was McKnight the best player he'd ever coached? Curtis refused to go there, but he did say that McKnight would be the most heavily recruited player he'd ever coached. With the 2006 season over, he knew a massive rush was heading the 18-year-old's way. Curtis said he was confident McKnight could handle it.

All of the Internet recruiting gurus were predicting that McKnight would sign with LSU. That's what pretty much all of the bluest of the blue-chippers from the Bayou had always done. The previous year's top tailback, Keiland Williams, had talked about wanting to leave home, and he flirted with USC and Ole Miss. But two days after Signing Day, he signed with LSU.

Another Bayou kid, Jai Eugene, the nation's top cornerback in the 2006 recruiting class, had been committed to Michigan; on the eve of Signing Day, he switched to LSU. And the year before that, the state's top player, QB Ryan Perrilloux, had switched to LSU from Texas on Signing Day, capping off that recruiting season's biggest soap opera.

Thanks in part to Curtis' strong guidance, McKnight hadn't said much to the Internet recruiting media. Like most recruits, he told reporters from whichever team sites called him what he thought they wanted to hear, but not much else. Back in June, however, McKnight had told a reporter from USCfootball.com that he was in Los Angeles to visit a female friend. The girlfriend angle, along with McKnight's admiration for former Trojans star Reggie Bush, had the online community speculating that USC was the biggest threat to LSU. (McKnight later laughed about that tip, saying he'd broken up with his girlfriend in LA by the end of the summer.)

Then, in September, the USC Rivals.com site stated with confidence that "USC, LSU, Florida State, Notre Dame, and Miami are the only schools McKnight will keep under consideration before making a commitment."

But Wilson and Orgeron refused to give up the battle for McKnight. With Wilson leading the way, Ole Miss' recruiting in the Bayou seemed to be going better than ever. The Rebels had targeted about 20 Louisiana kids for the 2007 class, and heading into the December "contact" period, they felt they were in good shape with a bunch of them. Wilson already had commitments from Rishaw Johnson, whom the Rebels believed to be Louisiana's top offensive lineman, as well as OL Alex Washington, TE David Rue, and DT Drake Nevis. Wilson also thought the Rebels had a shot at landing Lionel Breaux, a speedy wide receiver, and Rolando Melancon, the defensive tackle whom Orgeron loved so much.

McKnight, of course, would transform the entire Ole Miss recruiting class. More than that, he had the talent to alter the balance of power in college football the way Reggie Bush had done at USC. This is how Wilson put it: "In the last couple of years, we've gotten some good guys from down here. But I still haven't caught that really big fish, and that's Joe McKnight. If he comes here, some kid who may be on the fence will say, 'Joe McKnight could've gone anywhere in America, and he picked Ole Miss.' Getting Joe would mean that the recruiting plan that Coach O put in place for us had paid off."

Over the course of the season, Wilson had developed a good rapport with McKnight. Not an easy task, getting close to a kid who was being bombarded virtually 24/7 by phone calls and text messages from Internet reporters and recruiters and college football junkies of every stripe. By December, McKnight's monthly cell phone bill had quadrupled, peaking at $268. Everywhere McKnight went around New Orleans, he was inundated with pro-LSU comments. Wilson sensed at one point that McKnight was actually getting turned off by all the fawning.

Wilson opted for a low-pressure pitch, text-messaging the tailback only once a week. According to McKnight, the tactic seemed to be working: "I like Coach Wilson a lot. He's from where I'm from, and we grew up similar. I like how he coaches. My grandmother really likes him too."

Reading a kid's personality is the most underrated part of the recruiting process. All-America prospects get dozens of pitches from visiting college coaches who show up in their golf shirt with the school logo, wearing a toothy grin, and carrying a boatload of promises. The kids look for the school that provides the best fit, but that's seldom obvious to 18-year-olds. Usually the coach with the deepest insight into a recruit's personality has the best chance to make a connection.

McKnight was tough for Wilson to gauge. The young man's life experiences hadn't exactly conditioned him to trust men. His biological father had never been involved in his life. And by the time McKnight was 12, he and his mother had already been crushed by men they thought they could count on too many times. His big sister, Johanna, said that was probably why McKnight had always been quick to remind her that he was the man of the house.

Wilson had also grown up without a father, as his dad had died in a car crash when Wilson was in the fifth grade. Being a high school coach in inner-city New Orleans had made Wilson adept at understanding how certain experiences shape kids, and he said he was often able to learn from kids' grandparents, frequently the de facto caregivers in single-parent homes, what the children were too scared or proud to reveal.

"I never wanted to pry into Joe's past," Wilson said just before Signing Day. "I felt like if he wanted to talk about things, he would've brought them up. He didn't. I just tried to present him with an image of someone he would want to model himself after, without saying it. I simply tried to behave in a respectable manner so he would say, 'That's how a man should handle himself.'"

Wilson said he first realized he'd connected with McKnight in late September. He'd sent McKnight a text message wishing him good luck in Curtis's nationally televised game against Alabama's Hoover High, the nation's top-ranked team, and McKnight called him.

"Coach Frank, I'm gonna do my thing," McKnight started off. "You're gonna be proud."

"It was the first time we started breaking down barriers," Wilson said later. "Before, it had been me talking and him listening. But when he called me that time, his tone was different."

To boost the Rebels' chances with McKnight, Orgeron decided that Ole Miss should also recruit Colby Arceneaux, a 5'8", 185-pound DB at John Curtis. The best thing Arceneaux had going for him? He and McKnight were best friends. The two had been tight since they were 9. In coaching circles, it was the definitive calf-cow deal, in which a program takes a calf in order to get the cow.

But Arceneaux was no stumblebum. He was a four-year starter, a rarity at Curtis. And according to his coach, he had great quickness and hit like a truck. Arceneaux was also on the honor roll and was the vice president of the student council.

"Colby could make a really good strong safety," Coach Curtis said. "He's very physical and a really tough kid."

Plus, there were connections. Orgeron had known Bryan Arceneaux since they played high school football together. Later, they were on the same defensive line at Northwestern State. The icing on the cake? Orgeron had introduced Bryan to his future wife, Colby's mother.

As the Rebels started to believe that maybe, just maybe, they had McKnight in their crosshairs, Orgeron couldn't help but think that maybe this crazy connection was part of some mysterious grand design. Really, what are the odds that one of Orgeron's best friends from South Lafourche would have a son who turned out to be the best friend of the best recruit in America if there wasn't *something* going on in the cosmos?

Another good sign: Bryan Arceneaux had been telling Orgeron that McKnight didn't want to go to LSU. In fact, after Curtis' 41-7 victory over St. Charles Catholic at the Superdome to win the 2A state title, McKnight had said as much. Actually, he sang it, right there in the locker room during the Patriots' postgame celebration. When he spied an LSU recruiter in the distance, McKnight began to say, "Ain't goin' to LSU! Ain't goin' to LSU!"

McKnight later explained that he wanted to "get away" to go to school. Wilson said he wasn't surprised to hear that, considering that McKnight's sister had decided to play college basketball "way up north" in Virginia.

Ole Miss' first big coup was persuading Curtis to let Wilson and the Rebels get the first home visit with McKnight. Curtis conceded to wedge an Ole Miss visit in between McKnight's trip to Arizona for an awards banquet and a weekend trip to New York City, where he was promoting the U.S. Army All-American Bowl.

"J.T. was reluctant at the time because he was trying to protect Joe," Wilson said of Coach Curtis' concession. "They'd just come off the season, and he didn't want the kid to be exhausted. I was like, 'Come on, J.T., I need it! Come on!'"

For Orgeron, the timing of the visit with McKnight, his mother Jennifer, and Curtis was a gamble. Most head coaches save their one in-home visit until later in the recruiting process. Ideally, Orgeron would prefer to be the last coach in the house before Signing Day. But he knew the Rebels had to stay fresh in McKnight's mind, lest they get big-footed by the top-20 programs when they filed in. It was a calculated risk; in most cases, a visiting coach was looking to get a commitment. Orgeron was just hoping to persuade the tailback to make an official campus visit to Oxford.

The fresh hope of reeling in McKnight sent a lightning bolt through the war room.

"Everyone is talking about Joe around here," said Rebels recruiting secretary Amanda Gilpin in mid-December. "It sounds like a lot of good things are happening now. It's very exciting."

Two weeks had passed since the Egg Bowl, during which time there'd been quite a shake-up of the Ole Miss recruiting board. McKnight was the biggest news, but there was a lot more.

The formal announcement that Stephen Garcia, long the Rebels' top priority, was going to play QB for Steve Spurrier in South Carolina caused barely a ripple in the Ole Miss war room. Everybody there already knew the bad news. But at his press conference, Garcia mentioned something interesting. He said that Dan Werner, along with Carolina assistant David Reaves, were the two best recruiters he'd dealt with.

Words like that typically ring hollow in recruiting circles, where coming in second means you got beat. Yet the Rebels preferred to look for a silver lining.

Then ... an omen?

A few days later, Werner received a call from a high school trainer in Stephenville, Texas, who wanted to talk about a quarterback named Jevan Snead. Werner had pursued Snead a few years earlier back while at Miami, so he was all ears. The trainer said the kid had really liked Werner. He went on to say that, after spending his freshman year in the shadow of budding Longhorn star Colt McCoy, also a freshman, Snead had decided to transfer. He was looking for schools with a senior starting quarterback in the 2007 season so that when he became eligible in 2008, he'd have a shot at the starting job.

Next the trainer popped the question: "Would you guys be interested in Jevan?"

Werner almost jumped through the ceiling. Normally, such a call would come from a high school coach, so Werner asked the trainer to put him in touch with Chad Morris, Snead's coach at Stephenville High School. Sure enough, Snead—rated one of the nation's top-15 recruits in 2006—was available. Morris asked Werner if he wanted him to send some film of Snead.

Don't bother, Werner replied. We want him.

"When I got off the phone, I went right to Ed and told him the whole situation, and he got all excited too," Werner explained. "It was unbelievable. *Bam!* The timing was perfect."

In January 2006, Snead had enrolled a semester early at Texas in hopes of winning the Longhorns quarterback job which had recently been vacated by Vince Young. But in spring practice, Snead never could catch McCoy, who'd gotten a head start digesting the Texas offense. Most observers expected Snead, who was faster and had a stronger arm, to eventually pass McCoy, but it didn't happen. McCoy thrived in the UT passing game, setting school records.

Snead never felt comfortable in Austin. The kid from tiny Stephenville, a town of 15,000 that calls itself the Cowboy Capital of the World, had a hard time adjusting to living in the biggest college dormitory in the nation. Austin simply felt too big for him.

On December 1, Texas granted Snead his release. One week later, just a day after he'd gotten that call from the Stephenville High trainer, Werner was on his way to Texas to visit Snead in his hometown. This time, the Rebels' competition included Hawaii, Louisville, TCU, and Houston.

Hawaii and Louisville had potent offenses, but both presented potential timing problems for Snead. They had talented junior QBs (Colt Brennan at Hawaii, Brian Brohm at Louisville) who were toying with jumping to the NFL after the season, and they most likely wouldn't decide until around the same time that Snead would need to enroll somewhere.

The two Texas schools represented bigger threats. TCU is just an hour away from Stephenville, while Houston was coached by Art Briles, the former head coach at Stephenville High, where he won several state championships. Houston also had a few of Snead's former teammates on its roster, including his old center.

Werner based his pitch on things Ole Miss could offer that the other two schools lacked. Oxford is a small-college town, and Snead could play in a pro-style offense. He would be playing in the SEC, the most competitive league in college football.

Said Werner to Snead and Morris: "It's the best of all worlds."

The Rebels coaches who had scattered after the Egg Bowl reconvened every weekend to host their on-campus visits.

Their first big recruiting weekend of the season was December 1 to 3. Among the 14 visitors were three DTs (D'Angelo McCray, Justin Sanders, Drake Nevis), two players (OL Mike Dykes, DB Da'Norris Searcy) who had committed to North Carolina before the Tar Heels fired head coach John Bunting, prized OL commit Rishaw Johnson, Louisiana speedster Lionel Breaux, and Robert Elliott, the pride of Okolona.

Afterward, Orgeron said he believed the weekend had gone great. He'd hit it off with Sanders' father. The whole staff had grown closer to Johnson's family. And Breaux had told Wilson he was planning on committing.

The downside? Orgeron came away a little concerned about Elliott. Not about whether the star running back was still committed to Ole Miss, but whether Elliott had the toughness and personality to be a feature back in the SEC. Elliott had hardly uttered a word the whole weekend. He'd seemed meek, withdrawn. To Orgeron, shyness is a red flag.

That's what these visits sometimes reveal, Orgeron said. They provide an up-close-and-personal look at a player's makeup: how he carries himself, how he reacts to coaches, and how he deals with his peers in a social setting.

The Rebels had already backed off of six other prospects who had committed to them earlier in the year, in almost every case because of academics or character issues. A couple of other recruits (DE Rufus Williams, LB Stevan Ridley) had bailed on Ole Miss.

That sort of shifting perfectly illustrates the tenuous nature of modern-day recruiting, where an offer is always conditional, a commitment doesn't necessarily mean committed, and nothing really counts until National Signing Day.

Within 10 days of the Egg Bowl, the Rebels snared Breaux, the New Orleans receiver who said he became a believer after watching Ole Miss go toe to toe with LSU.

But then, a week after telling Wilson how much he'd loved his visit, the previously committed, New Orleans-area DT Drake Nevis called back to say it was his calling to spread God's word to the people in Louisiana and that therefore he must be an LSU Tiger.

But in recruiting, as in football, you win some and you lose some: The day after Nevis bailed, the Rebels parlayed some of that Egg Bowl momentum into flipping Jamariey Atterberry, the top in-state cornerback on their board.

Atterberry is a native of Kosciusko, Mississippi, the town where Oprah Winfrey grew up. Kosciusko is Bulldog country, and Atterberry had committed to Mississippi State seven months before. But after his official visit on December 8 to 10, he decided that Oxford was the place for him.

Another December visitor, Atlanta-area LB Scottie Williams, had committed to Auburn but now said he was rethinking his commitment after taking note of Ole Miss's late-season improvement.

And despite some apprehension, Orgeron wasn't backing off of Elliott. He couldn't, not with Joe McKnight's being far from a lock.

The most troubling news following the December 1 to 3 soiree had to do with one recruit who never got a chance to visit Oxford: highly regarded JC LB Chris Patterson. The Rebels figured that the only thing standing in his way was the formality of getting the SEC to waive its three-semester residency rule for junior college transfers, which McLeod didn't see as a problem. But just before Patterson's scheduled campus visit, SEC commissioner Mike Slive notified Ole

Miss that he was not going to grant the waiver. The ruling left Ole Miss with no choice but to drop Patterson.

"I wonder if Mike Slive even understands why that rule is in place," said McLeod, noting that it was on the books because former Mississippi State coach Jackie Sherrill had been notorious for steering junior college players to JCs with laxer standards after their season ended so that they could get qualified before going to MSU.

Worse still, word leaked in early December that linebacker Rory Johnson, coming off a strong first season at Ole Miss, had signed with an agent. If that turned out to be true, his college career was over, and Ole Miss' linebacking situation instantly would become desperate. Everything was in limbo because no one could get in touch with Johnson.

(Fast-forward: Johnson wasn't taken in the 2007 NFL draft, but he later signed with the Green Bay Packers.)

Less than two weeks after his November 26 war room edict about sticking to the plan, Orgeron decided to call an audible.

The Rebels' original plan was predicated on luring Stephen Garcia to Oxford. Now it was time to move to Plan B.

So rather than spend another day with Wilson scouring Louisiana for junior candidates for the 2008 recruiting class, on December 12 Orgeron and Werner hopped on a charter flight for a Texas detour to meet Jevan Snead's parents and high school coach in Stephenville and then Snead himself in Austin.

As much as Orgeron hated changing directions, he knew that Snead could be a cover boy for his program. He was sure of it. After all, Snead had been good enough for both Mack Brown and Urban Meyer to chase, which would give him enough of an Internet rep to help Ole Miss lure blue-chip receivers and maybe even seal the deal with Joe McKnight. Snead wouldn't help boost Ole Miss' position on the recruiting rankings, which by their own rules don't factor in

Division I transfers. But Orgeron was *positive* that Jevan Snead would boost Ole Miss.

Recruiting Snead was a bit different from pitching your average high school prospect. He was older, and he already had two bad college experiences under his belt. Since having spoken with Morris, Werner understood that the trust factor was vital.

Snead had committed to Florida during his junior year of high school, after Gators coach Urban Meyer told him they weren't going to be recruiting any other quarterbacks. Great—just what a blue-chip recruit wants to hear: no one standing in his way to becoming as good as he can be.

Then later that fall, Snead clicked on ESPN's *Outside the Lines* and caught a segment on Tim Tebow, a touted quarterback recruit from Florida. Interesting, he thought. Cool to see a guy going through the same stuff he'd gone through. But when the cameras panned up into the crowd at Tebow's game and focused on Meyer and his offensive coordinator, Dan Mullen, Snead was stunned.

Snead called Meyer the next day and asked about Tebow.

"Oh, don't worry about that," Meyer assured him. "We're only recruiting him as a linebacker."

Snead wanted to believe him because he wanted to go to Florida, but at that point, his high school coach interceded. "We may have been born at night, but it wasn't last night," Morris said later, recalling the situation. "Jevan was too dear to me to let something like that happen to him."

And it would have. The 6'3", 229-pound Tebow ended up playing quite a bit as the Gators backup quarterback in Florida's national title run in 2006. Subsequently, Meyer called him an ideal fit for Florida's spread-option offense.

"We knew Coach Morris and Jevan's parents had to trust us," said Werner. "And we knew they felt like they'd been burned. So we had to convince them absolutely that whatever we told them was going to happen."

Orgeron had intended to return to New Orleans the night after he saw Snead's parents, but as he and his offensive coordinator were leaving the Texas campus for the airport, Werner got a text message from the pilot: low clouds, can't leave 'til tomorrow morning. The bad weather turned the Snead visit into a two-day trip, which is two days more than the Rebels had initially budgeted to spend of their precious contact period in the Lone Star State.

When Orgeron finally got back to Louisiana, he faced two huge days: home visits to meet Breaux and Melancon on December 13 and a meeting with McKnight, his mother, and J.T. Curtis on December 14.

The Rebels were hoping to make up for lost ground with Melancon, the big DT from Lutcher, Louisiana. He'd been unable to get to Oxford for the December 1 to 3 visit because, like McKnight, his team had still been alive in the Louisiana state play-offs. Back in October, the Rebels' staff actually had anointed Melancon a higher priority than even McKnight. After the Egg Bowl, Wilson had said the Rebels had a 70% chance of landing Melancon, but their odds since seemed to have plummeted. Word on the street was that Tennessee now had a big lead.

Ole Miss had been the first school to offer Melancon a scholarship, a fact that loomed in the young run-stuffer's eyes. "I love Coach O," said Melancon, when asked about what that first offer meant to him. "He was the first one to jump out for me."

Melancon also liked that Orgeron had coached Warren Sapp, his idol and the reason he wore No. 99. "Coach O says I do some of the things that Sapp did, but I really don't buy into all that," Melancon said. "I think that's probably just recruiting talk. Warren Sapp, man, he's a great NFL player, and I'm just this little high school

248

dude living here in this trailer, tryin' to make it."

Melancon demonstrated an interesting personality, one that flip-flopped between cocky and humble. His goal, he said, was to make it out of Lutcher. Why? "Because nobody ever makes it out of Lutcher." In one breath, while talking about his hopes and goals, he boasted that "pain don't really hurt me," but then allowed that he'd been plagued by migraine headaches for years. The pain got so intense, he said, that it usually caused him to vomit. He said he planned to get a CAT scan "one of these days." For the time being, he'd cope with Tylenol.

Despite his affinity for Orgeron, Melancon said he thought the Vols wanted him the most. They told him he could come in and play right away since they were losing some starters. Getting Melancon to make his first official visit to Knoxville had apparently paid off for the Vols.

"It was my first time ever seeing mountains," he said. "It was my first time ever flying on a plane. I've been to LSU home games, and they don't compare to Neyland Stadium. It was great."

Orgeron, who is nothing if not a believer in his powers of persuasion, thought he could make up distance on the Vols once he saw Melancon, but that proved to be a challenge.

Unfortunately for the Rebels, when Orgeron and Wilson came to Melancon's trailer, they found him sprawled on the sofa with the lights off, suffering from another migraine. Twenty minutes later, an infant began to wail. Then Melancon's 15-year-old sister came out, screaming, "You woke up my baby!"

The one in-home visit Orgeron had been permitted with the most coveted defensive player on the Rebels board was over almost as soon as it had begun.

Orgeron and Wilson didn't have time to fret, because the next day they were in Curtis' house, making their case to Joe McKnight.

Naturally, they hit hard on all the good things McKnight would encounter when he got to Oxford, from the Rebels' academic support system and good graduation rate, to the beauty of the campus and the fanatic loyalty of the Ole Miss alumni, to how he would be featured in the Ole Miss offense as the perfect complement to BenJarvus Green-Ellis, their returning tailback.

Green-Ellis, also a New Orleans native, was a 220-pound inside runner, Orgeron told McKnight. The plan was for the Rebels offense to be similar to how USC had paired Reggie Bush's outside game with LenDale White's bruising style. And when Green-Ellis left, after 2007, McKnight would be the Rebels' featured back, not an interchangeable part of some backfield-by-committee approach. (The Rebels had heard that one of McKnight's problems with LSU was that the Tigers tried to rotate three tailbacks, so even their star back didn't get full-time work.)

Wilson also pointed out that the Rebels had a proven track record for developing blue-chippers: "Two years ago, Michael Oher, our left tackle, was a freshman All-America. This year, John Jerry, our right guard, made freshman All-America. Next year, it'll be you."

Best of all, Wilson said, Ole Miss would allow McKnight to experience life away from home, but he'd still be close enough so that his family could see him play.

McKnight was impressed. "I like those guys a lot," he said later. "They gave me a lot to think about, but I wanna see what happens on my visits. I need to go to a school and find a comfort zone."

Like the Ole Miss coaches, Jevan Snead had been busy working the road.

The day before Orgeron came to Stephenville, Snead had driven over to Fort Worth with Morris to observe TCU as the Horned Frogs prepared for the Poinsettia Bowl. A few days later, the Stephenville crew made the five-hour ride to Houston to visit the Cougars as they prepared for the Liberty Bowl.

On December 15, the following day, Snead boarded a plane in Houston to fly to Oxford.

As a rule, Orgeron preferred not to have individual visits on a weekend between semesters because campus was empty and the town was dead. Werner suspected that the empty campus might not be such a bad thing in Snead's case, because he'd said he was looking for a laid-back, casual setting.

Empty campus or not, the Rebels had the red carpet treatment lined up. The reigning Mississippi Miss Most Beautiful—a school ambassador, of course—gave Snead a golf cart tour of campus. It also didn't hurt that it was a warm, sunny December day in Oxford. Snead later said that he couldn't help but wonder how beautiful the place must be on a game day.

"I think we're in good shape with him," McLeod concluded. "He says he's looking for a place where he can let his dog run around, and I know he can do that here."

Snead was sufficiently intrigued by Ole Miss that on Friday night he called Morris, his high school coach, and asked him to fly to Oxford for a second opinion. Morris arrived in Oxford the next day before dinner, just in time for Orgeron and Werner to show off Vaught-Hemingway Stadium all lit up on a Saturday night.

Morris later said that while the glitzy facilities and comely coeds had caught Snead's eye, the young man from Stephensville, Texas, was mainly looking for a place where he felt comfortable with the coaches and the quarterback situation.

After watching Snead interact with his staff, Orgeron was dead certain that Ole Miss was just that place. Snead said that before making a call, he wanted to sit down with his parents and weigh the pluses and minuses of each school. He told Werner he'd decide by Monday night.

For Werner, that meant Sunday would be another sleepless night. The past 12 months had been brutal for the Rebels offensive coordinator. He'd been fired at Miami. He'd relocated his family (wife, two small kids) to Oxford, where he'd presided over the SEC's worst offense. Werner also knew better than anyone that he was working for the most demanding coach in the country when it came to recruiting, and the one recruit he was personally most responsible for, Stephen Garcia, had opted for another SEC school.

Another punch in the gut: Robert Marve, Werner's Plan B quarterback option from the previous summer, had become the fastest-rising QB prospect in the country after throwing for a Florida state record 48 touchdowns while leading his high school to a state championship—only now he was no longer thinking Ole Miss.

Werner realized he could've landed Marve six months earlier, but at the time Orgeron only had eyes for Stephen Garcia. The irony was that now Marve was thinking of de-commiting from Alabama to, of all places, Miami.

The one thing Werner didn't want to see was the look on Ed Orgeron's face if Jevan Snead called on Monday to say that the recruiter had finished second again.

For the Rebels, it had been a good weekend, much better than they'd first thought. Not only did they feel great after Snead's visit, but on Monday morning Chris Rippon got a call from Justin Sanders, who had just returned with his father from an official visit to South Carolina. The Rebels had worried that Steve Spurrier's aura might sway Sanders' old man, but Sanders told Rippon that he wanted to commit to Ole Miss then and there.

Orgeron howled his approval over the phone to Sanders.

"It's gonna be a great day for the Ole Miss Rebels," Orgeron said, handing the cell phone back to Rippon. "I can feel it. *Wooooo!*"

The early contact period was over for the Rebels. But before the staff left for Christmas break on December 20, Orgeron wanted them to complete one last chore: send out all the offers to juniors for the class of 2008. That meant that while they awaited Snead's decision—*the* decision, save for McKnight's, in terms of the class of 2007—Orgeron's coaches would be spending the next three days in the war room reviewing eval tapes.

By midafternoon on Monday, they had watched eval tapes of 83 juniors and made offers to 43. Just when Orgeron had gotten the feeling that the staff was starting to lose steam, he grabbed Snead's eval tape from the table.

Werner winced: "I don't know if I wanna watch that right now."

Orgeron: "You're not superstitious, are you, Daniel?"

Werner, like a spooked preschooler, nodded his head up and down, up and down.

Orgeron glanced around the table and slammed the tape into the VCR. As Snead's name appeared on the screen, Orgeron hit pause. "This just goes to show how important it is how you treat people," Orgeron said. "You just don't know what's gonna come around. This right here—I don't know, it's just a gift from above."

The tape opened up with Snead calmly surveying the coverage downfield and then firing to an open receiver. "*Wooooo!*" Orgeron purred. "He looked somebody off! *Ho-ly shit!* What do you think about that, Frank?"

"Love him, Coach," Wilson replied.

"Yes, sir, you can tell a trapper by his furs," Orgeron said. "And this right here is a really big fur."

Twenty minutes later, Werner's cell went off.

Snead.

Werner and Orgeron stepped out into the hallway. No one in the war room made a sound. The other assistants just looked at each other, hoping to hear …

"*Wooooo! Wooooo!*"

Orgeron charged back into the war room holding the cell up in the air so that the rest of the staff could formally welcome Jevan

Snead to Ole Miss with a big, loud, heartfelt Rebels yell.

Meanwhile, as the rest of the Ole Miss coaches screamed their heads off like pepped-up frat boys, Werner stood quietly by the door. His face was pale. His eyes were glassy. He had the look of a man who'd just spent all night waiting for his wife to go through labor.

It's a quarterback!

Chapter 15

HOME
STRETCH

T HE NCAA MANDATES that each year from mid-December through early January college football recruiting programs observe what it calls the "dead period," during which they may not host any prospects on their campus for an official visit.

Fearful that other programs might beat him to the punch, Orgeron designated the beginning of the dead period as the time to beef up Ole Miss's offer pool for class of 2008 kids.

A dozen times over the past month, he'd told the staff that Christmas break wouldn't begin until junior recruiting was "where it needs to be." Consequently, much of the "contact period" had been a juggling act between actual contact—home visits, school visits, recruiting weekends—and sifting through game tape so the Rebels could get their offers to top juniors before Christmas.

On Sunday morning, December 17, while Orgeron and Werner were wrapping up Jevan Snead's visit to Oxford, Ryan Nielsen was sitting alone in the defensive line room watching tape after tape of high school games in Southern California looking for blue-chip juniors. Armed with a remote and a list of prospects graded on a 1-4 scale from a California recruiting service, Nielsen spent three hours working his way through 11 candidates from the list's highest-rated names. Sometimes, Nielsen got lucky and found games where he could scout three players in the same game.

Sometimes he liked a kid but couldn't find enough plays to justify making an eval tape to be shown in the war room. Interior linemen were easiest because you could track them on most plays; receivers and defensive backs were the hardest.

And sometimes, if things weren't developing fast enough, Nielsen did a little coaching: "Why won't you throw him the damn ball? He's your best player. Throw him the ball!"

Other times, as in the case with one defensive end, he saw enough to get intrigued. In this instance, he kept watching for 15 minutes until a play made him physically cringe. The DE rushed into the opposing backfield and ended up grasping at air as the tailback deked him out of his jock and scooted upfield.

"That's it, right there, the telltale sign," Nielsen said with disgust. "The guy comes in unblocked and still can't make the play."

Fifteen minutes shot to hell.

All the eval tapes that needed screening kept Orgeron and his assistants grinding hard in the war room for three straight days. "This would've been an ugly Christmas around here if Snead had called and said, 'Thanks, but I'm going to TCU,'" observed one assistant. "Coach O's a lot more relaxed now. At least for him."

All but two of the 85 tapes the Rebels staff screened the first two days of the dead period were of juniors. The exceptions: two senior defensive linemen, one of whom was a St. Petersburg player whom Matt Lubick was pushing Orgeron to watch.

Orgeron had hoped he'd been shown everyone the Rebels needed to target for 2007 by now, but given the tenuous nature of his defensive line board, with so many academic question marks, he couldn't afford the luxury of leaving stones unturned.

Lubick, the son of longtime Colorado State head coach Sonny Lubick, told the group his new discovery was Scott Lawson, No. 75.

"He used to be 340 pounds, and they didn't have a coach there in the spring," Lubick announced to the group. "But he got down to 300 pounds, and they say he just tore it up in the Pinellas County All-Star Game. They say he's a whole new kid."

It's never quite clear who the "they" is. Maybe it's a high school assistant coach, or a teacher or a rival coach. But what "they" say often seemed to rank second in importance only to film among recruiting tools. In this case, the film was a bit grainy, but the big No. 75 did make a bunch of plays. "They" may be right.

"He's a frickin' load," Kehoe said. "I like him."

Orgeron: "We gotta get him! He makes plays. Nobody else has offered this kid?"

Lubick: "I think Wake Forest is about to."

Orgeron: "Got his phone number?"

Lubick: "You bet."

Orgeron: "Call him right now. Hurry up and sign that motherfucker or else your daddy will get him. You watch, I got 24 hours before Colorado State goes down there."

(The CSU dig was a reference to Lubick's dad getting commitments from QB T.J. Borcky and center Tyler McDermott, a pair of Floridians the Rebels had passed on.)

Lubick got the kid's coach on the line: "We were very impressed with Scott on film. He really plays hard, doesn't he?"

Lubick then proceeded to fire more questions at the St. Petersburg High coach: "Is he a good kid? Does he have both of his parents? Think he'd like to come play in the SEC? Who do we have to beat to get him? So we'd be the first to offer him?"

Lubick became visibly more excited with each answer. The new lineman was a good kid and a *great* student. Almost a 4.0 GPA. Humble. Tireless worker. Lubick said a formal scholarship letter would go in the mail today.

Five minutes later, a little problem popped up with Scott Lawson:

He didn't seem to exist. According to a 2006 roster that Rebels graduate assistant Matt Saunders pulled off the Internet, there was no Scott Lawson on the St. Petersburg High football team. For a few awkward moments, the Rebels were perplexed—dumbfounded—by what had just happened.

"You sure we're not interested in this other guy, Lawon Scott?" Kent McLeod asked as he looked at the roster.

"Are you sure you're not dyslexic?" Orgeron asked Lubick.

Sheepishly, Lubick buried his face in his hand.

The other senior making a late appearance on the Rebels board was LaMarcus Williams, a 285-pound defensive tackle from Bastrop, Louisiana. Back in June, Williams had committed to Alabama. But after the Crimson Tide fired head coach Mike Shula in November, the Rebels took a closer look at some of the Tide's commitments and re-opened their case file on Williams.

Sifting through another program's commitment list after a coaching change is common. Most new regimes were going to re-evaluate their prospects anyway. The Rebels had already locked in on three players (S Fonterrian Ingram, DB Da'Norris Searcy, C Mike Dykes) who'd committed to North Carolina before the Tar Heels canned head coach John Bunting in midseason. Maybe Bama commit LaMarcus Williams would join them on the Rebels' wish list.

Ole Miss had an in with Williams: Rebels return man Marshay Green was one of Williams's best friends. And unlike North Carolina, which appeared to have stabilized under new coach Butch Davis, the Crimson Tide coaching search was ongoing. One more clue that Williams might be in play: In the Shula purge, Charlie Harbison, the Tide assistant who recruited Williams, lost his job as well.

Much of Williams's eval tape came from film Wilson had shot of the lineman going through spring drills at his high school. The tape showcased the kid's agility and his ability to use his hands as he

258

bounced between bags lined up on the ground. Wilson noted that Williams was a onetime tailback, which would explain the agility.

Nielsen: "I like him a lot."

"This is another mistake by the big guy," Orgeron said, referring to himself. "Frank had this guy early, and I screwed him all up. I didn't wanna go on him."

But he did now: Williams got an Ole Miss offer.

Orgeron and his Ole Miss recruiting team had blown a few over the course of the year. Orgeron lamented "gonging" prospects he now thought he should've been more open to. He said he wished he'd kept some of them "by the fire." Welcome to the bust side of his boom-or-bust personality.

Measuring up to the SEC's heavyweights had been an issue for Orgeron from the moment he even thought about becoming the head coach at Ole Miss. But now he was interested in knowing if what his assistants had seen this year on the field in the SEC—and heard in the war room—had altered their perceptions about their recruiting criteria. Were they being too choosy for their own good?

A few hours earlier in the day, he had asked each coach to write down his prototype attributes of what they are looking for in a prospect. He wanted a realistic picture of a player they believed was a quality SEC starter, not necessarily a high NFL draft pick. Green-lighting no-brainers didn't require shrewd evaluating. Orgeron was more interested in being able to sort out and grade raw, underdeveloped prospects.

For instance, the Rebels' two top big-play threats on the current roster, receiver-returnmen Dexter McCluster and Marshay Green, were eye-catchers on film. Each was a shifty, quick, smurf-size darter, capable of producing a video highlight every time he touched a ball. But could that type of player carry a team to an SEC championship? After all, the 5'9", 158-pound McCluster amassed a staggering 268 all-purpose yards in his college debut, but then got drilled on the opening kickoff against Vanderbilt on October 7 and was lost for the season with a shoulder injury.

Lesson: Little guys can't take a pounding; approach with caution.

"Do we want to bring in more Dexters?" Orgeron asked after the room had gotten fired up watching back-to-back McClusteresque juniors, but then dismissed another player more in the mold of BenJarvus Green-Ellis, the Rebels' rugged 1,000-yard tailback.

"Our guys make that 12-yard gain," argued Wilson, "but they don't turn them into the 40-yard gains by making that second-level defender miss."

But to Orgeron, the downside of the waterbug-type player was not only fragility (see Dexter's shoulder) but also inherent limits on what a 158-pound player can do for a team. Consider Green-Ellis: If he weren't the Rebels' best ballcarrier, he probably could play linebacker or maybe fullback. Dexter McCluster and Marshay Green, as much as the staff loved them, were too small to shift to, say, defensive back.

Orgeron admitted he was torn on the subject. He loved speed as much as any football coach in America. Yet former USC star LenDale White, a sloppy 240-pounder who became the Trojans' career touchdown leader, was Orgeron's all-time favorite big back: "He ran hard, he had quick feet, and he was mean. I loved him."

Despite his feelings for White, Orgeron said he wasn't blown away by Green-Ellis when he first saw his eval tape three years earlier. He didn't think the big kid had the burst he wanted to see in an SEC running back.

Now after having just watched Green-Ellis pound his way to 1,000 yards in the 2006 season, Orgeron felt differently about him. He was the player he'd build the Ole Miss offense around in 2007.

There's a lesson there, and it goes something like this: It's fine to have an ideal in mind when you go out looking for football players—

in fact, you should—but always remember that, almost always, you're going to have to settle for something less. The trick is to make the best choices from a flock of less-than-perfect options.

Orgeron proceeded to share his version of the ideal defensive tackle prospect. First he reeled of the three core stats. Height: 6'2". Weight: 285. Time in the 40-yard dash: 4.8 seconds. Then he read from his notepad: "Great hips and feet. Great at using his hands. Great leverage. Great work ethic. Gives great effort."

Fine, but there was one problem: The only defensive tackle on the current Ole Miss roster who met those criteria was sophomore Peria Jerry, and he was out with an injury for part of the 2006 season.

Make that two problems: the only defensive tackles on the Rebels' recruiting board that came close to Orgeron's ideal DT profile were Ted Laurent and Rolando Melancon. And if you talked to coaches from Melancon's area, they'd question the "great work ethic" and "gives great effort" parts.

If you hold out for the ideal in the real world, you won't be able to field a football team. LaMarcus Williams was close on the size side of the equation but probably four-tenths of a second off on speed. According to a Web posting McLeod found, Lawon Scott ran a 40 at 5.5 the preceding spring, almost a full second over the speed Orgeron coveted. And yet, Orgeron would swear off Red Bull as his New Year's resolution if he could get both of them.

The two senior DT prospects were just the latest of a dozen or so new names that popped up on the Rebels' board in December, in some cases because a position need developed, as a result of injury or academic problems or poor performance.

In the case of wide receiver Rashad Mason, his absence from the board until December was mainly a consequence of his having missed his junior season. No matter how good a kid's sophomore season, missing his junior year leaves a huge gap in his résumé that makes coaches understandably wary.

Just three weeks earlier, Hugh Freeze had been driving to Nashville when he called the Ole Miss football office and asked Matt Saunders to take a look at a highlight tape from Pearl-Cohn High, an inner-city school in Nashville. "Can you see if I need to go there today?" Freeze asked.

Saunders found the tape and was so stunned by a 6'6", 215-pound receiver making acrobatic catches that he yelled across the hall to Dave Corrao, the defensive grad assistant: "Dave, you've gotta see this. Come over here right now."

In most cases, Corrao said, he gets hauled over to Saunders' office to see some blooper play or maybe a 350-pound referee trying to run backward downfield. Not this time.

"This Mason kid looked like a faster version of Marcus Monk of Arkansas," recalled Corrao. "He was obviously the type of player you'd have to redesign your pass defense to account for."

Within 10 minutes, Saunders was back on the phone with Freeze: "Go to that school and take an offer letter with you."

Saunders found almost nothing about Mason on the Internet recruiting sites. "How come nobody else knows about this kid?" Corrao said to Saunders. "That blows my mind."

Mason's reemergence turned out to be the best comeback story of the recruiting year. In September 2005, Mason and four of his buddies, all athletes at Pearl-Cohn, were heading to a Labor Day cookout on I-65 when their Ford Explorer swerved to avoid an 18-wheeler. The SUV flipped twice, skidding almost 200 feet before hitting a cement median, and then flipped again and toppled over the median into the southbound lane. Police reports said the SUV skidded another 50-plus feet before it finally came to a stop.

One of Mason's teammates, Jonathan Patton, the driver of the Ford Explorer, was killed. The other three passengers suffered minor injuries.

Mason, who hadn't been wearing his seat belt, suffered a fractured skull, bruised lungs, and a chipped disk in his neck. Rushed to Vanderbilt University Medical Center, he was listed in critical condition. After three days, Mason's family was told that he would survive, but that he might have a learning disorder. His brother, Darryl Mason, said that his younger sibling lost 30 pounds.

As Mason recovered, doctors told him he shouldn't try to play football anymore. Mason pleaded with them: "You can't take my favorite sport away from me."

By the spring of 2006, Mason was fully recovered and raring to go. He went to summer camps at Tennessee and Louisville, but neither school offered him. But that fall, once he started making eye-opening touchdown catches and his team headed to the Tennessee state playoffs, the coaches at Pearl-Cohn sent four dozen highlight DVDs all over the country.

By the time Matt Saunders saw him, Mason had caught 26 passes for 610 yards and 13 touchdowns. The Rebels were one of the first five schools to offer Mason a scholarship. The other four: Michigan, North Carolina, LSU, and UCLA.

Mason, who'd grown up wanting to play for Tennessee, admitted he was hoping USC would jump into the picture. "That's my dream school now," he said. "I like the environment and the climate." The distance from Nashville would also be a plus: "I don't want to be too close to home. I've been here for 17 years. I'd really like to see something new."

Considering that Ole Miss and UNC were the closest schools to Nashville, that wasn't something the Rebels wanted to hear.

Mason had also expressed a desire to go to a school known for throwing the ball, an understandable preference for a wide receiver with NFL ambitions. But that didn't bother Ole Miss much, despite the fact that in 2006 the Rebels finished last in the SEC in passing offense and 112th out of 119 Division I-A teams. After all, they now had Jevan Snead coming in to throw the ball.

At 2:32 p.m. on Tuesday afternoon, five days before Christmas, the Ole Miss staff was almost done watching junior wide receivers in the war room when Freeze's cell rang.

"What's up, big Jerry Franklin?" Freeze yelled into the phone after reading the caller ID.

Franklin was the speedy linebacker from Arkansas whom Ole Miss had been trying for months to flip from his home-state Razorbacks. The Rebels had Franklin in their summer camp and thought he was dynamite. He looked sharp, played hard, and ran the fastest 40-yard dash in camp. One geographical plus: Franklin's hometown of Marion, Arkansas, is three hours closer to Oxford than to Fayetteville. The Rebels were also convinced they had pursued him harder and shown him more love than had Arkansas. From talking to Franklin, his mom, and his sister, Freeze had learned that the Razorbacks coaches hadn't come to see the recruit often or been especially diligent in talking to his family.

For a few minutes Freeze listened to Franklin talk about how his basketball season was going.

"How 'bout if we play a game of H-O-R-S-E, and if I win, you come here?" Freeze asked with a chuckle.

"Tell him I got two scholarships left," Orgeron bellowed from the background. "Do I need to save one for him?"

"Coach O says he's got one scholarship left," Freeze told Franklin. "Does he need to save it for you?"

Freeze turned to Orgeron: "Jerry says probably."

Orgeron: "Ask him, Is he 'probably' going to make that open-field tackle for us? No, wait—ask him if Houston Nutt or any of his coaches has been to the Motel 6 to see his mom at work?"

Freeze nodded at Orgeron, who could hear Franklin laughing on the other end of the phone at his not-so-subtle dig at the Razorbacks coach for his lack of attention to the top recruit.

"Okay, Jerry, remember your deal. You said whoever recruits you the hardest is who you'll sign with, and I know you're a man of your word," Freeze said. "Look, I've been to your high school, and I know there's Hog stuff everywhere. And I know it's gonna be hard to say no to all those people there. But you remember this: Those people don't have to go over there, you do."

After Freeze said goodbye to Franklin and put his phone back on the table, he said to Orgeron in a neutral, subdued tone, as if he were afraid to jinx matters by displaying too much enthusiasm, "I think we got a shot. I really think we can get back in on him."

Near the end of the day, Freeze's good spirits got another boost. To goose the competitive vibe of the war room, Orgeron called his crew to attention and offered up $20 to the first coach who could get a junior to call him back. To a man, everybody in the room started thumbing their BlackBerrys, flooding the ether with text messages. Not five minutes had passed when Freeze, a grin splitting his face, handed his phone over to Orgeron. A junior linebacker high on the Rebels' 2008 board was waiting on the other end.

Freeze was $20 richer.

A few minutes later, Freeze was on the phone with Cedric Miller, Roderick Davis's high school coach in Memphis. Davis was one of the highest-profile players on the Rebels' 2007 board. Unanimously anointed a four-star blue-chipper by the Internet recruiting mavens, he was an explosive 5'11", 190-pound receiver-return man, a bigger, stronger version of Dexter McCluster. He was considered the best football player in Memphis. The Rebels were battling Oklahoma, Tennessee, and Texas Tech for him.

For months, Freeze had been telling Orgeron that he felt that Davis was leaning toward Ole Miss. Early on, Freeze cultivated his relationship with Ced Miller and had also developed a pretty good bond with Davis' mother, Trishonna Jackson. Oxford's proximity to Davis' Memphis home was also important, because he had a 15-month-old daughter, Jakiyra, who lived with him and his mother, and he wanted to stay close to her. Oxford is a little more than an hour's drive; Tennessee's campus is six hours away.

"We'd love it if he wants to announce it tomorrow," Freeze told Miller. "Don't you think he's wants to pull the trigger, Ced? You know big Rod wants to end this."

"Come on, Freeze," Orgeron said softly, leaning over his assistant's shoulder. "Reel him in, Freeze. Come on, baby!"

Freeze nodded his head a few times, and gave Orgeron a thumbs-up before saying good-bye and hanging up the phone.

"We might get some good news from big Roderick Davis tomorrow," Freeze announced to the room. "Ced thinks he's ready, but we'll have to see tomorrow."

The next day, December 20, kicked off with important news: Matt Lubick told Orgeron that he had accepted a job as recruiting coordinator and safeties coach with Dennis Erickson at Arizona State. This didn't come out of the blue. Lubick and Orgeron had talked several times over the previous six weeks about how the 36-year-old receivers coach, a guy who'd spent most of his life in the West, didn't seem to be meshing with his players or feeling comfortable in the deepest part of the Deep South.

Orgeron and the rest of the staff would miss Lubick, but they knew that Tempe was a better fit for him than Oxford.

That wasn't the only headline of the day. The Rebels had received word that Jessie Bowman, the junior college nose tackle who was the first recruit Orgeron visited after the Egg Bowl, was going to follow through on his initial commitment to the Mississippi State Bulldogs. The Rebels had figured that Bowman was probably heading to MSU the week after he no-showed on an official visit to Oxford, but now they'd heard that he was going to make it official and sign scholarship papers on December 20, the first day junior college players could sign binding scholarship offers.

But there was more. At 6:30 a.m. that morning, Orgeron got a call from Kent McLeod telling him to check out *The Clarion-Ledger*. Orgeron did so and learned that Bowman was spending the week in the Lincoln County Jail after pleading guilty to misdemeanor charges of trespassing and simple assault.

According to *The Clarion-Ledger* story, Bowman had told Mississippi State coaches the preceding Thursday that he was going to sign with them. One day later, Bowman was sentenced to 180 days in jail, with all but five suspended, for his part in a July 3 altercation. His jail sentence had started that Monday, December 18.

"He may just sign it in the jail right now, I don't know," Bowman's attorney told the paper. "He doesn't have to be anywhere specific to sign it."

In the story, Mississippi State coach Sylvester Croom declined to discuss Bowman's incident in detail. "All I can say is I'm aware of the situation," Croom said. "It has been handled by the coach and administration and the staff down there."

Orgeron read the story quietly in the war room and then put down the paper. He wasn't interested in gloating about the slime shower his rival at MSU was about to take for possibly having a star recruit sign his letter of intent in the Lincoln County lockup. Instead, he was pondering how it would've felt had if *he* had been the lucky winner of the Jessie Bowman lottery.

A few moments later, linebackers coach David Saunders, the assistant who had been the point person on Bowman's recruitment, walked into the war room. Saunders, 47, had close ties in the Ole Miss football community. He had worked there previously (1998-2002) as the Rebels director of recruiting for two seasons and then as the coordinator of high school and community college relations under head coach David Cutcliffe. He had also introduced Orgeron to the woman who would become his wife.

Now Orgeron asked him if he had known about the Bowman mess. Saunders admitted that he had, at least to some degree.

The story Saunders said he'd heard was that Bowman had been dating a woman in her 30s and that he'd caught her sleeping with another man. Bowman then broke down the bedroom door and beat the guy up. Saunders, sounding apologetic, said, "They had hoped it wouldn't get out."

So, obviously, had Saunders.

Orgeron stood up, scratched his head, put the newspaper in the rubber trash can, and walked out of the war room without saying a word.

The staff had hoped to be out of the office by noon to begin their Christmas vacations. But Orgeron wanted to use the day to review all the prospects they were still actively recruiting for the class of 2007. He'd had Matt Saunders and Kent McLeod put five dozen eval tapes in plastics bins by his VCR in the war room. After each position group was evaluated, Orgeron wanted the staff to rank the prospects top to bottom. The meeting wasn't supposed to start until 8 a.m., but since Kehoe and Wilson were already at the table, Orgeron began by putting in the tape of Rishaw Johnson, the top plate on the Ole Miss offensive line board.

Johnson's stock had continued to rise ever since Wilson got him to come to their summer camp. Florida State had been trying to pull Johnson away all year, but the Noles appeared to be slipping since rumors got out that FSU was about to dump the offensive line coach who had recruited Johnson. Orgeron was more concerned about LSU turning up the heat on the Louisiana native; the Rebels still hadn't beaten the Tigers for a local player they really wanted.

Wilson had been diligent in building a bond with Johnson and his parents, striving to gain the trust of a family that had been devastated by the tragic car accident of the lineman's childhood, not to mention by Hurricane Katrina. Wilson even brought Johnson's girlfriend, Jasmine Brown, into the process. "I think Coach Frank really called me to see if I was a good influence on Rishaw," said Brown, who planned to study biomedical engineering at Louisiana Tech. "He asked what kind of grades I get and how often we spent time together and things like that. I like Coach Frank a lot. I could tell he cared a lot about Rishaw and he'd be good for him."

The Internet sites listed Johnson as only a "three-star" recruit. Wilson thought that was a reflection of Johnson's having had to switch schools three times in the wake of Katrina. "If he stayed at St. Augustine, where he was as a sophomore," Wilson said, "he'd have been a national recruit."

Orgeron thought that if recruiting analysts had seen what he had of Johnson in person and on tape, they'd make him a five-star guy. Orgeron replayed one shot of Johnson hustling downfield, tracking down an undersized linebacker, and flattening him three times.

"Fuuuuuck!" Orgeron roared. "This guy is such a stud! He is gonna be an All-America. Ain't no doubt in my mind. I'd put Rishaw right up there with Chris Strong and Jerrell Powe. And Jevan Snead. And obviously Joe McKnight."

Orgeron then cued up the Rebels' other OL commit from Louisiana, Alex Washington. He was listed on the Rebels' eval tape at 6'4", 363, 5.39. Orgeron was thinking he had a steal, but then he saw a play that made him worry about the guy's flexibility. Now, he wasn't quite as sold.

Orgeron: "We gotta get him in the squat rack."

Kehoe: "He's got some toughness to him."

Orgeron: "I wanna see him in the squat rack with his heels on the ground."

Washington's tape also contained a play similar to the one Johnson made in which the 300-pounder ran 15 yards downfield to maul a defensive back.

Orgeron: "I do like how he comes off the ball."

Kehoe: "That is a huge thing for me right there seeing a guy that big being able to chase and get on little guys."

Orgeron: "We're scrappin' for second-team linemen right now, and he's a great kid. We'd love having him around. Are we the only people recruiting him?"

Wilson: "Yes."

Orgeron: "Great job getting him to camp. Mass kicks ass, right Bro?"

Freeze entered the room, and the trio moved through the other two 360-pound O-linemen on the board: in-stater Bradley Sowell and junior college transfer Mark Jean-Louis. Almost on cue, McLeod told Orgeron that Jean-Louis' letter of intent had arrived.

"Ole Miss got a nice Christmas gift today," Orgeron said.

Because of Jean-Louis's experience, the staff rated him second after Johnson among OL recruits. Later, outside the war room, Orgeron said that if the Rebels could keep Johnson on the hook— and, of course, that was a big if—he would be very pleased by the Rebels' O-line haul in the class of 2007.

The bulk of the morning's evaluation time was split between two positions, defensive line and linebacker. Not coincidentally, those were the two groups that were the biggest need areas and the ones with the most question marks.

From time to time over the course of the year, Orgeron had joked that he might sign 15 defensive tackles. But right now he'd be thrilled to have four of the names on his board suited up and ready to take wind sprints come August, when fall camp began.

The Rebels had 10 defensive tackles on their board, four with blue (as in "committed") nameplates—Ted Laurent, Jerrell Powe,

Justin Sanders, and JC transfer Larry Dennis. Only Sanders was a certainty to be academically eligible.

After watching all of the tapes, Orgeron agreed to put Laurent as their top DT. Orgeron had been expecting Powe to rank No. 1, but he was disappointed at how often the big kid was on the ground in film from his senior year at Hargrave Military Academy.

The collection of defensive ends was even more troubling. The top two talents, JC transfer Dion Gales and Rufus Williams, were both flagged by the Ole Miss staff as potential attitude risks. Orgeron was really high on Texan Von Miller—"a power-packed frickin' freak"—but it was a long shot that he'd opt out of his commitment to Texas A&M. Kenny Rowe, an undersized end from Long Beach, played hard, but the only time the Rebels had been able to get him to visit was in early December after school was out and the campus was desolate. Probably not the best setting to woo a West Coast guy whose e-mail moniker is "Imsohood."

All this meant that the Rebels might not sign a defensive end, unless you counted Chris Strong. A middle linebacker who was regarded as Mississippi's top high school football player, Strong would probably end up at DE because he appeared to have already outgrown linebacker. But Strong was no lock to qualify.

Still, Strong got the nod as the Rebels' top linebacker prospect ahead of Franklin. Of the nine players on the board, four of the bottom five prospects were the ones the Rebels felt they had the best chance to sign.

"Auburn's fallen off Scottie Williams," Freeze said about an Atlanta-area linebacker who'd reportedly been told by the Tigers that he might not be able to qualify. The Rebels took that as a sign that Auburn had lost interest, since they'd seen his transcript and that of another player also committed to the Tigers, and McLeod determined that the linebacker was in better academic shape.

"It's us and South Carolina," Freeze said, "and I'm gonna beat them."

Minutes after Freeze's prediction, his cell started spinning on the table. It was Roderick Davis.

"What's up, big Rod," Freeze said. "You got some good news for me man?"

Freeze rocked back in his chair and pumped his fist in the air.

"*Wooooo!*" Orgeron yelled in the background. "It's gonna be Snead to Davis! Just like Manning to Harrison. Way to go, Freeze! How about that? He goes up against Tennessee, Auburn, and Oklahoma, and he fuckin' beats all three!"

11:41 a.m. All the coaches in the war room had hoped the meeting would've wrapped by now. Many had cars packed and families waiting. It had been a long season. But the news from Davis? That was worth hanging around a little longer to celebrate ... at least to one person in the room.

Orgeron jumped out of his chair after Freeze snapped his cell shut and started circling the table. Shoulders rolled forward, neck thrust out, head bobbing up and down. The preferred posture, evidently, for yelling:

Wooooo!

Freeze hopped up and took his own victory lap around the table in the other direction. He and his boss came together back by his chair, where they collided in a mighty chest bump that sent tremors all the way to Memphis.

The Rebels still had plenty of holes in their class of 2007 recruiting board. The job wasn't done yet, not by a long shot.

But thanks to Jevan Snead and Roderick Davis, it was going to be a very Merry Christmas in Oxford.

Chapter 16

COUNTDOWN

T HE COUNTDOWN TO National Signing Day 2007 began in earnest on New Year's Eve 2006, when Joe McKnight arrived in San Antonio to play in the U.S. Army All-American Bowl.

An annual showcase for the nation's top high school prospects, the game itself is a sideshow to a weeklong feeding frenzy by an insatiable media pack. Led (of course) by Internet recruiting site reps, the pack stalks its prey—80 dazed 18-year-olds—before and after practices, in hotel lobbies and restaurants, and on the streets of Old San Antone.

Think of the Army All-American Bowl as a flea market where parents whose sons have already committed to a school spend their waking hours lobbying other parents whose sons have committed somewhere else to flip-flop. Meanwhile, committed recruits try to pressure uncommitted prospects, their new best friends, to come join them at old State U.

(No college coaches allowed, per the NCAA recruiting calendar: New Year's Eve falls into the dead period.)

"I know there's a whole lot of recruiting goin' on down there," said Orgeron, referring to the college coaches who instruct their recruits to befriend uncommitted top players. "That's become a big thing now. Everyone is gonna be after Joe."

Orgeron was correct. By the second day of team practices, McKnight, one of the few uncommitted players on-site, had distinguished himself as the top talent in the game. A trio of Texas Longhorns recruits were so enamored with McKnight's skills that they dialed up UT coach Mack Brown as they rode the bus back to the hotel and told him he had to get the New Orleans star.

"Coach Mack offered him right over the phone," said John Chiles, a future Longhorns receiver, citing the Texas coach's no-brainer move after the UT recruits handed their cell to McKnight.

McKnight did his part by offering up the juiciest sound bite of the week when he gave a reporter from BamaOnline.com his thoughts regarding Alabama's recent hiring of Nick Saban, which had made LSU, USC, and Ole Miss fans wince. "He's Coach Saban," McKnight said of the coach who led the LSU Tigers to the 2003 national championship. "If he was still at LSU, I'd be an LSU commit right now."

The game itself was a yawner—West 24, East 7—although McKnight did score the game's first touchdown for the victors. Afterward, amid an on-field postgame celebration with a country music concert kicking off at the 50-yard line, McKnight told reporters he planned to visit USC, Ole Miss, and LSU, with Texas, Alabama, Arkansas, and FSU in the mix for his final two trips.

USC fans who had visited McKnight's MySpace page to find it plastered with photos of Reggie Bush believed he couldn't possibly pass up that legacy. They also loved that a few of the Trojans' top recruits, players who had been teammates of McKnight's at the Army game, had posted on his site. Alabama and LSU fans bombarded McKnight with pitches for their schools—and with anti-USC pitches, warning the recruit about the Trojans' possible sanctions, stemming from an investigation into Bush's career at USC.

Frank Wilson said he didn't put any credence in all the Internet noise: "Joe says we're good with him, and he's always been truthful with me."

As the Rebels waited with their fingers crossed for McKnight's January 12 visit to Oxford, the staff's newest full-time coach, Dave Corrao, believed he might have found the answer to the team's middle linebacker problem.

The 32-year-old Corrao's elevation from graduate assistant to linebackers coach had been the first of several postseason staff moves by Orgeron, who had also hired his old mentor from Northwestern State, John Thompson, as his defensive coordinator and brought in 25-year-old Chris Kiffin, the son of NFL defensive guru Monte Kiffin and younger brother of new Oakland Raiders head coach Lane Kiffin, as his defensive graduate assistant. He had also moved cornerbacks coach Tony Hughes to tight ends, with Freeze moving from TEs to wide receivers.

As a graduate assistant, Corrao had spent most of his 16-hour days breaking down tape of rival offenses and the Rebels' own defense. He'd also coached the Ole Miss scout team offense that gave the first-team defense the various plays it needed to see during the practices that led up to each weekend's game.

Orgeron: "Dave's the yin to my yang."

Corrao's first big move for the Rebels was a consequence of his having scrutinized the Internet recruiting site lists as if they were tea leaves foretelling the future. He knew most of the top JC linebackers were already committed, but he went down a list from Rivals.com anyway, and sure enough, he found one guy who was open: Tony Fein from Scottsdale Community College.

Fein, 24, had quite a story, the Scottsdale coach told Corrao. He grew up in Port Orchard, Washington, then spent three and a half years in the Army, including a year in Iraq that he refused to talk about. He left home an immature, 200-pound high school quarter-back and returned a hard-nosed, 245-pound linebacker.

In his first season with the Scottsdale CC Fighting Artichokes, Fein struggled to adjust to defense. He played outside linebacker and was, by his own estimation, "only okay." But in 2006, after settling in at middle linebacker, Fein set a school record for tackles with 136.

Corrao couldn't get him on the phone fast enough.

"Coach, I'm so glad you called," Fein told Corrao. "I was all set to commit to Michigan State tomorrow."

Fortunately for the Rebels, Michigan State had just gone through a chaotic 2006, in which head coach John L. Smith was fired at midseason. New Spartans coach Mark Dantonio pursued Fein hard after he was hired, but the former cavalry scout was intrigued by the possibility of playing in the SEC and being the man to replace Butkus Award winner Patrick Willis. He told Corrao he wanted to learn more about Ole Miss before he made his decision.

Two days later, Ole Miss had the linebacker's transcripts and game tape, as well as contact info for everyone connected to him. Fein's highlight tape from Scottsdale ran so long and contained so many good plays that Corrao didn't even make it to the end before Orgeron pulled the trigger and offered the ex-GI a scholarship.

"We loved the way he attacked the ball," Corrao said. "A MIKE, and he was making plays on the sideline. He's got that violent streak. He was making the plays we want out of the position."

And then: "If this works out, it'll be a hell of a nice late Christmas present for all of us."

The Joe McKnight college tour officially began on January 12, 2007, when McKnight, along with Curtis High teammate Colby Arceneaux and Colby's father, arrived on the Ole Miss campus along with 13 other prospects who had scheduled on-campus visits that weekend.

The Rebels assigned tailback BenJarvus Green-Ellis as McKnight's host. As the weekend progressed, McKnight and Arceneaux spent time with a collection of Rebels players as they toured campus, hit parties, and hung out. Orgeron stressed to McKnight that he would be showcased in the Rebels system, re-emphasizing everything that he and Wilson had told McKnight a month earlier.

Orgeron knew USC was the school he had to beat, but he shot straight and didn't try to discourage McKnight from considering the Trojans: "I will never say a bad word about USC. I respect the program, and I respect Pete Carroll. You will play there right away. There is no doubt in my mind."

Orgeron's hope was that his no-BS pitch and a built-in support system in not-too-far-away Oxford might be enough to tip McKnight's decision. From what McKnight had told the Arceneaux on the ride back, it sounded like it might have been.

"It was a lot better than I expected," McKnight told his friend. "Ole Miss definitely increased my interest in their program."

"They did a terrific job," said Bryan Arceneaux, Colby's father. "Joe had a great time. He knows it's a good fit for him."

Colby Arceneaux was sold on Ole Miss too. "I haven't had that much fun in a long time," the hard-hitting, 5'8" safety told RebelSports.net. "The whole scene was exciting because everything we did had so much energy. It was electric, man."

Naturally, McKnight's Ole Miss visit was the talk of college football in that part of the world, and it had a negative effect on Robert Elliott, the tailback who had been committed to the Rebels for 11 months. Elliott's uncle Ronald told Hugh Freeze he wasn't thrilled that the Rebels were chasing McKnight at his nephew's expense.

For all of the strides Orgeron believed his program had made in Louisiana, California, and Tennessee—not to mention in the Rebels' own backyard—he was still frustrated by his staff's inability to woo Florida talent.

Orgeron had expected that the arrival of old pals Dan Werner and Art Kehoe from Miami would give the Rebels a stronger connection in South Florida and that it would help Matt Lubick bring in more prospects. But it had become evident to Orgeron that the attention to detail he demanded from his assistants seemed to have been lost in translation to Kehoe.

As much as Orgeron loved what Kehoe had done—developing a young offensive line and transforming an afterthought guy like Andrew Wicker into a quality SEC lineman and the team's best blocker, he knew that his former Miami colleague hadn't really absorbed his recruiting philosophy.

That became evident when, en route to seeing Lawon Scott, the defensive tackle from St. Petersburg whom the Rebels expected to sign, Orgeron dropped by three other South Florida football hotbeds (Pahokee, Belle Glade, Lakeland) to scout juniors. While at Glades Central Community High, Orgeron was approached by Ernest McCoy, a 6'5", 330-pound senior offensive lineman already committed to LSU.

"Hey, Coach O," McCoy asked, "how come y'all stopped recruiting me?"

McCoy said he was interested in getting a better look at Ole Miss, so the Rebels bought a plane ticket for $513 and booked the trip. But then, a flag on the play: The next day, McCoy's mother told Kehoe she wouldn't permit her son to take the visit because she was afraid LSU might get mad.

The plane ticket was nonrefundable.

The McKnight tour pulled into Los Angeles on January 19.

To no one's surprise, Pete Carroll played the Reggie Bush card at every opportunity. For instance, McKnight's player-host at USC was reserve linebacker Thomas Williams, Bush's old roommate and best friend on the Trojans. USC also made sure that several other top committed prospects who knew McKnight from the Army All-America game were in the same group of weekend visitors and would show the tailback some love. The only down note of the trip came when McKnight got stuck in the airport for four hours and didn't get home until the middle of the night.

The Monday after his (late) Sunday return, McKnight declined to give many details about the trip to reporters. He said he was coping just fine with all the pressure and attention, but the process was clearly wearing him down. He was getting calls on his cell at all hours from all sorts of people he didn't know. His MySpace page, which he'd started as a lark, had turned into an Alabama and LSU message board studded with postings by college football's most fanatic fans.

McKnight to his big sister, Johanna: "All those people have no right to tell me where I should go."

Johanna: "He's getting a little aggravated and upset."

As McKnight tried to cope with the madness, Robert Elliott and his family were looking back on a wonderful visit to Florida State on January 19 to 21.

"I would say it was a 9.7 out of 10," Elliott told the FSU fan site Warchant.com. "It was great, very exciting. For the first time visiting a campus, I really enjoyed myself a whole lot ... As far as atmosphere, players, coaches, and facilities, Florida State beats them all by just a little bit. All the schools are neck and neck. I have a leader with Ole Miss, but the rest of the schools are right alongside one another right now."

Ominous news for Ole Miss?

Maybe not.

January 22—another day, another interview for Robert Elliott. Only this time it was with an Ole Miss fan site, and he softened his earlier comments about the FSU trip. "Ole Miss is still the leader of the pack by a lot," Elliott told Rebelsports.net. "My trip to FSU was okay. It was a pretty long drive, but the visit went well."

Elliott also told Rebelsports that Joe McKnight was "not a factor in my decision-making process at all." Uh-huh. The Rebel coaches had heard otherwise from members of Elliott's family.

The negative feedback spooked Orgeron, who'd been losing faith in Elliott since he'd caused the Rebels to have second thoughts following his December on-campus visit.

"It's worried me," Orgeron said. "It sends up a lot of red flags, poses a lot of questions."

Among them: "Can Robert Elliott take the demands of this program? Is this the type of person I want running the football for me? Does he have enough confidence? Can he handle the SEC? I mean, come on. If a kid is worried about the depth chart or whoever you're recruiting—those are red flags."

And he continued: "I think Robert is a very nice young man, but we've heard a lot of conflicting stories the whole time."

Inside the war room, the out-of-state targets had been shifted to the in-state boards to make room for the class of 2008 nameplates. Only two senior plates remained: Joe McKnight's and the one belonging to Rob Gronkowski, a blue-chip tight end from Pittsburgh.

Orgeron opted to leave McKnight's up because he didn't want to jinx anything by disturbing the apparent good karma with which the tailback's recruitment seemed to be infused.

Gronkowki's plate remained atop the board as Orgeron's not-so-subtle way of teaching Kehoe a recruiting lesson. In December, one of Gronkowski's high school teammates, Mike Dykes, visited Ole Miss and told Kehoe that he'd loved it so much, he was going to come back with his more highly touted buddy. But when Kehoe talked to Gronkowski on the phone, the big tight end showed no real interest in a visit. Even so, Kehoe had flown up to Pittsburgh to make a plea. Gronkowski cold-shouldered him, saying he was more intrigued by Clemson, Ohio State, and Arizona (the school he eventually signed with.)

The Pittsburgh trip really annoyed Orgeron. "All of those schools up north are trying to come down south to find players, so why would we do the opposite?" he told the staff. "It makes no sense." Orgeron believed that was time—and travel money—that would have served his program better in Florida, where he was convinced they'd missed out.

In fact, the Gronkowski trip served as a launch point for Orgeron's newest motto: "Planes don't fly north!!"

On January 24, *The Clarion-Ledger* reported that Chris Strong had transferred to Genesis One Christian School, a boarding school 180 miles from his Batesville, Mississippi, home, in hopes of becoming eligible to play college football.

Strong, the state's top recruit, had always appeared to be a long shot to qualify. The story quoted Strong's former high school coach, who said he felt that the private school would provide a better setting for the linebacker to prepare for the ACT. The cost? $10,000, which Strong said his family would pay.

The *Clarion-Ledger* story added that Genesis One, a school with 225 students in grades K through 12, was one of dozens of non-traditional schools nationally whose academic practices had been questioned in 2006 by the NCAA. The school was cleared in July for use in the NCAA initial eligibility process, but only for prospects entering college in the fall of 2006. Genesis One, the story said, would remain subject to ongoing review by the NCAA.

The story about Strong surprised Kent McLeod, who said there was a definite stigma attached to any transfer move in the final high school semester by an athlete.

"Any time an athlete transfers now," McLeod said, "it triggers him getting looked at more closely."

Tony Fein, the last Ole Miss class of 2007 recruit scheduled for an on-campus visit, arrived in Oxford on January 26.

"Y'all know how much we need this guy to come here," Orgeron told the staff the day before. "Let's make sure we get a good feel for what kind of guy we're dealing with."

It didn't take long for Fein, who was hosted by defensive tackle Brandon Jenkins, one of the oldest players on the team, to get the royal treatment from many of the Ole Miss students who noticed him at the Library, a local bar.

"People kept coming up to me, saying, 'Ole Miss needs you,' and talking about how glad they were that I was there visiting," Fein said afterward. "I was really impressed with how involved the students were, how much they cared, and how much they knew about me. I guess that's why the SEC is so different."

As Orgeron and some of the Rebels staff ate lunch with Fein, Frank Wilson was at a Chili's in Oxford with Werner. Wilson's mind, understandably, was 350 miles away with Joe McKnight, who was in Baton Rouge on his official visit to LSU. Rishaw Johnson was in Baton Rouge too. Wilson hoped Johnson would connect with McKnight and firm him up with Ole Miss.

Before Wilson's lunch was served, he received what he thought was a great sign—a text message from McKnight, ripping on his counterpart, LSU assistant Larry Porter: "YOUR BOY PORTER IS SO FAKE!"

Wilson smirked at the message. McKnight had bashed LSU and its staff to him before, but the fact that this had come during an actual visit to the Tigers campus carried heavy weight with Wilson. Surely, he thought, McKnight must feel pretty connected to us to have sent such a message. He then spent a few minutes pondering an appropriate response. Nothing too malicious, and nothing too forgiving, which might give McKnight a reason to look at Porter or LSU in another light. Werner chimed in with a few suggestions before Wilson thumbed back his reply: "OK. JUST BE RESPECTFUL AND KNOW THAT I GOT YOU."

Wilson couldn't stop smiling for the rest of the afternoon, but toward the end of the day, his demeanor changed. He got a call from Johnson that gave him considerable pause. The big lineman said he was having a great time at LSU; he'd seen teammates he'd been separated from since Katrina. This wasn't something Wilson wanted to hear. Suddenly, Wilson started to worry that both McKnight *and* Johnson would jump out of the Rebels' boat.

He learned that Johnson's old teammate and fellow LSU recruit Chad Jones was giving him the hard sell: "Everything you need is right here. Why would you want to go anyplace else? You could be real close to your family and your friends. We'll have a great time."

Later that night, after Wilson spent an hour on the phone with Johnson's mother, she called her son. "Coach Frank is pretty worried," Johnson's mother said she told Rishaw.

Johnson then got a little heart-to-heart from his girlfriend, Jasmine, whom Wilson had also been working on. "Don't do anything drastic up there," she said. "Wait 'til you get back home so you can sit down and talk it out."

Before flying back to Arizona, Tony Fein had a sit-down with Orgeron. He told the coach that the visit had blown him away.

"You're a man, and I'm not going to bullshit you," Orgeron told Fein. "We need you to come in and play middle linebacker right away for us."

Fein said he wanted the challenge of coming in and being the one to replace Patrick Willis.

Orgeron told Fein he would like to fly out and visit him in Arizona the following Saturday, the last possible day to see a prospect, but only if the linebacker was planning to come back to Oxford.

"Coach, I think you should come to Arizona," Fein told Orgeron. "I think it'll be worthwhile for you."

Later on Sunday night, Robert Elliott, back from his visit to Mississippi State, told the school's fan site Bulldogblitz.com that he was "still solid with Ole Miss," but he added that there was a chance he might end up someplace else.

"The timing has to be right and the opportunity, and I got to have my jersey number," he told the MSU site. "If that can't happen, I'm probably not coming. I want a single-digit number. I got to get me a single-digit number."

Told of Elliott's latest comments, Orgeron just rolled his eyes.

Eight days before Signing Day. On one of the white boards in the war room, the Rebels' committed list was filled with 25 names. Included were the four newcomers who had already arrived in Oxford: Texas transfer Jevan Snead and junior college transfers Mark Jean-Louis, Ashlee Palmer, and LaDerrick Vaughn, a linebacker from Memphis who'd signed with the Rebels the previous year.

To the right of the list were seven other names: Johnathon Frink, Tommy Walker, Joe McKnight, Tony Fein, Maurice Harris, Jerry Franklin, and Rashad Mason. By NCAA rules, the Rebels could bring in only 25 new scholarship players each fall. Like most schools, Ole Miss planned to "oversign" a few players, knowing that some prospects wouldn't qualify and that they'd have to be rerouted to a junior college or prep school.

In a morning meeting with McLeod and Ole Miss AD Pete Boone, Orgeron was pleased to report that he had 17 prospects who already were full qualifiers, which was probably a half-dozen more than he'd had at this stage the previous year. The Rebels, however, did have a handful of recruits who were going to have Orgeron holding his breath until they became eligible.

Unfortunately, four of them were among the core group of guys he needed most: junior college wide receiver A.J. Jackson and defensive linemen Ted Laurent, Chris Strong, and Jerrell Powe.

Boone was opposed to oversigning.

McLeod understood the AD's thinking: "It looks bad if you end up having to tell a kid who committed to you and whom you signed, 'Um, we need you to grayshirt a semester.'"

Later, as Orgeron and McLeod sat in the war room and stared at the boards, the Rebels head coach said he was sure it was a moot point: "I've been doing this for 15 years, and it's never happened once. We played with 64 scholarships last year. The NCAA allows 85 max. It's okay for us to push the envelope a little."

On Tuesday, Orgeron and Freeze were back in the air, en route to Nashville.

Orgeron opted to use his one contact visit with Rashad Mason to watch the 6'6" wide receiver play basketball. Back when he was at USC, Orgeron saw another big high school wide receiver play high school basketball, and that performance by Tampa's Mike Williams convinced the Trojans that they were watching a future TD maker.

"Mike was so aggressive and quick," Orgeron said. "He was just going up over people to get rebounds and had these instincts where he was making no-look passes. It was really something."

Mason's hoop skills didn't impress Orgeron as much. Still: "He's a legit 6'6", and we'd love to have him." But the visit left Orgeron believing that the Rebels were second to North Carolina in the running for Mason: "I hope I'm wrong, but I just don't have a great feeling about him."

Orgeron and Freeze finished off their swing through Tennessee in Memphis, where Coach O's once-ridiculed "Build a fence around Memphis" mandate no longer seemed like a joke. In addition to visits at area high schools, this trip included two in-home stops. The first to wide receiver Roderick Davis, the top player in the city. But it was the second stop that proved to be more memorable.

For six months, the Rebels had a Memphis-area offensive lineman named Tommy Walker on their board. He was a slightly undersized lineman who the Ole Miss assistants uniformly agreed was a solid player. The only school they had to beat to get him was Memphis. But with the Rebels' list filling up, Orgeron had been searching for more red flags. During the in-home visit to Walker, he found one.

Orgeron was impressed by the rapport Freeze had built with the recruit and his mother. But he was also irked by the tone Tommy took when he asked how many commitments Ole Miss had received. Instantly, Orgeron suspected that Memphis coaches had told Walker the Rebels already had 32 committed recruits. Perhaps they'd gone so far as to hand him a printout of the Ole Miss commitment list that the Internet recruiting sites had posted.

Freeze, as a matter of course, had already explained to Walker (and any other Rebels targets who asked) that those lists were inaccurate, and that they reflected the status of prospects whom Ole Miss had dropped from consideration months earlier because of bad grades.

"I don't know," Walker countered, looking at the coaches. "How can I trust y'all?"

Before Freeze could even begin to answer, Orgeron stood up, shook Walker's mother's hand, and thanked her for opening her home to them. Orgeron then turned to her son, wished him good luck, and headed for the door, Freeze following right behind him.

If Orgeron had any residual sour feelings from the Walker visit, they were washed away the next morning when Tony Fein called Corrao to tell him he had committed to Ole Miss.

"I got my first fur!" exclaimed Corrao with a fist pump as he delivered the good news to his boss.

Orgeron high-fived Corrao as he assembled his things from the war room. Orgeron was driving up to meet Dan Werner and John Thompson at the Memphis airport, where a plane was waiting to take them to Gulfport. From there they'd drive down to Biloxi for the annual Mississippi state high school coaches convention.

At 10:55 a.m., just 10 minutes after he left the Rebel football complex in his Hummer, Coach O pulled up at a convenience store off Route 6 and picked up a four-pack of Red Bull, a small bag of pork rinds, and some mixed nuts. The drive to Memphis lasted an hour, about five minutes longer than it had taken for Orgeron to guzzle down all four cans of Red Bull and polish off the pork rinds. His mind, meanwhile, had shifted from the learning curve of the new middle linebacker to the battle Frank Wilson was waging over in Louisiana.

"Can you imagine the sea of alligators Frank's swimmin' in right now?" Orgeron said into his car phone as he chatted with McLeod, the intensity pulsating in his voice.

At the Memphis airport, Orgeron met up with Werner and Thompson for their flight on an eight-seat private plane, courtesy of FedEx founder Fred Smith, a friend of Hugh Freeze's.

As the co-pilot completed his pretakeoff spiel, Orgeron clicked off his cell. He'd just spoken with Wilson, who was in New Orleans preparing for the last scheduled in-home visit with McKnight. Wilson sounded confident, Orgeron told his assistants. But Orgeron was not. He knew this was a huge day. Both Pete Carroll and LSU head coach Les Miles were doing in-home visits with McKnight.

"I'm a little worried," Orgeron muttered as the flight lifted off. "Pete's good in the home. Really good."

The flight to Gulfport was a bumpy 70 minutes, and the two rental cars McLeod had arranged for weren't ready when the coaches deplaned. Orgeron used the waiting time in the cramped two-room terminal to hop on the Ole Miss Rivals and Scout sites at a computer station and surf for recruiting updates. Nothing new on McKnight. Ten minutes later, the coaches were on the road to the Beau Rivage, the posh, Vegas-style casino hosting the convention. Tony Hughes, who'd driven over from recruiting in southern Mississippi, had already checked in.

For the Rebels coaches, the convention was a place to slap backs and get better acquainted with the state's high school and junior college coaches, who'd come down to the Mississippi coast to hear about the latest variations on the spread offense, check out the newest weight room equipment, and be courted by their college brethren. Most, of course, were there primarily to get drunk with their buddies and to try to win a fortune at blackjack.

After working the convention's lobby and showroom for three hours, Orgeron jumped back in his rental car, picked up another four-pack of Red Bull, and drove west to New Orleans to meet Kehoe and Wilson for an in-home visit with Rishaw Johnson.

The hour-long visit with Johnson and his parents went well. ("We think the Ole Miss coaches are really like family now," said Gaynell Jenkins, Rishaw's mother.) Their mission accomplished, Orgeron and Kehoe headed back east, arriving at the Beau Rivage by 10 p.m. While the rest of his staff mingled with other coaches in the casino, Orgeron, fresh off a mind-scrambling eight-Red Bull day, headed back to his room.

His last bit of business before calling it a day was to ask the front desk for a 5:30 a.m. wake-up call.

Before checking out of the Beau Rivage at 10 a.m. on February 2, Orgeron pored through the latest recruiting news, which had been faxed to him from Oxford. In the stack of pages was a story on McKnight's growing interest in Ole Miss. *Yes!* Orgeron got a special kick out of a passage that mentioned that the Rebels "actually got in on recruiting McKnight late."

The morning's first flight was to Huntsville, Alabama. On board, Orgeron had a treat for his assistants: a sack of po'boy sandwiches he'd had the flight crew pick up for the trip. From the Huntsville airport, Orgeron and Thompson drove to New Market, Alabama, 30 minutes away, where they met up with Chris Rippon at the home of Justin Sanders, the big lineman who had committed to Ole Miss right before Christmas.

The Sanders' home visit turned up something that none of the coaches, each with two decades of recruiting stories, had ever encountered before: a cockfight.

While making polite conversation, Justin's father, Tim Sanders, mentioned that he raised gamecocks for fighting. Cockfighting isn't legal in most states, Alabama included, but Sanders said the fines were "pretty small" and it wasn't hard to find a "derby." Usually, it cost about $200 to enter, but some derbies paid over $50,000 to the winner's owner. (The most the elder Sanders said he ever won in a cockfight was $15,000.)

"It ain't like fighting dogs," he said. "They don't have personalities. A lot of people don't know this, but Abraham Lincoln kept roosters out at the White House."

The elder Sanders mentioned that Justin had been handling the roosters since he was 13, then he told the coaches that the cages were out back if they wanted to have a look.

Thompson couldn't help himself: "Let's do it!"

They all headed out behind the trailer and trudged through the muddy yard to the cages. Tim Sanders lifted up the gate to one of the cages, and a five-pound rooster strutted out. Then he lifted up another gate, and another one stalked forward.

The two roosters circled each other for a few seconds, and then, in a stunning, explosive burst, they soared three feet off the ground and collided breast to breast, beak grabbing beak, hackles flaring.

"*Wooooo!*" Orgeron howled. "*Gahhh-daayam!*"

The roosters bounced off each other for 20 seconds while the Rebels coaches watched in amazement. Then Tim Sanders gave his boy a nod, and the 275-pound teen calmly moved into the scrum of flailing birds, grabbed them by their feet, and put them back in their cages.

"I say we gotta get our defense to compete like them birds," Orgeron said, punctuating the thought with another "*Wooooo!*"

Later, after they said their good-byes, Orgeron elaborated on what they'd just witnessed: "Well, you know, we're in the South, and it's all kind of a cultural toughness thing."

The Rebels coaches arrived back at the Huntsville airport muddy and spent but still thrilled with how their visit had gone. All of them might have been thinking about the one program they knew they had to beat for Justin Sanders, but no one mentioned it.

The South Carolina Gamecocks.

On Friday, February 2, when Frank Wilson turned up at Joe McKnight's place for the Rebels' last in-home visit, he encountered an entirely different person from the one he'd been courting for nearly six months. The 18-year-old sat slumped on the sofa in his living room, looking spent and worn-out. The young tailback, who had worked so hard to keep all of the grown men who had been coming after him at arm's length, seemed to have finally cracked.

"Coach Frank, I'm twisted," McKnight told Wilson. "I gotta get my mind right. I gotta think this out."

"I applaud the way you've handled yourself, Joe," Wilson responded calmly. "I know you feel right now like the weight of the world is on your shoulders. But if there's anybody you know you can confide in—your mom, your grandparents, your coaches—go hear what they have to say. You don't have to make this decision all by yourself. Pray about it, and you'll make the right call."

Wilson's visit was the shortest he made during the whole contact period. Still, Wilson knew that McKnight would be spending the weekend palling around with Colby Arceneaux.

Maybe spending time with a close friend would calm him down.

Orgeron's home visit to see Tony Fein turned out to be more of a crash course in the Rebels' Cover 2 defense than a pitch session. Fein told Coach O he didn't need any more convincing. "I felt like this was meant to be because so many pieces had fallen into place," he said afterward. "It's a perfect situation for me."

The day's real drama had taken place just an hour down the road at Robert Elliott's house. Freeze, Wilson, and Werner had driven to Okolona at 10 a.m. to make sure their running back recruit was all set for Signing Day, now only 92 hours away. Things seemed fine. Robert's mother, Bridgett, was working at the hospital in Tupelo; Robert said they could go see her there. Then he invited the three Rebels coaches into his bedroom to watch his highlight tape. He also had them read the speech he was going to give at his kid brother's Pee Wee football banquet later that night.

Before the coaches left to visit his mother at work, Elliott called her and reiterated that he didn't want to have any more visits with other coaches.

Freeze felt good about the trip, but after meeting with Robert's mother, he became apprehensive. He noticed a change in her tone with them. She'd always been friendly and bubbly. This time she was curt. She told Freeze she'd be off work at 2:30 and that if the coaches came back to the house then, she'd talk to them.

"Something's changed with her," Freeze told Wilson and Werner as they left. The coaches went to get lunch, and when they returned and sat down with Bridgett Elliott in her living room, she told them that she and her son were going to talk Sunday night and make his decision.

"Well, Robert just told us that he's made his decision and it's final," Freeze said. "He told us he's sticking with his commitment."

"Well, whatever Robert wants to do is fine," Bridgett Elliott said, "but we'll sit down tomorrow night and talk about it."

Something had to be going on, Freeze thought. He was determined that he, Wilson, and Werner would be the last coaches to see Robert Elliott on Saturday.

Robert wasn't at the house, and he wasn't answering his cell. Freeze believed another program had been scheduled to make a home visit that afternoon. The coaches sat in the driveway for 20 minutes, then Freeze went back into the house. Bridgett Elliott's mood was distant; she let Freeze into her home but had little to say to him. His mind was racing: Someone must've snatched Robert Elliott away from them.

Sure enough, at 3:30, another car pulled up. J.B. Grimes, the offensive line coach for Mississippi State, came to the front door and was ushered in by Bridgett Elliott. It was an awkward moment for all three people.

The two rival coaches greeted each other cordially. Freeze then explained what Robert Elliott had told them earlier that morning. Grimes said that he'd "dropped off" Bulldogs head coach Sylvester Croom but didn't say where. This led Freeze to conclude that the visit wouldn't last long because Grimes had to go pick up his boss, who must've been recruiting somebody else close by.

"We're going to let you visit with Miss Bridgett," Freeze told Grimes. "But we're going to come back, and we're going to be the last ones in."

The Ole Miss coaches drove around the block a few times, then parked outside and waited. A few minutes later, Freeze's heart sank when two cars pulled up. One contained Croom and Elliott's uncle Ronald; the other, Melvin Smith, a Bulldogs assistant.

"We got issues," Freeze told Wilson and Werner. "Real issues."

The Mississippi State coaches talked with Bridgett Elliott and Robert's uncle for half an hour, then left. Still no sign of Robert.

The Ole Miss coaches figured that at some point he'd have to come home to change for the banquet, so Werner and Wilson left Freeze at the Elliotts' house to wait while they drove over to Robert's grandmother's house to talk with Uncle Ronald.

That visit didn't go well at all. Wilson and Elliott's uncle got into a heated exchange over Ole Miss' pursuit of Joe McKnight. "We know how it's gonna be," the uncle railed. "McKnight's from Louisiana. You're from Louisiana. Coach O's from Louisiana. Robert won't get a fair shot."

Back at Bridgett Elliott's home, Freeze confronted the tailback's mother: "Miss Bridgett, can you be honest and tell me what's going on?"

Elliott: "I don't know. I haven't seen Robert today, and I don't know where he is."

Freeze: "Can we go to the banquet?"

Elliott: "I don't know. I don't even know if he's gonna be there. It's all the way across town."

The Ole Miss coaches went to where the banquet was being held. Freeze opened the door and saw Robert inside. Wilson got his attention and motioned for him to come over. Robert started toward the door, but then a man the Rebels coaches didn't recognize stopped him. Another man came outside. "Sorry, this is a private party, and y'all weren't invited. You have to leave."

The Rebels coaches rode back to Oxford pretty sure, despite what Robert Elliott had told them, that the tailback wasn't going to be signing with Ole Miss.

SUNDAY, FEBRUARY 4: 68 HOURS UNTIL SIGNING DAY

The contact period was over. The Internet was buzzing. And so were the traditional media.

The most intriguing buzz came in the *Northeast Mississippi Daily Journal*, which reported that Joe McKnight had spent the weekend in Tuscaloosa visiting Alabama and Nick Saban.

Wilson, who had come into the Ole Miss office with two of his young children, showed no ill effects from the previous day's soap opera in Okolona. Then McLeod informed him of the McKnight rumor. Wilson's face scrunched up a bit, but he promptly dismissed it: "I talked to Joe last night; he was with Colby. We're fine. I don't know where people come up with this stuff."

But the Rebels' recruiting ranking was just about to take a big hit. Nielsen reported to Orgeron that Jerrell Powe was still waiting for BYU to send out his exams for the courses he'd been taking and that he wouldn't be at the academic benchmarks Ole Miss had set for him to reach by February 1. That meant Orgeron couldn't sign him. He knew Powe was no sure thing to get admitted even if he were able to sign him, but now the odds had just become even longer.

The disappointing Powe news seemed to have faded a few hours later as Orgeron settled in on his couch with his wife and kids to watch the Super Bowl. Or maybe watching a football game simply took his mind away from work.

Monday, February 5: 48 Hours

Two hours before the Rebels' 8 a.m. staff meeting, Orgeron was in the war room screening junior tape. A few of his staffers sat around the table.

All anybody wanted to talk about was Joe McKnight: "What's the latest? Have you heard anything? Do you think that … ? I wonder if … ? Could he possibly … ?"

Orgeron said he felt confident. Bryan and Colby Arceneaux had been with McKnight for much of the weekend in Louisiana, and they'd told him that McKnight was definitely coming to Ole Miss.

Orgeron then broached something that many inside the IPF had also been thinking about.

"I know if we get Joe, we'll get investigated," Orgeron said matter-of-factly, referring to his coaching brethren's instinct to suspect an upstart program that lands an all-world recruit of having done something shady. "Hey, we didn't do nothing wrong. But I still know it's comin'."

Then he gave the staff a little pep talk: "I couldn't be more pleased at how things are goin', but we've got to close the deal. We've got that championship blue marlin on the line, but he ain't in the boat yet. We finish. They say it's the dead period, and I know coaches can't be out there, but somebody's workin'. So we ain't taking nothin' for granted."

Orgeron turned to Corrao: "Find out what's going on with Tony Fein. Michigan State is gonna call him. I guaran-damn-tee it. Call his parents."

Then Orgeron turned to Nielsen: "You need to stay on Lawon Scott like white on rice. Wake Forest has come after him. You know they're into negative recruiting, telling him that 'Ole Miss has signed five defensive tackles' and how we cuss out our players. Talk to his mama."

As his assistants pecked away at their BlackBerrys, Orgeron reminded them of the lesson of Jevan Snead. "Just remember this on Wednesday: Take the high road. Don't burn no bridges with these kids."

And one more thing: "Don't forget *nobody*. John Brown and Rolando Melancon goin' off to JC don't mean we forget about 'em until next spring. Let's track these guys and call them once a week."

Oh, and in case you forgot: *"We gotta build a net!"*

Monday, February 5: 40 Hours

Wilson's cell buzzed. It was LaMarcus Williams, the defensive tackle from Louisiana who had de-committed from Alabama so he could come to Ole Miss. Wilson told Orgeron how upbeat the 285-

pounder sounded. But when Orgeron got on the phone, he got a bad feeling after he asked Williams, "LaMarcus, you *are* coming to be an Ole Miss Rebel, right?"

Williams: "Coach, I'm just having me a good time."

Listening in, Wilson thought—hoped—that Williams just didn't quite understand what Orgeron had asked. Orgeron handed him back the phone; he knew better.

Meanwhile, the soap opera in Okolona continued to unfold. According to Robert Elliott's high school coach, the star tailback hadn't come to school on Monday, and no one knew where he was. Freeze estimated that he'd made 800 phone calls trying to reach Elliott since Saturday. He even asked if the superintendent of the school would go check up on him.

Bridgett Elliott wasn't taking Freeze's calls either.

"She promised me, 'Coach, I'll never not answer your call,' " Freeze told Orgeron, who sounded amused by the farce of it all. "And that was yesterday. Right now, I'm just trying to open the lines of communication."

"Open the lines of communication?" Orgeron said, starting to laugh. "It sounds like we got us a hostage situation or something."

A few feet away, Rippon was on his cell with Justin Sanders' father: "Yeah, Tim, we all really liked that chicken fight."

Running with that, Orgeron yelled out, "*If we can get our defense to play as fast as them roosters, we're gonna be okay!*"

Freeze's phone buzzed. It wasn't Robert Elliott calling back. It was Cedric Miller, Roderick Davis' coach.

Freeze listened for a minute and then turned to Orgeron: "Coach Ced says he's guarding all the back doors, Coach."

MONDAY, FEBRUARY 5: 36 HOURS

Much of the suspense in the war room centered on players Freeze was recruiting. In addition to his highest-profile target, Roderick

Davis, Freeze was on the hook for Robert Elliott, Jerry Franklin, and Johnathon Frink, an Oxford High linebacker with great grades who the Rebels figured would have committed to them by now but hadn't. Like Elliott, Frink wasn't returning calls.

Freeze called Bradley Sowell, another Ole Miss commit who had befriended Frink during the year. "Come on, Bradley, Frink's making the decision tonight," Freeze said. "You gotta get in his ear. Get him on the phone, whatever. Just talk to him."

Ten minutes later, Freeze was giving Roderick Davis pointers on how to handle his Signing Day press conference.

"Don't forget good ol' Coach Freeze, your new position coach, when you talk to those newspapers," Freeze told him. "You do want to see that ball thrown to you, dontcha, Big Rod?"

In hopes of reaching Frink, Freeze asked Tony Hughes to send his son Jamison, one of Frink's best friends, to talk to his pal. Twenty minutes later, Jamison called his dad from outside Frink's home.

Hughes: "Jamison just told me that the Frinks won't let him come through the front door tonight."

Orgeron: "How about the window?"

TUESDAY, FEBRUARY 6: 14 HOURS
Orgeron's suspicion that Ole Miss needn't worry about over-signing had, unfortunately, come true.

A handful of "maybe" guys announced that they'd committed elsewhere. Rashad Mason was signing with North Carolina. Maurice Harris was signing with Florida State. Kevin Bryant, a 380-pound lineman from South Florida, was signing with North Carolina.

Things were looking increasingly bleak for Frink, Franklin, and Elliott, too.

Orgeron warned the staff that there also might be some night-before-Signing-Day defections. On the white board, he scrawled four names under a "Make Sure" list: Rishaw Johnson, Lionel Breaux, LaMarcus Williams, and Roderick Davis.

Suddenly, the general feeling in the war room was that the Rebels might end up one player under the 25 max, so Orgeron asked the staff to ID other prospects who might still be available.

Freeze sent one of the grad assistants out to fetch the tape of a 280-pound offensive lineman who'd committed to Mississippi State, a kid the Rebels hadn't been too impressed by the first time they saw him on film.

Orgeron: "Would he come?"

Freeze: "I know if we'd asked a week ago he would have."

Didn't matter. When Orgeron watched the tape again, he became annoyed: "We don't want this. Forget him."

Next Wilson offered up a 6'5", 240-pound defensive end from Louisiana who'd already committed to Oklahoma. He was a prospect the Rebels had been on the fence about some months ago and had never really pushed to recruit.

"He came here for our basketball camp," Wilson said. "And my mom is married to his dad's first cousin."

Then somebody remembered why they'd been on the fence about him: not bad, but not somebody worth chasing. Then or now.

TUESDAY, FEBRUARY 6: 12 HOURS

"*Wooooo! Wooooo! Wooooo!*"

Just back from his kids' basketball game, Orgeron burst back into the war room, stalked around the big table, and rolled his shoulders to loosen up, as if it were game day: "We got us a case of Red Bull and some pork rinds, and we are *competin'* tonight!"

But soon, more bad news: Orgeron's queasy feeling about LaMarcus Williams turned out to be well-founded—Williams was signing with Mississippi State. He was following Charlie

Harbison, the assistant coach who'd once recruited him for Alabama and had just taken a job with the Bulldogs. The assurances Wilson had been getting from Williams's high school coach had proved worthless.

Wilson had an idea. He popped in a tape of Jonathan "Tank" English, a 5'11", 325-pound nose tackle who happened to be teammates with Joe McKnight and Colby Arceneaux. Wilson liked English but could never get Orgeron to pull the trigger. English really wanted to come to Ole Miss. He'd e-mailed Wilson to try to make his case, and he'd given him an updated highlight DVD when they met a few weeks later.

In late January, English had committed to Arizona State, where, ironically enough, former Ole Miss assistant coach Matt Lubick was the new recruiting coordinator.

Wilson put in the tape. This time around, English's quick feet and effort caught Orgeron's eye. He liked what he saw.

"Let's call J.T.," Orgeron told Wilson, referring to J.T. Curtis, English's high school coach.

"Man, Matt Lubick is gonna be *so* pissed," Orgeron said as Wilson dialed the number. "But all is fair in love and recruiting."

"I love Big Tank," piped up Brad Villavaso, a former Louisiana high school coach who was one of the Rebels' new graduate assistants. "I coached him in camp. Man, he played hard."

"We ain't going to bed 'til we get him," Orgeron pronounced.

TUESDAY, FEBRUARY 6: 8 HOURS 51 MINUTES
Orgeron threw up a Hail Mary and called all-everything defensive tackle D'Angelo McCray, who had been committed to Illinois for almost two months.

"Come on, D'Angelo," Orgeron told him. "You knew we weren't gonna quit."

McCray said that he was set but that he appreciated the call.

TUESDAY, FEBRUARY 6: 8 HOURS 42 MINUTES

Word came in that a fight had broken out at McKnight's younger brother's basketball game—and that nobody could find Joe.

Colby Arceneaux, who had permission from his dad to stay out late and was expected to be with Joe McKnight, couldn't find his friend. Bryan Arceneaux, Colby's dad, told Orgeron that nobody knew where Joe had gone. The curious thing was that McKnight didn't have a car, and he wasn't answering his cell.

Fourteen minutes later, Wilson got his callback from English. The young nose tackle was excited, but also confused: Why now? Why not before, when I hadn't already committed to Arizona State?

Orgeron was having second thoughts too. He wondered how J.T. Curtis would view the last-minute offer to one of his players. Would it somehow anger the longtime high school coach and turn him—and perhaps McKnight—off of Ole Miss? Was it worth the risk?

Wilson passed his cell to Orgeron.

"Tank, you think we're too late, or do we have a shot to get you?" Orgeron asked English, who replied that yes, he was interested.

"Well then," said Orgeron, "we're gonna talk to Coach J.T. Curtis and do this thing right."

Wilson got English's mother on the phone. She was upset. *Very* upset: "Jonathan prayed on it, prayed that Ole Miss would give him a scholarship, and you didn't, you overlooked him. Dennis Erickson, he came in, and he said Jonathan reminds him of Warren Sapp."

Wilson backpedaled, trying to explain that the Rebels had not misled English and that his prayer had come true: He'd gotten his offer from Ole Miss. He'd gotten it late, maybe, but he'd gotten it.

Uh-uh. Tank English's mother said that she would *not* let her son de-commit from Arizona State.

TUESDAY, FEBRUARY 6: 8 HOURS 1 MINUTE

Freeze finally, *finally* got through to a member of the Elliott family. Robert's 11-year-old brother, Devin, answered the phone.

"Devin, my man, you are my *hero*," Freeze said. "Can you please do me a huge favor and go beg your mom to get on the phone with me for two minutes?"

Bridgett Elliott picked up and said that she had nothing to say.

No Robert Elliott—*Where is he? What's he gonna do?*—but at least this exhausting, frustrating, energy-sucking, roller coaster of a day was almost over.

Ninety minutes later—six hours and 18 minutes before the official start of Signing Day—after enough waiting by their cell phones, the staff had emptied out of the war room.

WEDNESDAY, FEBRUARY 7: 1 HOUR 10 MINUTES

Twenty minutes before Orgeron pulled into the parking lot next to the IPF, he had given Pete Carroll a little wake-up call. Orgeron knew his old boss would be sleeping in the office; that was a National Signing Day eve tradition at USC. After a brief exchange of pleasantries, the Trojans coach told Orgeron what the big Cajun had feared he was going hear: Carroll said he believed McKnight was going to be a USC Trojan.

"Guess we'll find out soon enough," Orgeron said. "G'night, Pedro."

NATIONAL SIGNING DAY
6:02 A.M.

Two minutes after the official start of Signing Day, with Freeze and Nielsen flanking the fax machine, the Rebels got their first fax from a recruit. It was from Lawon Scott, and it settled a bet about which coach would get a recruit in first, Freeze or Nielsen. Freeze dug out his billfold and gave Nielsen $20.

Chris Kiffin walked over to the big bass drum on the floor and started to pound on it.

6:41 A.M.

At his desk, Frank Wilson was more on edge than ever. "He was supposed to call me last night," Wilson said, "but he didn't. I think maybe that's good."

"He," of course, was Joe McKnight.

Wilson had reasoned it out that the prize tailback would have made the call if he weren't coming to Ole Miss because he was a thoughtful kid and would want to let Wilson down easy.

The noncall, Wilson was sure of it, meant that Ole Miss was still in the hunt.

7:10 A.M.

Good news from Louisiana! Rishaw Johnson was in, although his mother called to ask for another form to fill out and refax; she'd accidentally written down her birthday instead of the date.

8:02 A.M.

Wilson clicked off his phone. He'd been on with Colby Arceneaux, his old friend's son, in hopes of—what else?—getting an update on Joe McKnight.

"Colby said, 'My nerves are so bad right now, I'm pretty much speechless,'" Wilson told the room. "He hasn't seen Joe since they got kicked out of the gym last night."

8:14 A.M.

Less than two hours before McKnight was to make his announcement on ESPN, Orgeron's cell rang.

"What's up, Pedro?"

It was Pete Carroll.

Orgeron stepped out of the war room. Wilson shook his head. He feared the worst. Three minutes later, Orgeron reentered. He didn't say a word. He just walked over to the recruiting board, grabbed McKnight's nameplate, and tossed it onto the table.

"He signed with USC," Orgeron announced, as if he needed to say the words and be done with them.

Everyone's worst fear had come true. Make that *almost* worst: Some of the coaches were even more worried about Orgeron's reaction to McKnight's decision. After all, Orgeron had been the biggest believer among them. For another 90 seconds no one said anything, and they turned back to watching junior film.

Orgeron then clicked off the projector and sat back in his seat.

"The work and the thought process were there, and that's all you can do," he said in a subdued voice. "This is just like us almost beating LSU last year. We were down after coming up short, but then we came right back and beat Mississippi State. We *are* going to keep going after the best players, and we *are* going to get them."

He paused, but he wasn't through.

"Let's not forget all of the great players we've signed today," he continued. "Tony Fein is really gonna help us. We got Jevan Snead. Roderick Davis is going to be a great player for us. We love Big Ted Laurent, and Rishaw Johnson is as good as any offensive lineman in the country."

Coach O said those words and meant them with all his heart, but there was one word he did not say:

Wooooo!

8:21 A.M.

Another cell phone rang. The call was from Gavin Hardin, one of the top junior linebackers in the country. Freeze handed his phone to Orgeron.

Hardin's timing couldn't have been better: He told Orgeron he wanted to be an Ole Miss Rebel. Orgeron stuck the phone up in the air, and the rest of the staff roared their approval.

12:02 P.M.

Tiffany Wilson looked crushed. She and Kelly Orgeron and a few other coaches' wives and family friends had been waiting in the IPF as the fax machine cranked out the news.

Yes, Frank Wilson had finally beaten LSU for two local kids whom the Tigers really wanted, but he had convinced himself he was going to reel in Joe McKnight, too. Said Tiffany, in a halting voice: "I know how much he is hurting right now."

4:14 P.M.

Freeze had just watched the footage of Robert Elliott's press conference on the Internet. As Ole Miss had pretty much figured out during the week, Elliott had signed with Mississippi State.

"At first I was going to go to Florida State or Ole Miss," Elliott said from behind a podium, his smiling mother standing right beside him. "But then Coach Croom told me I could come in and wear No. 2. It was really where I could go and feel comfortable and rock my No. 2. I've been wearing it since Pee Wee, and that's the only number I can rock. If I put something else on, it won't look right on me. I figure, you've got to look good to play good. I can't wear those double-digit numbers."

Freeze just laughed.

"Crazy, isn't it?" he said. "This whole dang thing's just plain crazy."

THE
FUTURE
IS NOW

THE MORNING AFTER Signing Day almost always signals the start of a four-day weekend for coaches in college football programs all across the country. It's been a long haul, and everybody's pretty much tapped out.

At Ole Miss, Orgeron scheduled a staff meeting for 8 a.m. on Thursday, February 8, the morning after Signing Day 2007.

Tired? No time to be tired. No time for any four-day weekend. Too much work still to be done. Too much junior film to evaluate. All those senior recruiting lists to update to find out who went where—and to see who might've fallen through the cracks.

Inside the war room, the heartbreak from not landing Joe McKnight and a few others was still fresh. All that carping from Orgeron's boss Pete Boone about being sure not to sign too many kids lest the Rebels not have scholarship space now seemed laughable. National Signing Day had come and gone, and Ole Miss still had two scholarships left.

"Find out who's out there. Find out if there's someone who just got asked to grayshirt," Orgeron told his staff. "Call all the JCs and prep schools for the No. 1 guys still available. Get all the newspapers and go through the analysis of the signings. Are there walk-ons out there? We got two scholarships to give!"

At the very least, Orgeron wanted his staff working to identify top players to bring to the Rebels' Junior Day and to their summer camp: "We're competing to get them here to see what we have. Big Ted Laurent was worth it. Rishaw Johnson came here. That's why we got them."

The meeting was equal parts pep talk and postmortem. Orgeron made no mention of a controversy that flared up after McKnight said at his Signing Day press conference that he'd heard from Reggie Bush regarding an on-going NCAA investigation at USC involving the Heisman Trophy winner. McKnight later denied that the two had spoken, which would've been a recruiting violation. And while newspaper columnists and talking heads had a field day with the speculation, Orgeron didn't believe there was anything there to get worked up about.

In their final national rankings of the Class of 2007, the Internet recruiting sites dropped Ole Miss about 10 places below where the Rebels had been ranked in January based on likely signings. Rivals.com ranked the Rebels No. 26 nationally. Scout.com had them at No. 31. Neither sites included the signing of Texas transfer Jevan Snead, who probably would've bumped the Rebels up five or six spots had he been factored in. Ole Miss also fell because it wouldn't sign blue-chip JC defensive end Dion Gales and because it hadn't yet signed Jerrell Powe, probably the first "15-star" prospect in the short history of Internet recruiting analysis.

(A five-star recruit, Powe had failed to qualify for three consecutive years and subsequently kept re-signing and boosting the Rebels' recruiting ranking, hence the "15 stars.")

McKnight, of course, was the biggest reason for gloom in the war room, but the Rebels also would've loved to have landed linebacker Jerry Franklin, Rolando Melancon, and T-Bob Hebert, all coveted blue-chippers whom the Rebels thought they had a shot at.

But Orgeron was still convinced this class was the best crop he had brought in during his three years at Ole Miss. After all, he did get his potential franchise quarterback in Jevan Snead; he landed the top player in Mississippi (DL Chris Strong) as well as the best player in Memphis (WR Roderick Davis); and he signed the best junior college receiver in the country (A.J. Jackson). He nabbed a junior college middle linebacker (Tony Fein) to replace Patrick Willis; he persuaded the top defensive tackle in the Southeast (Ted Laurent) to come to Oxford; and he beat out LSU for two top Louisiana kids (lineman Rishaw Johnson and speedster Lionel Breaux) whom the Tigers really wanted.

If Orgeron is right, and the 2007 Class is his best yet, Ole Miss should be in position to challenge for a bowl bid in 2007. His 2006 Class (ranked No. 15 by Scout.com and No. 16 by Rivals.com) looks to be better than advertised. Through the spring of 2007, 10 of those signees were starters and 16 were on the two-deep depth chart. Four Rebels (OG John Jerry, DE Greg Hardy, DL Marcus Tillman, K Joshua Shene) made freshman All-America teams.

The 2005 Class (ranked No. 29 by Scout and No. 30 by Rivals), a group that was snapped together in just a month, hasn't been as productive, despite some successes. Marshay Green blossomed into one of the nation's most lethal return men, while much-ballyhooed OL Michael Oher is a two-year starter. Peria Jerry is the most talented member of the Ole Miss D-line; Mike Wallace was the team's leading receiver in 2006; and Reid Neely was the team's most improved player in the spring and won a starting job.

But by the spring of 2007, the bulk of the 28-man 2005 Class had already washed out. Orgeron booted many of those players from the program within their first three semesters at Ole Miss for a variety of disciplinary issues. Others left voluntarily rather than endure the intensity of yet another Orgeron practice. Others flunked out. And Powe, the marquee name of that 2005 recruiting class who never finished high school and whom Orgeron had hoped to squeeze into the 2007 class, remained in admissions limbo.

Orgeron wrote it off as part of the learning process. This past year he yanked guys off his recruiting board because of red character flags whom he would've gladly pursued a year or two earlier.

One prospect the Rebels had hotly pursued all year but lost to Steve Spurrier's South Carolina Gamecocks had already made national headlines—for all the wrong reasons.

Stephen Garcia, the cocky Tampa quarterback who spurned Ole Miss and enrolled early at South Carolina, was arrested twice in a three-week span. On February 17, 2007, he was arrested and charged with drunkenness and failure to stop for a police officer. Then on March 3, Garcia was arrested on charges of malicious injury to personal property after a professor reported that Garcia had used a key to scratch the man's car.

Spurrier suspended Garcia for the Gamecocks' spring practice.

The incidents served to remind people in Oxford how fortunate they were with how things fell in their big QB chase. Jevan Snead, ineligible until the 2008 season, had been so impressive in spring drills that Orgeron delighted in showing him off on April 17 in the Rebels' annual intrasquad game, the Grove Bowl.

Cliff Davis, the rocket-armed, former minor league baseball player known as Talladega Nights, who some Ole Miss staff members the previous fall had tabbed as the Ole Miss QB of the future, didn't take a snap in the game. At the start of the fourth quarter, Talladega Nights walked off the field. After the game, he told Werner that he was quitting the team.

The biggest news from the Ole Miss spring game was that starter Brent Schaffer, the heavily hyped junior college QB recruit who struggled in 2006, might've been overtaken by understudy Seth Adams, a 6'4" 225-pound senior who came to Oxford in the spring of 2006 as a walk-on after playing at Gulf Coast Junior College. Adams connected on 16 of 20 passes and made a case to Rebels coaches that he, not the enigmatic Schaeffer, might be their best hope to lead them to a winning season.

The obvious irony? The fate of master recruiter Ed Orgeron might end up resting in the hands of … a walk-on.

The time had come, Orgeron said in a short press conference after the Grove Bowl, for the Rebels to become a winning team. No more talk about being so young or making improvements or lacking enough depth to stave off teams in the fourth quarter.

No, in 2007, there had to be tangible results in the win column:

> We *need* to have a winning season. We *must*
> have a winning season. Is that a goal? No. We're
> shooting for the Sugar Bowl every year. But we
> need to have a winning season, go to a bowl
> game, and win. That's where we must go to get
> to the next step of our program.

The contract extension that Orgeron signed in the winter took his deal to 2010. In spite of the two losing seasons, it was an endorsement of his progress in rebuilding Ole Miss into an SEC contender.

But the time has come, as Coach O knows better than anyone, when progress will no longer be measured by the number of prime prospects he and his Ole Miss staff manage to snatch away from other big-time schools. The time has come when progress will be measured by his W–L record.

If Ole Miss doesn't win, Ed Orgeron's only solace will be that he stocked the fridge for his successor.

First and foremost, I am grateful to Coach Ed Orgeron for his help, encouragement, and openness from Day 1. Coach Orgeron endured all of my questions and random interviews, and never made me feel out of place. I can't thank him enough for opening up his war room to me.

I also want to thank the Ole Miss staff: Kent McLeod, Frank Wilson, Dan Werner, Art Kehoe, Chris Rippon, Ryan Nielsen, Dave Corrao, Hugh Freeze, Matt Lubick, John Thompson, Tony Hughes, Matt Saunders, Barney Farrar, Maurice Harris, David Saunders, Kyle Strongin, Brad Villavaso, Grant Heard, and Chris Kiffin. They were kind enough to take the time to answer yet another question and to field a phone call that was supposed to take five minutes and inevitably lasted a half-hour. I can't imagine a better group of tour guides.

In addition, I appreciate the generosity of sports information director Langston Rogers and the entire Rebels support staff.

My agents Greg Dinkin and Frank Scatoni deserve credit for pushing this project, as does Chris Raymond at ESPN Books for jumping on it, and even more so for giving me Glen Waggoner as an editor. Huge thanks to researcher Dale

Brauner, who was invaluable in checking my X's and O's. A doff of the helmet also to *The Mag*'s copy chief, Steve Horne, and his eagle-eyed copyedit crew: Ethan Lipton, Roseann Marulli, Margaret McNicol Robbins, and Dave Sutter. They made sure I hit the right holes. ESPN Books summer intern Erin Peterson obviously has a bright future in publishing. Thanks also to Henry Lee and John W. Glenn.

I would not have been able to manage this project without the support of my colleagues at *ESPN The Magazine*: J.B. Morris, Gary Hoenig, Neil Fine, Seth Wickersham, Eric Adelson, Chris Berend, Ryan Hockensmith, Gary Belsky, and Perry van der Meer.

Many colleagues at ESPN.com were a great source of encouragement and insight as I sought to balance the demands of book and blog: John Hassan, David Duffey, Keith Hawkins, Dave Albright, Bill Curry, Rod Gilmore, Jim Donnan, Pat Forde, Ivan Maisel, Craig Haubert, Tom Luginbill, Wright Thompson, and Mark Schlabach.

I am also indebted to a large team of Bristol-based ESPN colleagues, especially those suited up with ESPN college football, who have been helpful in more ways than they can ever know for making my job so easy: Howie Schwab, Jim Bowdon, Mike Epstein, Michael Kim, Dave Revsine, Rece Davis, Eric Kuselius, Chadd Scott, Colin Cowherd, Doug Gottlieb, Chris Fallica, Beano Cook, Brad Edwards, Chris Spielman, Chris Fowler, Kirk Herbstreit, Mike Tirico, Brian Kenny, Bob Davie, David Salerno, Scott Turken, Michael Fountain, Lee Fitting, John Skipper, and Michael Rooney.

Thanks to my brethren on the college beat who make everything in between the games and trips such a pleasure: Stewart Mandel, Pete Thamel, Dennis Dodd, Ralph Russo, Chris Dufrense, Teddy Greenstein, Ted Miller, Wendell Barnhouse,

Spencer Hall, Thayer Evans, Andy Staples, Larry Williams, Tom Dienhart, Matt Hayes, Tom Shatel, Vahe Gregorian, Bryan Curtis, John Bianco, Shawn Schoeffler, Ryan Abraham, Chris Huston, Austin Murphy, Jeff D'Alessio, and Gary Klein.

I am also grateful for the candor and cooperation of many other individuals who helped breathe life into this project. Among them: Micheal Antonescu, Bryan Arceneaux, Aaron Ausmus, Andy Bark, Broadway Joe Barnett, Greg Bukowski, James Bryant, Pete Carroll, Ginny Crager, Nathan Jew, J.T. Curtis, Manny Diaz, Bridgett Elliott, Paul Finebaum, Gary Garcia, Jim Hofher, Gaynell Jenkins, Joe McKnight, Fred Stroock, and Gary Treangen.

And, most of all, I want to thank my family and Christie for their patience, support, and understanding.

Bruce Feldman
July 2007